Contesting Patriotism

PRAISE FOR *CONTESTING PATRIOTISM*

"Peace movement organizations operate in a diverse social and political climate, one distorted by rhetoric of fear and lies. That's why the peace movement has hungered of late for an informed, analytic framework to assess where we are and where we go next. Woehrle, Coy, and Maney provide rich, deep, but fully accessible research that will sharpen our focus, increase our effectiveness, and provoke our community to "smart growth" through self-reflection. This is a very timely gift."—**Mark C. Johnson**, executive director, Fellowship of Reconciliation–USA

"In an era when U.S. nationalism and unilateralism are arguably the biggest threats to world peace and security, Woehrle, Coy, and Maney offer an important analysis of how culture can be used as a strategic tool for those seeking to promote a more peaceful and just world."—**Jackie Smith**, director, Center for the Study of Social Movements and Social Change, University of Notre Dame

"Those who advocate for peace have too often had their patriotism questioned. This carefully reasoned and richly researched book provides a set of tools to help reshape the discourse about who speaks for America in matters of war and peace. This timely book is vitally important for all who seek new ways to turn this country away from the catastrophic policies that, in the name of patriotism, have deeply harmed Americans' interests at home and abroad." —**Andrew L. Barlow**, University of California, Berkeley and Diablo Valley College, author of *Between Fear and Hope: Globalization and Race in the United States*

Contesting Patriotism

Culture, Power, and Strategy in the Peace Movement

Lynne M. Woehrle, Patrick G. Coy, and Gregory M. Maney

ROWMAN & LITTLEFIELD PUBLISHERS, INC.
Lanham • Boulder • New York • Toronto • Plymouth, UK

ROWMAN & LITTLEFIELD PUBLISHERS, INC.

Published in the United States of America
by Rowman & Littlefield Publishers, Inc.
A wholly owned subsidary of The Rowman & Littlefield Publishing Group, Inc.
4501 Forbes Boulevard, Suite 200, Lanham, Maryland 20706
www.rowmanlittlefield.com

Estover Road, Plymouth PL6 7PY, United Kingdom

Copyright © 2008 by Rowman & Littlefield Publishers, Inc.
First paperback edition 2009

All rights reserved. No part of this publication may be reproduced, stored
in a retrieval system, or transmitted in any form or by any means, electronic,
mechanical, photocopying, recording, or otherwise, without the prior permission
of the publisher.

British Library Cataloguing in Publication Information Available

Library of Congress Cataloging-in-Publication Data
Woehrle, Lynne M., 1965-
  Contesting patriotism : culture, power, and strategy in the peace movement /
Lynne M. Woehrle, Patrick G. Coy, and Gregory M. Maney.
    p. cm.
  Includes bibliographical references and index.
  1. Peace movements—United States. 2. Patriotism—United States. 3. Political
culture—United States. I. Coy, Patrick G. II. Maney, Gregory M. III. Title.
JZ5584.U6W65 2008
303.6'60973—dc22

                                                                          2008032578

ISBN: 978-0-7425-6447-3 (cloth : alk. paper)
ISBN: 978-0-7425-6448-0 (pbk. : alk. paper)
ISBN: 978-0-7425-6572-2 (electronic)

Printed in the United States of America

∞™ The paper used in this publication meets the minimum requirements of
American National Standard for Information Sciences—Permanence of Paper
for Printed Library Materials, ANSI/NISO Z39.48-1992.

This book is dedicated to all those who have engaged others in discussions about peace during times of war.

Contents

Acknowledgments

All three authors contributed equally to the research, writing, and production of this book. While we readily accept responsibility for this book's shortcomings, we cannot take sole credit for its virtues. A research project of this scope would not have been possible without the generous assistance of the following institutions: the American Sociological Association's Fund for the Advancement of the Discipline, the National Science Foundation's Sociology Program (SES-0423289), Hofstra University, Kent State University, and Mount Mary College. The opinions expressed in this book are those of the authors and do not necessarily reflect the views of the funding agencies.

We are indebted to several colleagues for their insightful advice on earlier drafts of various chapters. They are Jeffrey Anderson, Robert Benford, George Cheney, Morten Ender, Mark Cassell, Ed Kinane, Louis Kriesberg, David Meyer, Erin O'Brien, Manfred Stegner, Jackie Smith, Lee Smithey, and Sidney Tarrow. Thanks to their comments, this book is more rigorous in its data analysis and more refined in its argumentation.

In terms of data collection, we thank Wendy Chmielewski of the Swarthmore Peace Collection for her assistance in gathering statements from the Gulf War period. Staff from several peace movement organizations also responded graciously to our many requests for their official statements. In addition, Patricia Leahan, Linnea Mersberger, Dave Robinson, Ethan Vesely-Flad, and Bob Wallace generously assisted us with photographs.

We also appreciate greatly the long hours of dedicated work that several student research assistants put into collecting or helping to code data. They include Christopher Bellas, David Castillo, Denise Dollar, Tiffany Johnson, Douglas McKinzie, Michelle Prescott, Rebecca Quirk, Mekha Rajan, and Musa Tuzuner.

We have tried to make this book visually compelling as well as accessible to those not firmly entrenched in the ivory tower. Any success in this endeavor is partly due to those who have assisted us in its production. In this regard, we thank the patient assistance of editors at Rowman and Littlefield, especially John Green, Alan McClare, and Alden Perkins. Anne Holzman also has our gratitude for producing a good and useful index.

Last but certainly not least, we express tremendous gratitude to Holger, Karin, Mary, and other family and friends who have not only gracefully supported our efforts in ways too numerous to mention, but have also inspired us through their suggestions and through their own work for peace. Your unfailing support gives us the courage to attempt to speak some truth to power.

A note to our readers: Much of chapter 1 was originally published in *Sociological Research Online*, 13:4, www.socresonline.org.uk/13/4/3.html, under the title "A Typology of Oppositional Knowledge: Democracy and the U.S. Peace Movement." It is included here with their kind permission. Much of chapter 5 also appears in volume 29 of *Research in Social Movements, Conflicts and Change* and is included here with the kind permission of Emerald Publishing Group.

I

PEACE DISCOURSES IN A WAR CULTURE

1

Creating Oppositional Knowledge and Promoting an Active Democracy

> They have always taught and trained you to believe it to be your patriotic duty to go to war and to have yourselves slaughtered at their command. But in all the history of the world you, the people, have never had a voice in declaring war, and strange as it certainly appears, no war by any nation in any age has ever been declared by the people.
>
> —Eugene Debs, speech on June 16, 1918

A firm voice drifts over the crowd: "The people united, will never be defeated." The chant echoes down the line while hands hold high in the air placards with the slogan "peace is patriotic" stamped across the background of an image of the United States flag. After a pause the voice begins a new chant: "Support our troops, bring them home now." Meanwhile a competing chant begins further back in the line: "No war for oil, stop the bombing, stop the war."

What is the bystander to make of this set of repeated catchphrases? Some might take momentary notice of it as an attempt to play out the well-protected right to free speech, and continue walking in the other direction. Others might see it as a threat. Still others might hesitate and begin to wonder, What is best for our country? Is war the only option?

If you stand for a moment in that third set of shoes, open to more than one explanation of "how things are," you are one of the people that those who are collectively marching down the street want to reach. But it is unlikely that you will be persuaded by this simple set of catchphrases, which helps explain the great depth and breadth of arguments put forth by peace movement organizations active in countering foreign policies that lead to war.

In the United States, public opinion and broad-based participation in public policy formation are widely regarded as important aspects of our sociocultural

3

heritage. Far from being unusual, issue-oriented debate and dialogue on domestic policies, whether among individuals, in the media, or through expressions to local, state, and national officials, is expected. However, active, open discussion of foreign policy is less likely to be viewed as commonplace, and more likely to remain in the shadows of closed-door discussions among elected officials. Influence and sway over foreign policies can be asserted more easily by powerholders (all those who occupy influential positions in society such as corporate leaders, media moguls, military officers and the like) than by most members of society. Powerholders tend to support and reproduce existing social and political relations. Thus, as is the case in all countries, rules of access have attached themselves to the political and policymaking institutions of the United States. Whose voice is listened to and taken into account by policymakers is a critical issue. In March 2006, for example, Congress commissioned the Iraq Study Group to evaluate U.S. policy in Iraq and to propose substantive alternatives. Cochaired by former secretary of state James Baker and former congressman Lee Hamilton, the group's membership was made up entirely of former high-ranking members of the Washington political establishment. No voices from outside the Washington beltway were heard. National government commissions studying domestic issues—like health care or transportation policy, for example—typically include experts and activists beyond the Washington policy elite. But this is decidedly not the case with regard to the one issue which cuts to the core of national identity: the decision to wage war. This is indeed unfortunate as public input into policy formation and evaluation—especially on this issue—is critical in a democracy. The role of peace movement organizations in promoting public dialogue and official accountability on matters of foreign policy is central to this study. The leadership offered by organizations included in our study in pressing for public dialogue about foreign policy decisions around war and peace serves as an important practical example of fulfilling the democratic vision.

In this chapter we introduce the idea that such practices of persuasion are rooted in two dynamic processes central to the peace movement. One process (which is the central focus of this chapter) is the creation and dissemination of *oppositional knowledge*. A second, equally important process involves responding to hegemony by harnessing it, challenging, or a combination of both (elaborated more in chapter 2). Together these concepts allow us to examine the discourse work of peace movement organizations (PMOs) as they address issues related to peace and war. We begin in this chapter by defining what makes knowledge oppositional and then analyze peace movement discourses about democracy as an example of oppositional knowledge.

CREATING VOICE, CREATING CHANGE

Social movements exist partly to bring about social change. They also exist as a place for maintaining alternative ideologies. To achieve these objectives, movement organizations aim to capture the hearts and the minds of the populace. Often efforts at persuasion are done not only with the intent to widen organizational membership, but also to shift the meanings of dominant ideas in society at a particular juncture in history. Rhetoric, argues Leland M. Griffin, has a "vital function as a shaping agent in human affairs" (Griffin 2001, 10). Thus participation in creating and changing discourses in a society can be a political act. We define discourses as ways of talking and writing that carry a set of underlying assumptions about how the world does and should work. Our particular interest is the role of peace movement organizations in shaping discourses around United States foreign policy.

To change dominant political discourses, a movement needs to regularly and systematically provide the populace with new ways of talking and writing that mix criticism of conventional thinking with alternative ways of making sense of the world and human behavior. It is this clearly articulated social and cultural criticism coupled with alternative viewpoints that forms oppositional knowledge. Participation in creating discourse is an important measure of power in society. Traditionally, powerholders have privileged access to communication and, therefore, disproportionate control over political discourse. This control over language and explanations further supports their continued dominance (Van Dijk 1993). As a result, discourse becomes an important site of contestation and form of resistance by social movements. Meanings in society emerge from the tug and pull of discourse. This means the work of social change includes engaging the public in processes of discourse (Muhlhausler and Peace 2006). An engaged public can create pressures that shift meanings that, in turn, inform policy.

One important action that social movements pursue is challenging powerholders' control of discourse. This work is in itself deserving of study and analysis.[1] Engaging in producing alternative discourses serves the movement by chipping away at control by powerholders. Creating discourse also has important influences on social movement organizations internally, including developing a sense of efficacy. In addition, Gary Fine (1995) and Richard Gregg (2001) argue that group cohesion is enhanced through the process of creating contributions to social discourses.

Discourse analysis demonstrates that how problems are constructed, explained, and understood is a source of real and considerable power in politics (Armstrong and Bernstein 2008; Edelman 1988). Peace movement organizations engage from below the dominant political discourses that influence the public's understanding of foreign policy. As Michel Foucault (1978, 101) argued, "Discourse transmits and produces power; it reinforces it, but also undermines and exposes it, renders it fragile and makes it possible to thwart it." While existing power inequalities are present and in some ways reproduced in the discourses generated by oppositional groups like the U.S. peace movement, challenges to those inequalities are also present (Naples 2003).

Discourse analysis offers one set of insights into how ideas emerge and change. Another important approach to understanding the ideational work of social movements is frame analysis. While discourses are the large bodies of language and ideas arising from multiple instances of contestation, we think of frames as specific instances of identifying and contextualizing "a view" of a particular situation. Frames offer individuals a "schemata of interpretation" so they have a means "to locate, perceive, identify, and label" what surrounds them in a given moment (Goffman 1974; Snow et al. 1986; Gamson 1988; Snow and Benford 1988, 1992). Frames present a view of the situation upon which the person or organization relaying the information wants others to focus. For social movement organizations this means that with framing, they actively put into the eye of the public their interpretations of specific events. How they frame an event or the issues that surround that event frequently aligns with their organizational mission, the group's collective identity, and their ongoing discourse.

The process of framing makes more central a particular, partial view of the situation so that what is centered in the "frame" becomes the focus of attention. There are, for example, many ways to define or describe the concept of "peace." Standing at an antiwar demonstration holding a sign that reads "peace is patriotic" frames opposition to a specific foreign policy in terms of one's commitment and obligations to the nation as a citizen. Another protester at the same demonstration might hold a sign reading "no blood for oil." The slogan portrays the foreign policy as being based upon callous greed.

Though operating on different levels, discourses and frames are in a relationship of mutual benefit or dependence, that is, they are in symbiosis (Sandberg 2006). Each discourse created by powerholders and challengers helps to weave the fabric of a society. Together the various discourses help create the larger cultural context within which specific events of framing are introduced. The discourses may shift, but they continue carrying ideas forward even within a context of change. During discursive exchanges different ideas are debated. That pulling and tugging can shift the dominant discourse. At the same time, dominant discourses shape and constrain frames (Ferree 2003; Steinberg 1999). Furthermore, we argue that the presentation of a new frame—either by the challengers or the powerholders—is a contribution to the discourse around a particular phenomenon (Coy, Woehrle, and Maney 2008a). Most frames are not designed to make a radical break with the existing discourse, but rather are aimed at shifting the direction of the discourse (Tarrow 1992).

We argue that dominant discourses are reproduced, challenged, and transformed through an interactive, contested, and cumulative process of framing by multiple actors (see figure 1.1). Public information can emerge from either the dominant discourse or from oppositional knowledge. Each shapes and reshapes the information and makes it available to the public. Often they provide competing explanations or interpretations, aimed at recruiting support for particular sets of ideas. Sometimes language and ideas are used to challenge existing interpretations. At other times, language and ideas from the dominant discourse are harnessed but reworked into a different message

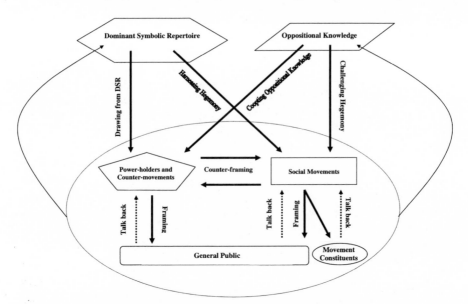

Figure 1.1.   Reproduction and Transformation of Political Discourses

(see more on this in chapter 2). There are also several opportunities for feedback, when political discourses may be reshaped and even transformed. Not shown in figure 1.1, but a significant player in the developing and filtering of information, is the media (Gamson 1995). If the media could be meaningfully represented in figure 1.1 without also causing a great deal of confusion, it would appear in multiple locations influencing, funneling, and filtering the content and the meanings of the discourses.[2]

Framing (and reframing) events and issues and putting them before the public is an influential tool for the movement organization that wants the public to think differently about an idea or a policy. Ongoing framing, along with other means of contesting dominant discourse, builds an alternate discourse. Thus creation of oppositional knowledge is done with the intent to subvert and transcend the discourse of the powerholders. We will establish in the next chapter that this subversion can take a variety of forms. Two important forms revolve around whether the oppositional knowledge is aimed at reworking the meanings and implications of already accepted symbols (i.e., harnessing), or if the goal is to rebuke and jettison those symbols entirely (i.e., challenging). In either approach the art of persuasion is central to legitimizing the alternative knowledge provided to the public.

Frames that resonate with the general public often do not appear widely through the dominant discourse in the exact form the movement proposed. There are feedback mechanisms that shape and modify the initial frame. Positive and negative feedback can lead to increased use, abandonment, or modifications. Frames that do not fit into the dominant discourse or attempt to shift it too quickly or too radically are likely to be at risk for negative feedback from general audiences.[3] When a frame does fit well, it resonates with the general public and its potency may be increased (Snow and Benford 1992). In addition, frames that are used consistently gain legitimacy and develop a deeper resonance. They develop a historical momentum and create a future trajectory reaching well beyond the initial framing act (Coy, Woehrle, and Maney 2008a). Thus framing can be used to harness or challenge the dominant discourse (Maney, Woehrle, and Coy 2005).

Studying the documents produced by a broad sample of U.S. peace movement organizations gives us insight into the ways the movement attempted to shape public awareness and understanding of certain actions taken by the United States government abroad between 1990 and 2005. Our focus is the rhetoric produced about the possibility and actuality of war or large-scale military action on foreign soil. Such actions possess significant ethical, political, and cultural ramifications. We are not attempting to measure the actual impact of the rhetoric on members of the peace movement or their opponents. Rather, we hold up for analytical scrutiny what peace groups had to say to powerholders, to potential supporters, to the general public, and to each other about U.S. foreign policy. We also analyze the content of their statements across organizations and across conflict periods; we are interested in both variations in forms of discursive contention as well as in the development of oppositional knowledge.

WHAT IS OPPOSITIONAL KNOWLEDGE?

We see oppositional knowledge creation as a necessary part of a dialogical process where social movement organizations discuss ideas with the intent of changing what is predominantly viewed as normal or acceptable. Social meanings have the potential to be altered at the intersections of oppositional ideas with the dominant symbolic repertoire of the society. Power disparities often limit institutional openness to oppositional expressions. Nonetheless, all societies produce symbolic cultural changes through the intersection of those ideas that are dominant with those that are oppositional.

Oppositional knowledge questions what is considered possible and what is considered impossible, what is considered desirable and what is considered undesirable. It injects criticism of assumed limits and it also provides a vision for what is outside "normal" practices. In some cases it takes the form of moral rebellion. It becomes both the basis and expression of a counterculture. For example, in a society where "patriotism" means being willing to use preemptive violence to defend the nation, connecting peacemaking with being patriotic produces an oppositional definition of citizenship (this is discussed in more depth in chapter 3).

HOW DOES OPPOSITIONAL KNOWLEDGE
RELATE TO SOCIETY?

Societies often produce familiar, authoritative conceptions of how the world does and should work. These conceptions are routinely applied to legitimate existing power relations and the policy agendas of the powerful (Gramsci 1971; Perry Anderson 1976; Raymond Williams 1982). For example, in the United States, when we talk about what it means to "be an American" we attach to that label a set of norms, values, and beliefs that shape our thinking, our behavior, and our understanding of who we are as a nation. Much of that social consensus shapes our lives in quiet and unassuming ways—so quiet that we may not even notice the influence. In times of crisis, however, the familiar cultural identity scripts rise to the surface of everyday discussion and action (Worth and Kuhling 2004). It is this cultural process that underpins social relations and policy formation. The production of oppositional knowledge is a response to this process of legitimization. Oppositional knowledge is created by individuals and organizations opposed to existing power relations and policies.[4]

FORMS OF OPPOSITIONAL KNOWLEDGE

We identify four types of oppositional knowledge. Two types describe "what is" and two describe "what could be." The first and perhaps most common type of oppositional knowledge is *counter-informative*, which aims to present the "untold story" and what is missing from the picture—what is not revealed. Information not otherwise available is offered to widen the discussion and possibly change the political assessment people make or the outcomes they desire. For example, providing evidence of disenfranchisement in those countries believed to be democracies to show that they have at best only partially achieved democracy is an instance of *counter-informative* knowledge. This oppositional view provides examples that show how the information available has been selectively offered and what other information should also be considered.

Another form of oppositional knowledge is *critical-interpretive*, which assesses the information that has been provided as accurate, but questions the moral or social basis for how that information is presented, interpreted, and used. It raises the questions "What is it all about, and what does it mean?" It presents an alternative interpretation of what the picture painted by the powerholders means. For example, accepting that democracy improves people's lives but challenging the idea that workable democracy can be successfully imposed by an outside force is an instance of critical-interpretive knowledge. Instead of simply providing alternative facts, a different perspective is articulated on the meaning of the information and on what is important.

A third type of oppositional knowledge is *radical-envisioning*, where what is regarded as the definitional root is made central in an attempt to change where society is headed. The goal is to raise what alternatives could and should look like if they are instituted. These instances tend to be forward looking and often rather optimistic about what is possible if the essence of the root can be revived. This approach paints a new picture that accounts for the knowledge and understanding exposed by *counter-informative* and *critical-interpretive* oppositional knowledge. An example would be encouraging people to think about the essence of democracy and what specifically makes it work, such as wide-based public participation. Oppositional knowledge of the *radical-envisioning* type might also argue for a global democratic polity where a community of nations would cooperate in the nonviolent, multilateral enforcement of international law. This approach asks us to consider what is at the root of democracy and how democracy would look if its original intent was reclaimed. For example, a popular chant among activists demonstrating for global justice is "This is what democracy looks like." This chant emerged during the 1999 antiglobalization protests in Seattle. The protesters were a historically diverse representation of contemporary social movements. The Seattle protests have come to be described as an example of true democracy in action (Jackie Smith 2001).

A fourth type of oppositional knowledge is *transformative.* In these instances, oppositional knowledge defines specific ways to achieve the alternatives that are envisioned by the movement. It shows how to paint a picture that embodies this alternative vision. For instance, transformative oppositional knowledge about democracy created by the PMOs included a range of recommended activities such as participating in electronic lobbying, signing e-petitions, joining street protests and street theater, participating in globally coordinated vigils, or taking action to disrupt congressional hearings. Since democracy is dynamic and responsive to the public voice, it only operates effectively when leaders acknowledge and respond to criticisms and concerns. The transformative approach lays out how to demand and achieve responsiveness from the powerholders.

Of course, these four types of oppositional knowledge might be intertwined in a statement or even in a single paragraph. Moreover, the four types build on each other in certain ways. *Counter-informative* knowledge provides *new* information that is not available as part of the dominant discourse in society. The *critical-interpretive* approach digs deeply into existing knowledge, raising critical thinking questions or analysis that often reinterprets the claims of the dominant discourse. And *radical-envisioning* knowledge goes beyond the question, what *does* it really look like? to ask, what *could* and *should* it look like? Meanwhile the transformative approach adds solution thinking to the envisioning process, clearly and convincingly showing how goals can be achieved. It is the four approaches working together in interlocking ways that make oppositional knowledge so powerful. This sort of knowledge combines the subversion of what is normative with the articulation of alternate ideological and strategic visions.

To offer up oppositional knowledge is to enter into a dialogue of ideas. Oppositional knowledge is deep-rooted in the vision of society as a collective where concepts and norms are developed through interaction, disagreement, and emergent consensus. Legally, in many societies oppositional thinking finds support in the constitutional protection for the freedom of speech. More generally, it is expressed as having a voice. We observe that it is in the discourse about what should be the normative framework for organizing society that the process of persuasion takes place.

Shifting the normative center of society is a slow and contentious process. Changing worldviews involves taking an oppositional stance against what those with power portray as the expected action. Radical pedagogy is central to creating a collective consensus willing to contravene establishment views. Social movements at their heart are about constantly educating the populace that there is additional information they have not heard, that there are options other than those commonly suggested, and that there is action that can be effectively taken by those who disagree with the status quo. The production and dissemination of alternative understandings and visions defines what we refer to as the creation of oppositional knowledge. To further develop the concept of oppositional knowledge we now examine in more detail PMO discourse around the concept of democracy.

DEMOCRACY AS A TWENTY-FIRST-CENTURY IDEAL

The definition of democracy is a critical twenty-first-century debate. National identity for the United States centers on its self-image as the deliverer and protector of democracy. The role of the United States in developing the large-scale use of democracy as a form of government is widely accepted domestically. However, whether the United States in its domestic practices and foreign policies embodies democratic principles is a point of contention for the peace movement organizations in our study. Our data reveals eight themes that together comprise the alternate analysis of democracy offered by PMOs. These themes depend upon *counter-informative, critical-interpretive, radical-envisioning,* and *transformative* approaches to shaping oppositional knowledge. They weave together an analysis that criticizes the established understandings of democracy, reclaims the concept, and optimistically portrays new possibilities.

COUNTER-INFORMATIVE OPPOSITIONAL KNOWLEDGE

The U.S. Government Represses Legitimate Dissent

Because states often practice social control rather than responding to the needs of citizens, government power is at times used to limit freedoms. This is

Table 1.1. Oppositional Knowledge

Type of Oppositional Knowledge	Key Words	What Understanding Is Added	Themes in PMO Democracy Discourse
Counter-informative	Declassify Expose hidden truths	What is missing from the picture	1) US government represses dissent 2) War weakens democracy 3) Democracy is a pretext for U.S. power plays
Critical-interpretive	Question the norms Redefine Provide context	Alternative interpretation of what the original picture means	4) Democracy cannot be forced upon others 5) The U.S. democracy project is in trouble at home and abroad
Radical-envisioning	Go to the root Get back to fundamentals Imagine alternatives	Paints a different picture	6) The power and promise of *true* democracy 7) Democracy should be rooted in broad-based political participation
Transformative	How social change can be realized	Explains how to paint the different picture	8) Democracy works when the public holds leaders accountable

quite familiar in totalitarian regimes, but PMOs aim to expand social awareness by pointing out that even the U.S. government at times acts to limit citizen power in order to protect the goals of its leadership. This information is offered in opposition to the familiar and often cited assumption that the United States is a completely open polity that protects the rights to freedom of speech and assembly. PMOs argue that national crises like war tend to increase political closure, thus limiting the freedom of expression. In discussing the war in Iraq in 2003, the Black Radical Congress (BRC)[5] said:

> Terrorism abroad has been accompanied by repression right here at home. This ruthless imperial thrust into Iraq is supplemented within the US by the neo fascist policies of Homeland Security as well as Patriot Acts I and II. These repressive laws roll back civil rights and civil liberties in the same way the US seeks to roll back the self-determination of the people of Iraq. (Black Radical Congress, March 20, 2003)

Like the BRC, other organizations in this study also argued that freedom to criticize the government, access to information, freedom of movement, and due process are suppressed when it serves the interests of the powerful. For example, the War Resisters League (WRL) argued that in wartime, powerholders narrow the space for dissent:

> We have experienced a small slice of the costs of war in the violation of our rights. On August 31, a day of direct action during the Republican National Convention in NYC more than 200 WRL identified activists as well as legal observers, journalists and bystanders near Ground Zero were illegally arrested. The War Resisters League plans to march again on November 3rd to assert our constitutional rights to free speech and assembly. (War Resisters League, November 3, 2004)

That such repression is not a characteristic of a healthy democracy was a message that the PMOs wanted to add to the public discourse. This helps explain why arguments against the USA PATRIOT Acts I and II (Uniting and Strengthening America by Providing Appropriate Tools Required to Intercept and Obstruct Terrorism)—which in many ways are domestic-focused—were commonly found woven among discussion of U.S. foreign policy.

War Weakens Democracies

According to the PMOs, the conditions that prevail during wartime typically do not enhance the democratic process either abroad or at home. For example, in March 1999 the bombings by NATO were negatively assessed in relation to the goal of eliminating authoritarian leadership in Serbia:

> The bombing has politically bolstered the repressive and unpopular Yugoslav President, Slobodan Milosevic, and reinforced his myth of the Serbs as a victimized and abused people. The Kosova Liberation Army (KLA), with its own vision

of an ethnic state, has also been fortified; while the democratic opposition in Serbia and the forces committed to nonviolence and pluralism in Kosova have all been undermined by the attacks. (Fellowship of Reconciliation, March 29, 1999)

Peace Action concurred that the NATO action had done "more harm than good" by rousing support for a regime that repressed the opposition (Peace Action, n.d., "Beyond the Bombs").

Moreover, the PMOs typically argued that powerholders decide to go to war despite popular opposition within the nation. To legitimate the decision, the populace is rallied to stand behind the commander in chief, and there is little patience for public or personal expressions of opposition. Reflecting on the onset of the Gulf War, WILPF (Women's International League for Peace and Freedom) wrote: "Within the United States, war fever has resulted in a chilling effect on public debate and dissent, the harassment of Arab-Americans by government agents and censorship of press reports" (Women's International League for Peace and Freedom, January 19, 1991).

Democracy Is a Pretext for U.S. Power Plays

In questioning the policies of the government, PMOs argued that the public is told one justification or cover story, but there is really another goal that remains hidden. Counter-information is provided by the PMOs to reveal the *real* motivations behind the policies. Moreover, the PMOs claimed that the idea of spreading democracy is often presented as one of these cover stories, typically for a wider imperialist agenda. The lofty goal of protecting or introducing democracy may also be a cover for something much more practical. For instance, Peace Action discussed the Gulf War as generated by a thirst for power over oil: "Now we are in a terrible mess. And the worst of it is, it's all for oil—to keep the supply plentiful and the cost of it low. . . . If imposing suffering on behalf of greed is right, what's left to be called wrong?" (Peace Action, August 24, 1990).

Or the policies of the leadership may be generally aimed at power consolidation and self-aggrandizing foreign policy, as the American Friends Service Committee suggested:

Today, the US has defied the will of the United Nations Security Council! Our diplomacy increasingly relies on acquiescence and threat. It is the noon of our arrogance. Members of the administration speak of our need for full-spectrum dominance and our militarism has risen to the point that relief organizations are labeled force enhancers and expected to report to the Pentagon. (American Friends Service Committee, March 27, 2003)

According to this presentation of U.S. policy, the government is hiding its aggression behind the popularity of democracy.

At times it may be in the interest of the state to use war to undermine popular resistance on seemingly unrelated issues. Peace groups raise awareness by exposing these actions for the public, deepening understanding of the situation. For example, during the Iraq War it was convenient for the national leadership to try to further weaken labor movements at home. As USLAW (United States Labor against the War) surmised, "He [George W. Bush] has proposed legislation that would enable him to suspend many union rights in the event of war. . . . His war against Iraq serves as a cover for a war against working people here at home. War will bring neither democracy to Iraq nor security to us" (United States Labor Against the War, "Why Labor Opposes War"). In a parallel move following the overthrow of Saddam Hussein, the U.S. government extended the dictatorial law prohibiting unions in Iraq.

CRITICAL-INTERPRETIVE OPPOSITIONAL KNOWLEDGE

Democracy Can Not be Forced upon Others

Critical-interpretive oppositional knowledge takes what powerholders say and delineates new and alternate meanings of their discourse. This kind of oppositional knowledge also interprets powerholders' intentions, presenting them with an edge of criticism. Oppositional groups ask, for example, what is behind the project of building new democracies around the world? Many of those supporting war argued that it is necessary to promote democracy abroad. While acknowledging the virtues of democracy as a system of governance, peace groups critically assessed that democracy cannot be pressed upon people. Moreover, in situations such as the Iraq War the critical-interpretive approach asks whether the military strategy is actually improving the Iraqis' quality of life and introducing democracy, as the powerholders claim.

PMOs recognize that democracy may vary from society to society. They stand behind the idea that democracy should be formulated from within a culture rather than imposed from outside. As the War Resisters League (WRL) argued in a statement released on March 21, 2003, "Every principle of democracy holds that regime change, whether in Iraq or in the United States, is the task of the people of that country, and not of any foreign power." Six months later, trying to help the general public critically assess the situation in Iraq, the American Friends Service Committee (AFSC) released the following statement from Peter Lems, their national representative for Iraq: "The central question remains: will Iraq be defined by military occupation and foreign control, or the emergence of a civil society guided by the Iraqi people?" (American Friends Service Committee, October 20, 2003). As Women's Action for New Directions (WAND) argued, "Democracy must have its source in the hearts and minds of the people involved. It cannot be forced through the barrel of a gun" (Women's Action for New Directions, May 20, 2004). The oppositional stance is clearly laid out for all to see: democracy is to be created by the people who are part of the nation, not by external factors. And when assistance is needed, the source for help should be the representative of the larger community of nations.

The U.S. Democracy Project Is in Trouble at Home and Abroad

The dominant discourse in the United States presents its government and people as authorities on the development and practice of democracy. Critical of this idea that the United States is a beacon to emerging democracies, the PMOs reinterpreted the U.S. democracy as failed or failing. They highlighted the shortcomings of the leadership and pointed out policies that contradict broad public participation. This theme surfaced in our data particularly after the start of the post-9/11 crusade to eliminate terrorism and terrorists. Civil liberties in the United States became a public issue with the passage of the USA PATRIOT Act. Debates around the validity of much of the "Patriot Act" emerged as the public questioned how much centralized oversight is appropriate in a democracy. For the PMOs this act raised two major issues, the first around treatment of people in the United States with Arab heritage, and the second regarding the protection of the constitutional right to dissent (see chapter 3 for further discussion).

A second flashpoint in the data concerned the decision to initiate the Iraq War. The PMOs frequently presented democracy as failed in light of the Bush administration's decision to ignore the popular majority that opposed military intervention, particularly after learning that there was no viable evidence of weapons of mass destruction in Iraq. As an example, consider the following statement from the online group, Moveon.org:

> President Bush believes he doesn't have to listen to the American public—which, even during war, has overwhelmingly been skeptical or strongly resistant to the idea of an American empire. He has decided that his faith in the military takes precedence over his faith in democracy. The election in 2004 is our chance to take our democracy back. (MoveOn.org, April 24, 2004)

Not only did this concern over democracy focus on what is happening in the United States, but it also considered the weaknesses of U.S. democracy projects abroad. This two-pronged attack suggested that the United States is hardly good enough at democracy itself to be offering advice abroad.

Classifying the U.S. attempts at democracy building as a failure, USLAW wrote about the situation in Iraq two months before the June 30, 2004, transition of power:

> Recent events demonstrate that [the] opposition is gaining support among ever wider sections of the population transcending religious and ethnic allegiances. US credibility is at an all-time low, both in Iraq and around the world. (United States Labor Against the War, April 30, 2004)

Several other PMOs shared this concern that it is neither appropriate nor possible for the United States to effectively create and mentor democracy projects abroad:

> The U.N. is equipped to build democracies; the United States government has neither the expertise nor the long-term political will to see such a process through. (Moveon, April 3, 2003)

CODEPINK challenged the claim by U.S. leaders that the attack on Iraq had improved the situation for women:

> the occupying authorities have failed to foster significant women's participation in the political process. . . . This speaks volumes to the lack of US commitment to hear the voices of Iraqi women. (CODEPINK, April 22, 2004)

And while commenting on assumptions about the value of the U.S. democracy project in Iraq, one group argued that "It [the U.S. war in Iraq] has brought neither liberation nor democracy, only death, torture, devastation and oppression" (New York City Labor Against the War, March 24, 2005). In these ways the peace groups confronted the normative assumptions about democracy driving U.S. foreign policy, and criticized them as inaccurate, counterproductive, and perhaps even dangerous.

RADICAL-ENVISIONING OPPOSITIONAL KNOWLEDGE

The Power and the Promise of True Democracy

Despite heavy criticism of the export of democracy, the statements indicate that democracy remains a significant ideal for the peace movement in the United States. The sticking point seems to be the failure to carry out democratic principles in good faith. The U.S. government is at times accused of bending those principles for self-serving purposes. While that is not acceptable to the PMOs, the premise that democracy is the preferred approach to social organization remains a mainstay, even within the peace movement. TrueMajority suggests that a different pathway to democracy is needed, but that the goal of democracy remains important: "We will attack world hunger and poverty as if our lives depend on it. Through compassion and generosity, we will reduce poverty and win over potential terrorists to the side of democracy and the rule of law" (TrueMajority, January 24, 2003). Furthermore, PMOs argue that even established democracies need vigilance to maintain democratic structures:

> The people of the world are watching and waiting to see how the government of the United States will respond to these acts of violence. Let us demonstrate that our strength is in our resolve to maintain a democratic and free society and to break with the cycles of violence and retribution. (Women's International League for Peace and Freedom, September 12, 2001)

Thus the peace movement acknowledges that democracy is not easy to achieve. It takes time and effort and a whole lot of compassion. But democracy is clearly embraced as an important route to achieving peace and justice.

Democracy Should Be Rooted in Broad-Based Political Participation

PMOs approached the concept of democracy by advocating for broad public participation as a core value in their vision of democracy. They redefined democracy as standing on the shoulders of compassionate, dedicated, involved citizens. The WILPF suggested that "concerned citizens" have a right and responsibility to go to the offices of their elected officials and "demand to know the position of your elected official regarding going to war with Iraq. Refuse to be brushed off. Let them know you will wait until a statement is made" (Women's International League for Peace and Freedom, Act Now, September 2002). Further evidence of PMOs advocating citizen action through providing oppositional thinking, is found below:

> Pax Christi begs all people of good will to scrutinize public policies as well as the actions of government and military leaders. In a democratic society such as ours, a government acts in the name of its citizens. No matter what actions are taken by other governments, we cannot, as a people committed to ethical and international standards, acquiesce in any military action that would compromise our moral integrity. Nor can we allow the winds of war ominously stirring in our land to silence the voice of moral responsibility required of peoples who pride themselves on the rights of citizen participation. (Pax Christi, August 22, 1990)

Speaking out to demand accountability was also encouraged when Peace Action[6] decried the move to war, saying:

> The American people demand that the US Congress live up to their constitutional responsibility. We demand answers to these questions. We demand that a full, open and informed debate on the use of US military force in the Persian Gulf be held before it is too late. (Peace Action, January 7, 1991)

TRANSFORMATIVE OPPOSITIONAL KNOWLEDGE

Democracy Works When the Public Holds Leaders Accountable

In this approach, the focus is on how to press for the will of the people to influence decisions by those who represent them. *Transformative* oppositional knowledge acknowledges the whole picture and shows how an active democratic citizenship matters. Building on the concept of a grassroots view of democracy, the PMOs push the idea that people must act to achieve their desired change. In other words, it isn't enough for citizens to make demands;

elected representatives must also respond positively to the will of the people for democracy to really exist.

CODEPINK rose to fame while resisting the Iraq War for their "pink slip" campaigns where leaders who they felt were failing to lead properly were confronted. In May 2004 they described participation in the "Fire Rumsfeld" campaign as "an example of CODEPINK's policy to 'speak truth to power.'" Typically the powerholders get to hand out the pink slips when workers become redundant, expensive, or otherwise problematic. In claiming the power to "pink slip" those in positions of power, CODEPINK turns to the premise of democracy that the power is among the people and those in power rule at the behest of the populace. In the same statement, CODEPINK urged people to demand accountability from government leaders, saying: "We encourage you to continue to be in the streets and speak to the outrageous behavior of those with power in this country" (May 7, 2004). In fact, just two and a half years later, Donald Rumsfeld's leadership over the U.S. strategy in Iraq ended when political pressures forced his resignation.

An imaginative action led by the Fellowship of Reconciliation (FOR) in opposition to the Gulf War shows that the PMOs provide concrete tactics for expressing one's opinion on foreign policy, even when not invited to do so. In 1991 FOR called on the public to send empty black plastic film canisters to the White House, labeled to represent oil barrels. They claimed that "the NO BLOOD FOR OIL campaign is designed to capture the imagination of U.S. citizens and our policy makers, and give the American people an opportunity to simply but effectively voice their opposition to U.S. military action in the Middle East" (Fellowship of Reconciliation, January 1991).

MoveOn, a cyberbased PMO, stressed the importance of speaking out and using the democratic process to demand changes to U.S. foreign policy. They worked to mobilize hundreds of thousands of people to sign petitions, write letters, conduct sit-ins, canvass their neighbors, and hold house parties, all in the interest of protesting the war in Iraq. In 2003 they argued: "It's Congress' duty to keep the President accountable. You can tell Congress to hold onto the $87 billion until the President changes his team and changes his course" (MoveOn, September 17, 2003). They insisted that transformation comes through the will of the people. That will needs to be made evident by voicing opposition.

METHODOLOGY OF THE STUDY

The data for our research consist of press and media releases, printed statements, editorials, and public calls to action from fifteen peace movement organizations, issued in the name of the organization as a whole (usually by the national office).[7] The data collected begin in August 1990, end in March 2005, and include 510 documents issued during five conflict periods. The collected statements were typically released to the mainstream media and/or posted to the organizations' websites. They not only represent the public face and voice of the social movement organization, but are arguably the best record of an organization's evolving official positions. Such statements provide a tangible representation of the organization's discourse and use of frames and as such can be effectively used in data analysis. They also create a partial but clear historical record of an organization's words and actions and demonstrate how these groups contribute to the discursive processes that create social knowledge and shape public policy. Just as important, the statements have the added benefit of not being subject to the vagaries of an individual's memory, or of the face-saving and after-the-fact reconstructions that often accompany later interviewing (Polletta and Amenta 2001).

The data set as a whole provides a unique collection of documents on the United States peace movement. The diversity and breadth of organizations represented, combined with the longitudinal nature of the data set, makes it an important contribution to the study of social movements. The inclusion of fifteen organizations and five conflict periods supports comparative analysis and interpretations that reveal the dynamic nature of peace movement discursive practices (see table 1.2). Conflict period one is the Gulf War with data from five national organizations and a total of 94 documents. Conflict period two is the 1998 bombing of Iraq; it includes seven organizations and 20 documents. The third conflict period is the 1999 bombing during the conflict over Kosova/o. This data set has 22 statements from six organizations. The next conflict period is the four months post-9/11 and it includes statements from nine groups for a total of 58 documents. The final conflict period is composed of data from the first two years of the Iraq War and covers fifteen groups and 316 documents. The data stretches across three presidential administrations encompassing both Republican and Democratic leaderships.

We found it was helpful to look closely at the interaction between the dominant discourse and the discourses of oppositional knowledge. To do this, we collected and coded White House transcripts of seventy-five statements issued by President George W. Bush. The statements focused upon (in chronological order) the events of 9/11, military intervention in Afghanistan, the USA PATRIOT Act, and progress in the war on terrorism. The speeches collectively embody the Bush administration's discourse in the months immediately following 9/11. The data allow for a more rigorous comparative analysis of document content compared to referencing relevant presidential speeches.

These publicly available PMO statements have the advantage of being easy to work with to produce conceptual analysis. In addition, the size of the data sets allows for greater generalizability of the findings. The five sets of organizational statements were issued during conflict periods that differed in terms of available political opportunities and national emotional climate, offering rich comparative opportunities.

Table 1.2. Peace Movement Organizational Data by Conflict Period

Conflict Period	Organizations Included
Gulf War	American Friends Service Committee*
	Fellowship of Reconciliation*
	Pax Christi*
	Peace Action*
	Women's International League for Peace and Freedom*
Iraq 1998	American Friends Service Committee
	Council on American-Islamic Relations
	Fellowship of Reconciliation
	Pax Christi
	Peace Action
	Women's International League for Peace and Freedom
	War Resisters League
Kosova/o	American Friends Service Committee
	Fellowship of Reconciliation
	Pax Christi
	Peace Action
	Women's International League for Peace and Freedom
	War Resisters League
9/11	American Friends Service Committee
	Black Radical Congress
	Council on American-Islamic Relations
	Fellowship of Reconciliation
	New York City Labor Against the War
	Pax Christi
	Peace Action
	Women's Action for New Directions
	Women's International League for Peace and Freedom
	War Resisters League
Iraq War	American Friends Service Committee
	Black Radical Congress
	Black Voices for Peace**
	Council on American-Islamic Relations
	CODEPINK
	Fellowship of Reconciliation
	MoveOn
	New York City Labor Against the War
	Pax Christi
	Peace Action
	TrueMajority
	United States Labor Against the War
	Women's Action for New Directions
	Women's International League for Peace and Freedom
	War Resisters League

* Obtained and used statements from this organization for each of the five conflict periods.
** Organization excluded from quantitative analyses due to small number of statements.

We suggest that social movement strategists, that is, those who monitor and respond discursively in resonant and potent ways to structural and cultural changes, are something like farmers. All successful farmers know that they not only have to monitor the weather but that they must also regularly test their soils. As the weather and the soil changes, so too must their tilling, planting, and fertilizing practices or they risk poor or unsustainable harvests. Similar principles also apply to social movement activists as they track cultural trends and monitor shifting structural conditions. One of the reasons why this dynamic relationship between structure, culture, and agency has been too seldom demonstrated empirically is because of the difficulty of collecting longitudinal data on the same social movement actors over many years and across multiple periods of contention. Our data set on the statements from five PMOs (American Friends Service Committee, Fellowship of Reconciliation, Peace Action, Pax Christi, Women's International League for Peace and Freedom) across five different conflict periods (Gulf War, Iraq 1998, Kosova/o, 9/11, Iraq War) over fifteen years (1990–2005) overcomes this difficulty. Whenever we present longitudinal analysis (across multiple conflict periods) in the following chapters, we base those findings only on the data drawn from the five organizations for which we have statements for all five conflict periods.

In our data analysis we used rigorous methods that combined the strength of weaving deductive and inductive thinking together as we moved through the phases of analysis. Additionally our research team combined quantitative and qualitative methodologies, allowing for triangulation at every phase of the data handling. Computer-assisted analysis eased the challenge of accurately analyzing rather large amounts of textual data.

The data-mining and analytical modeling program NVivo allowed us to work directly with each document. In NVivo, conventional (inductively based) coding is used to index the documents for ideas. The same codes were applied to all the data. The codes created a backbone for the analysis across and within organizations and conflict periods. The documents were also coded for various attributes defined by the researchers' knowledge of peace movement characteristics and by historical events. When the documents were fully coded they were queried for frequencies of codes. Files from NVivo can be exported to SPSS (directly) and to Stata (via Excel). These statistical packages were used to conduct descriptive statistical and regression analyses upon data weighted to control for variations in the amount of text produced by different organizations as well as across conflict periods (see appendix 2).

Our coding process involved a series of developmental analytical stages. Codes emerged inductively from the data and others were added from existing ideas in the literature. All three researchers participated in the coding process. To develop our initial coding strategy and promote consistency among coders, randomly chosen documents were coded by all three researchers and compared. Based on the resulting coding strategy, the data set was then split into three parts, and each document was coded by a primary coder who then sent it to be coded by a secondary coder. The secondary coder made suggestions for additions and deletions. The resulting dialogue between the researchers then established the final coding for each document. Since multiple rounds of coding are typical in content analysis, we believe our approach produces both reliable and verifiable coding that recognizes the conceptual richness of the documents.

OVERVIEW OF THE CHAPTERS

Each of the following chapters develops our analysis of how PMOs shape, hone, and change their messages about U.S. foreign policy. We show that the historical context in which the statements are released influences the production of oppositional knowledge. So does the organizational identity and the sort of audience the organization believes it might influence. Organizations vary their strategies. In times when dissent is less welcome they may emphasize building on dominant cultural themes. This strategy helps to keep them as cultural insiders. At times they aim to cut deeper, however, articulating a clear challenge as they work to "speak truth to power" by formulating a "truth" that counters the familiar, authoritative scripts for the situation.

Chapter 2 lays out the second theoretical framework used in the book. During times of war, the forces faced by the peace movement increase in intensity, particularly in the interplay between culture and politics. We rely on Antonio Gramsci's concept of "hegemony," which involves powerholders drawing on familiar, authoritative ideas to present issues in ways that benefit their policy agendas while also discouraging dissent. We explain in chapter 2 that when discursively engaging hegemony, social movement organizations (SMOs) have three primary options: they can challenge hegemony, harness hegemony, or employ some combination of the two approaches. Since it is such a fecund issue in all conflict periods, we use discourses around "supporting the troops" to introduce and explain in chapter 2 the three-part theoretical framework that we employ throughout the book.

"Supporting the troops" forms part of broader nationalist discourses. Chapter 3 takes an in-depth look at five nationalist ideas that have aided powerholders, not only in minimizing dissent to war, but also in generating high levels of popular opposition to peace movements. In turn, we examine both challenging and harnessing responses by U.S. peace movement organizations to each of these ideas. We find that the relative reliance upon these responses varied across conflict periods and between organizations. Collectively, PMOs were most likely to harness nationalism during the 9/11 period in the face of intense national pride. During the Iraq War period, more than other PMOs, the Council on American-Islamic Relations negotiated a stigmatized identity, attempted to blur identity boundaries, and used discursive opportunities to criticize the government for oppressing those identified as belonging to the group and living in other societies. Overall, our findings reveal adaptability in fashioning messages to take advantage of discursive opportunities as well as fidelity to core assumptions and beliefs. In the process, the U.S. peace movement has created a constructive form of patriotism.

Chapter 4 is focused on emotions and it proceeds along three lines of analysis. First, we discuss the trends present in the emotions discourse of the PMOs across the conflict periods. There we zero in on the presence or absence of emotional opportunities and how the movement responded to those shifting cultural conditions. Second, we analyze the ways that the PMOs constructed their discourse around the emotions of fear during the 9/11 and Iraq War periods. We show that they engaged the fear emotion on multiple levels. On the societal or macro level, the PMOs directly challenged the climate of fear. On the individual or micro level, they engaged the fear emotion by promoting the faculty of what we call "critical feeling," for example, counseling their members and the public about how to free the individual human heart from the tight grip of fear. Developing the faculty of critical feeling complements the critical thinking skills associated with oppositional knowledge creation and is a robust example of the important cultural roles played by movement organizations. Third, we analyze a movement cyberproject that promoted the public expression of emotions *other* than fear through the online posting of photographs directed toward the Iraqi people. We point out that this project was designed to enable Americans to break through the culture of fear by reclaiming both their emotional and their moral agency during war.

War and peace is sure to engage religion in manifold ways, as chapter 5 amply demonstrates. We first set the context for our analysis by discussing the influential role civil religion has historically played in the United States. Since George W. Bush has featured religious discourse heavily in his presidency, we focused this chapter on the two conflict periods associated with him: the 9/11 period and the first two years of the Iraq War. Following an overview of Bush's religiosity and a detailed analysis of his religious discourse, we show that he relied upon binary thinking and the repeated construction and demonization of a largely religious enemy. Our analysis of the PMO discourse reveals that the U.S. peace organizations had three primary responses. First, they directly challenged his reliance on binaries and his demonization of a broadly defined enemy. Second, they harnessed the president's use of religion and turned the power of these symbols against him and his policies. Third, many of the PMOs constructed oppositional knowledge by providing education about Islam. In addition, our quantitative analysis further reveals a close relationship between the peace movement's use of religious discourse and its identity-based talk. We also discovered a relationship between the movement's religious discourse and its support for extra-institutional, protest-based politics. Thus we argue that the movement's religious discourse was both strategic and expressive, meant to mobilize others even while providing avenues for authentic expression of deeply held beliefs.

In chapter 6 we take up questions about collective identity and its relationship to movement appeal and members' sense of belonging. Our focus is on four areas of identity: gender, race/ethnicity, class, and religion. Some of the organizations have collective identities that fit in these categories, and there we find regular use of identity to frame issues and (re)direct discourse. We also find that other PMOs make use of these four sources of identity. These instances are noticeably fewer, but still we find in general that the work of harnessing and challenging the dominant discourse and offering up oppositional knowledge often includes references to these categorical identities. Interestingly, a longitudinal analysis suggests that the "intersectionality" approach to understanding identity increased in later years. This suggests that not only was identity seen as an important vehicle for achieving resonance with bystanders, but the understanding and application of identity in movement discourse were increasingly complex and sophisticated.

Chapter 7 turns to a theme very prevalent since the attacks of 9/11: security. It is on the minds of people and a continuing issue in government and among political leaders. Our analysis uses a longitudinal lens to show that post-9/11 the theme of security also became markedly more common among PMOs. While taking up the issue might have been a reaction to the social environment, our analysis shows that the approach of the PMOs in addressing concerns about security was to focus on transforming the concept itself. Whereas governments often view security as protection from without, we find PMOs arguing that security is more likely to emerge from constructive global engagement. And that engagement, they argue, should be one that places human dignity and human rights as the central concern, even before national security. Security is a concept the PMOs harness from the dominant symbolic repertoire, and then they attempt to turn it on its head by transforming what it means, where it comes from, and who it includes.

Chapter 8 analyzes how the U.S. peace movement responds to the often contradictory logics of domestic and global contexts. The bulk of the findings make it clear that dismissing the impact of domestic cultures and polities upon social movements would be premature. The U.S. peace movement responds first and foremost to domestic considerations. Nonetheless, post-9/11 trends suggest that U.S. peace movement discourses will increasingly highlight global systems and their implications for conflict transformation. If these trends continue, we expect to see peace activists in the United States defining themselves more and more as part of a global polity that will obviate military intervention by creating a humane and just set of relations across borders.

The book concludes with chapter 9 where we explain ways that our two analytical frameworks should prove useful to peace activists as well as to social movements scholars. Like much else in the book, the chapter is meant to demonstrate the insights that both theory and practice offer one another.

NOTES

Much of the material presented in this chapter also appeared in Coy, Woehrle, and Maney 2008b. It appears as part of this book with the kind permission of the editors of *Sociological Research Online*.

1. Charles E. Morris and Sherry H. Browne's (2001) collection highlights especially the contributions of Leland M. Griffin and Robert S. Cathcart to developing theory and method for the study of social movement rhetoric.

2. Elizabeth Armstrong and Mary Bernstein (2008) offer a helpful discussion of the "multi-institutional" nature of what is often named as the dominant symbolic repertoire.

3. We elsewhere describe in more detail the feedback dynamics that may influence how and why certain movement discourses may come into common usage or fall out of usage over time (Coy, Woehrle, and Maney 2008a).

4. This discussion acknowledges only one part of Gramsci's framework. The other part focused upon the appropriation of oppositional knowledge by powerholders (Gramsci 1971).

5. See appendix 1 for detailed descriptions of the organizations included in this study.

6. At that time Peace Action was still called SANE/Freeze, but to avoid reader confusion we reference the group as Peace Action throughout the book

7. We have collected a large set of data. Although we utilize specific parts of that data set in different research projects, overall the data were collected, coded and analyzed in highly similar ways for our various publications. We, therefore, have written the methods sections of our different papers in similar ways. Consequently, some of the language in this methods section has also appeared in other publications (Coy, Maney, and Woehrle 2003; Coy, Woehrle, and Maney 2008a, 2008b; Maney, Woehrle, and Coy 2005; Coy, Maney, and Woehrle 2008).

2

To Harness or to Challenge Hegemony?

Peace Movements at a Cultural Crossroads

If those in charge of our society—politicians, corporate executives, and owners of press and television—can dominate our ideas, they will be secure in their power. They will not need soldiers patrolling the streets. We will control ourselves.

—Howard Zinn

One must speak for a struggle for a new culture, that is, for a new moral life that cannot but be intimately connected to a new intuition of life, until it becomes a new way of feeling and seeing reality.

—Antonio Gramsci

Most anyone who has ever announced to their family or to their surprised coworkers that they are going to take part in a protest demonstration has likely experienced reactions ranging from mild concern to disdain to active disapproval. Would-be protesters may be counseled that such actions are at best mostly meaningless wastes of time that seldom accomplish any policy changes. At worst, protesting is characterized as downright dangerous to one's health, reputation, and career. Such active, explicit attempts at persuasion are an important tool for cultivating acquiescence to the status quo and, therefore, limiting social protest. But indirect, implicit forms of persuasion are also omnipresent. Thus, perhaps the more interesting question is what day-to-day, hidden means of persuasion also convince people to accept things as they are, and not to collectively organize to change aspects of their lives that they wish could be very different?

THEORETICAL FOUNDATIONS

Hegemony is frequently thought of or defined as primarily having to do with domination in the international system through the projection of economic power and military might. People and places as far-flung as India, South Africa, the Philippines, Canada, Iraq, and Australia, for example, at one time or another came under the hegemonic influence of Great Britain. But such an understanding of hegemony tends to obscure important ingredients beyond the military and economic ones, namely deeply cultural components. The Italian social theorist Antonio Gramsci refers to cultural processes that aid in the reproduction of existing power relations and the maintenance of the status quo as hegemony (Gramsci 1971; Raymond Williams 1982; Carroll and Ratner 1994). Specifically, hegemony involves powerholders drawing upon a reservoir of familiar, authoritative ideas to frame issues in ways that are not only advantageous to their policy agendas but that also discourage dissent. For us, "powerholders" refers not only to government officials or those with influential positions in the policy establishment. We mean it in a much broader sense to include all those who occupy influential positions in society and who support and reproduce existing social and political relations. Similarly, our conceptualization of hegemony focuses upon the interplay between culture and politics. It is "cultural" in highlighting how widespread symbols, language, norms, values, and beliefs all contribute in interrelated ways to legitimate powerholders and their policies (Foucault 1980; Eley 1994). Yet it is also "political" in emphasizing the importance of power relations and political structures in shaping public discourse and policy preferences.

For example, when President George W. Bush claimed that those whom he calls Islamist extremists oppose democracy and hate "our" freedoms, he counterposed Muslim activists with two values—democracy and freedom—that are central to the identity of many living in the United States. These values are virtually beyond contesting in the U.S. political arena. The president framed the issue in such a way that openly working against his policies became more troublesome, both culturally and politically. Our approach to understanding hegemony in this book emphasizes the influence, control, and even domination that is cultivated and achieved through cultural processes and the conscious—or more commonly unconscious—consent that is the product of those cultural forces (Seidman 1998; Ku 2001).

THE CONTEXT OF THE
DOMINANT SYMBOLIC REPERTOIRE

When the president and other political actors invoke such terms as liberty, patriotism, democracy, equal opportunity, civil rights, or free enterprise, they are tapping into the persuasive capacities that have accrued over time to the ideas that these individual terms reference. Social theorists have many names for this phenomenon, including cultural tool kit (Swidler 1986), cultural themes and resonances (Ryan 1991; Gamson 1992a; Rohlinger 2002), and cultural reservoir (Tarrow 1992). These and other similar terms refer to enduring beliefs, images, narratives, and collective identities that are interactively created and circulating among the public. Within this vast symbolic repertoire, there exist discourses that, because of their frequent invocation by those with disproportionate access to and influence over the mass media, carry uncommon authority (Steinberg 1999; Ku 2001; Ferree 2003; Rhys Williams 2002). The widely and deeply resonant quality of these cultural materials reflects the extent to which they form part of taken-for-granted ways of thinking, writing, talking, and acting. These are the "social myths, language and symbols" that inform how people both understand the issues they care about and their opportunities for addressing them (Gaventa 1980, 15–16). Myths also obscure social issues by redirecting people's attention away from some issues and toward other problems and on to the "proper" solutions to those problems (Leatherman 2005, 3–27). With regard to social inequalities, for example, symbols and myths present the disadvantaged as responsible for their plight instead of as being worthy of sympathy (Loseke 1993).

Rhys Williams has variously used the term "cultural repertoire" (1995, 124–43) and "symbolic repertoire" (2002, 247–65). We use the term "dominant symbolic repertoire." This adds the qualifier "dominant" to indicate that there are cultural resources that occupy a particularly privileged position due to their frequent invocation by powerholders and by many others, and due to their widespread acceptance by the general public. The cultural resources that make up the dominant symbolic repertoire perform a constraining role insofar as it is difficult and sometimes unwise for challenging movements to attempt to operate completely outside of the dominant symbolic repertoire. To do so may compromise the cultural resonance of the movement's messages. On the other hand, challenging movements are far from completely constrained by the dominant symbolic repertoire, since it always remains available for appropriation and is vulnerable to challenges. They can reinterpret and refashion the meanings of elements in the dominant symbolic repertoire, thereby contributing to substantive cultural change in the process.[1] Insofar as powerholders and other political elites enjoy disproportionate access to mass media outlets, the mainstream media in the United States is not an equal opportunity venture. This fact, combined with the repeated and unquestioned use of the dominant symbolic repertoire by political elites, allows them to discursively link the state and their policies with cherished symbols as well as familiar, authoritative beliefs associated with these symbols. Opposing policies that are constructed and presented in this way is both difficult and demanding. Hegemony, therefore, provides powerholders with an advantage over social movements in mobilizing public support for their claims.

WAR AND THE DOMINANT SYMBOLIC REPERTOIRE

The institutionally advantaged position of symbols and ideas in the dominant symbolic repertoire makes their referencing almost second nature, particularly during crises, conflicts, and wars. During these historical moments when so much is uncertain and when ordinary people are often asked to risk so much, the dominant symbolic repertoire is the cupboard that gets opened first by policy makers; it is never bare and always well stocked. In addition, war itself offers an enormously powerful and potentially appealing symbolic terrain to all who are touched by it in any way (Hallin and Gitlin 1994). Songs, stories, and memorials that glorify past conflicts and wars and that valorize their participants become symbolic lenses for viewing a variety of collective public events as attacks on the nation. More ominously, they also serve as scripts for ethnocentrism and for responding violently to these perceived attacks (Coy and Woehrle 2000). Even just the prospect of war affects the interpretive and emotional climate; it generates negative ideas and strong emotions against the perceived enemy and positive feelings for the nation and the state (White 1970). This is essentially what the radical American social theorist Randolph Bourne meant when he opined on the eve of World War I that, for the state and its leaders, war is generally good.

> War is the health of the State. It automatically sets in motion throughout society those irresistible forces for uniformity, for passionate cooperation with the government in coercing into obedience the minority groups and individuals which lack the larger herd sense. . . . Loyalty—or mystic devotion to the State—becomes the major imagined human value. (quoted in Hansen and Bourne 1977)

In short, what we are calling the dominant symbolic repertoire becomes infused during protracted social conflicts and wars with an interpretive and emotional intensity that far exceeds its already considerable potency in times of normalcy.[2]

Long-standing beliefs in the dominant culture of the United States have aided political elites in minimizing domestic dissent to projections of military power, and to war itself. Many of these beliefs are associated with the armed forces. With regard to soldiers, for example, it is commonly believed that those who enlist in the armed services are selflessly serving the nation while protecting it from danger. In turn, soldiers who risk or sacrifice their lives on behalf of the nation and its ideals are seen as heroes worthy of the highest respect. Thus, the very image of the American soldier elicits a deep, positive emotional response in most U.S. citizens. Indeed, within popular culture, solidarity between the citizenry and "their" troops is central to the war experience (Hallin and Gitlin 1994). The perennially popular Hollywood war movie—with its intimate and often flattering portrayals of the GI—is only one manifestation of this social solidarity between the public and their troops. Policy elites have discursively exploited these emotions and other deeply potent beliefs to mobilize popular support for war and to delegitimate those who oppose war or militarism. During the Vietnam War, protest was equated with failure to support the troops, and protestors were marked as failing in their citizenship (DeBenedetti and Chatfield 1990; Huebner 2002; Fendrich 2003). During the Gulf War, war supporters were often characterized as "normal" and "typical" citizens while protestors were deviant rebels who were failing in their civic duty to rally round the flag (Allen et al. 1994; Kelman 1995).[3]

Nonetheless, our research shows that this discourse has not been confined to powerholders; the peace movement has engaged in discursive politics and talked back, using the "support the troops" mantra to their own ends, including to mobilize popular support against war policies. As Michel Foucault's study of power relations revealed, and as our research on the peace movement shows, there is always another side to the discursive coin. "We must make allowance for the complex and unstable process whereby discourse can be both an instrument and an effect of power, but also a hindrance, a stumbling-block, a point of resistance and a starting point for an opposing strategy" (Foucault 1980, 101). In other words, just as the U.S. government uses the symbolic power of the troops to marshal support for its wars, so too can a war's opponents use respect and concern for the troops' welfare as a rallying point for alternative policies, like the greater use of negotiation and the United Nations, increased

Photo 2.1. Peace march by Peace Action Wisconsin incorporates support for troops with war protest. (Photo by Lynne M. Woehrle)

multilateralism, adherence to international law and human rights, and troop withdrawals. Put more broadly, rather than rejecting the rhetoric and idea of supporting soldiers, PMOs discursively struggle over *how* best to support the troops, over *whose* policy proposals will best support them, and *whether* we ought to be concerned about supporting others beyond the troops—including civilian casualties, for instance (Coy, Woehrle, and Maney 2008a).

All of this, combined with the data presented in the following chapters, leads us to argue that when discursively engaging hegemony, social movement organizations (SMOs) have three primary options available: challenging hegemony, harnessing hegemony, or some combination of the two.[4] Each of these approaches employs frames, emotions, cognitions, and moral reasoning. Each of them is rooted in the agency of the movement activist and organization. The main distinction between them is their discursive positioning vis-à-vis the dominant symbolic repertoire.

Challenging Hegemony

On the one hand, SMOs can *challenge hegemony* through framing that contradicts the dominant symbolic repertoire (Roszak 1968; Raymond Williams 1977; Gamson 1992b). Challenging hegemony creates oppositional knowledge and sustains oppositional cultures (Carroll and Ratner 2001; Mansbridge 2001; Meyer, Whittier and Robnett 2002). While powerholders and their many allies tap into cultural predispositions and heightened emotions, hegemony challengers try to limit the resonance of elite discourses justifying war strategies and the domestic repression that normally accompanies war by calling into question the dominant symbolic repertoire. Challengers also try to decouple positive relationships between the dominant repertoire and the strong emotions of potential constituents.

As discussed in chapter 1, the belief that the United States is the world's greatest democracy is accepted uncritically by many Americans, and is a source of intense citizen pride. It also serves as a basis for the belief that the United States must bear the burden to export democracy to places such as the Middle East. A peace group that opted to challenge hegemony in this context might dispute the notion that the United States is a model democracy, citing low voter turnout rates, the corrupting influences of corporate contributions to election campaigns, and the disarray in vote counting that has marred many recent U.S. elections. They could argue that the United States first ought to attend to its own democratic shortcomings before exporting democracy, especially through military invasion. Antiwar framing like this that challenges hegemony counters not only specific prowar framing but also broader ideas from the dominant symbolic repertoire (like the democratic greatness of the United States) that give these frames their potency. Taken-for-granted beliefs are rejected, deference to the state is questioned, and traditions even give way to new rituals celebrating resistance.

Let's make this even more concrete. Every Labor Day weekend in Cleveland, Ohio, a large military air show is mounted from a downtown airport along the shores of Lake Erie. Many thousands of people typically turn out to witness the acrobatics of military jet fighters, to tour and even play on military equipment stationed along the lakefront, and to talk to armed services personnel. The event is particularly popular with families who picnic, play, tour, and simply make the day of it along the downtown lakefront. The peace community in Cleveland pickets this event with signs and banners which say such things as "fighter jets are not for entertainment," "tanks are not toys," "being bombed is not fun," and "war is not healthy for children and their families."

While they are often guilty of being overly optimistic, hegemony challengers generally are not foolish: they usually don't go up against deeply held cultural beliefs without having something else to offer or to rely upon. Consequently, in addition to the protests, the Cleveland peace community mounts an alternative "peace fair" at an adjacent park. Challengers typically draw upon existing oppositional knowledge to appeal to those belonging to social networks active in or sympathetic to the movement (Meyer and Staggenborg 1996; Coy and Woehrle 1996; Carroll and Ratner 2001; Mansbridge 2001). Thus, at the alternative peace fair participants might learn about values-based projects like using Lake Erie for sustainable wind power while a local organic community-supported farm distributes packets of organic seeds of native plants and wildflowers. Encouraging peace fair attendees to plant and nurture a wide variety of sustainable seeds of peace (from wind power to native prairie plants) rather than supporting unsustainable budget levels for the Pentagon is an example of including oppositional values and beliefs as part of a challenge to hegemony.

Although challenging hegemony is reactive in the sense that challengers are responding directly to the dominant symbolic repertoire, it is also proactive (Ferree and Miller 1985) due to its creation and maintenance of alternative practices and oppositional knowledge, as in the example above. However unlikely it may seem in the short run, challenging hegemony therefore holds out the possibility of substantive, long-range change as it attacks existing systems of thinking and being while proposing and building support for radically different alternatives (Ferree 2003). In the debate over war, challenging hegemony involves directly rejecting militarism, the nationalist identities associated with war policies (Hackett and Zhao 1994), and the legitimacy of some emotions like nationalistic pride. It also requires making explicit the implicit beliefs and hidden values that undergird war polices and then discarding them as misguided, undesirable, or irrelevant (e.g., as in saying that the United States would be better off being proud of its sustainable wind power systems than of its unsustainable military weapons systems). Those using this approach must climb a steep hill to achieve mass persuasion. That is why social movement activists frequently take a less strenuous approach, what we call harnessing hegemony.

Harnessing Hegemony

While discourse is a medium for hegemony, and while hegemony does restrict and structure discourse, it is always a matter of degree, thanks in part to the nature of discourse (Blain 1989; Melucci 1989). Discourse is multivocal. Its meaning, therefore, is inherently unstable (Steinberg 1999); it is always open to multiple meanings and interpretations that are socially situated and interactively constructed, even within a hegemonic context (Melucci 1996). Foucault (1980) referred to this phenomenon as the rule of the tactical polyvalence of discourses. Put more simply, the dominant symbolic repertoire becomes a social field where meaning is strategically constructed by various actors, yet it always remains vulnerable to interpretive contests, its strategic origins notwithstanding.

Consequently, SMOs can do more than directly challenge hegemony. They can also draw from the same reservoir of cultural materials that structure elite discourse, only this time to fashion alternative meanings that are potentially persuasive precisely because they have broad cultural resonance, even while they also support oppositional claims (Ferree and Miller 1985; Swidler 1986; Tarrow 1992; Nagel 1994; Hackett and Zhao 1994). We refer to this process of appropriation and recombination of dimensions of the dominant symbolic repertoire by movement organizations as *harnessing hegemony*.[5] The interactive dynamics of harnessing hegemony can be usefully compared to those of jiu-jitsu.

Richard Gregg (1935/1966) was the first nonviolence theorist to apply the principles of physical jiu-jitsu to the realm of ideas and morals. "The nonviolence and goodwill of the victim act in the same way that the lack of physical opposition by the user of physical jiu-jitsu does, causing the attacker to lose his moral balance. . . . He plunges forward . . . into a new world of values" (1966, 44). Gregg was concerned with the moral and practical superiority of nonviolence over physical violence, and so he called this "moral jiu-jitsu." Since we are focused on the arena of persuasive competition, we think that the harnessing hegemony dynamic present in this context is better thought of as "ideational jiu-jitsu." In other words, rather than trying to block the considerable weight and cultural resonance of ideas from the dominant symbolic repertoire, activists embrace and use this weight, going along with its momentum and flow, even while redirecting it and eventually turning it to the movement's advantage. If a peace activist wants to challenge and disengage a prominent trope in the dominant symbolic repertoire used to justify war, like patriotism, for example, she might argue that patriotism is destructive, dangerous, and should be rejected. On the other hand, if it seems more effective to harness the language and value of patriotism rather than to try and stand against its considerable cultural power, the activist could argue that dissenting from war and working nonviolently for peace is actually deeply patriotic. She would contest the meaning and definition of patriotism, harnessing patriotism as a persuasive force for peace, rather than challenging patriotism itself.

Like challenging hegemony, harnessing hegemony increases the horizon of potential successful outcomes for oppositional movements. One difference, however, is the route by which change is affected. For example, in the dialogic framing around the partial birth abortion policy debate in the United States, abortion rights activists failed to enact a new law, but effectively changed the social meaning of key abortion-related terms through what we are calling the harnessing dynamic, thereby influencing the ongoing policy debate (Esacove 2004). Likewise, the nuclear weapons freeze movement of the 1980s was able to shape policy discourse and redefine the meaning of key terms like "security" because organizers harnessed security concerns rather than rejecting them outright (Cortright 1991). While the peace movement may fail to stop a war, it still might alter in important and lasting ways the meaning of terms in the dominant symbolic repertoire that it effectively harnessed, such as "patriotism," "democracy," and "heroism." While harnessing hegemony appears to be practical and effective, it nonetheless poses both strategic and affective dilemmas for peace activists.

Dilemmas in Challenging and Harnessing Hegemony

Making clear the distinctions between challenging and harnessing highlights discursive dilemmas that strengthened hegemony poses for peace activists. By attaching different meanings to the same symbols and language that supporters of war regularly reference, harnessing hegemony risks confusing and demobilizing potential constituents who may become unsure of whom to believe (Gamson et al. 1992; Rohlinger 2002). Moreover, harnessing hegemony may inadvertently fuel hegemony by increasing the potency of symbols, language, and beliefs inextricably linked in the popular psyche with existing social relations (Ku 2001; Ryan 1991).

Another concern is that activists appropriating ideas from the dominant symbolic repertoire might find their demands diluted to the point that "winning" changes very little. In addition, activists who harness hegemony are vulnerable to allegations of co-optation (Benford 1993; Coles 1999; Tarrow 1992). Favorably referencing the dominant symbolic repertoire can easily upset traditional movement constituencies who assume that its elements are rigidly connected to power structures such that their use perpetuates undesirable mentalities and social practices. Those belonging to minority groups may especially perceive attempts to harness hegemonic and stereotypical representations of their groups as perpetuating their oppression.

On the other hand, challenging ideas from the dominant symbolic repertoire can invite incomprehension, ridicule, dismissal, and active opposition from policymakers and the general public. Statements that directly criticize hegemonic images of being "American" won't have broad appeal and are unlikely to gain new participants for the movement. Finally, even if oppositional knowledge is widely embraced, powerholders can co-opt and rework it to legitimate their policies, in effect, harnessing oppositional knowledge (Coy and Hedeen 2005; Naples 2002).

HYBRIDIZED APPROACHES TO ENGAGING HEGEMONY

Combining these strategic dilemmas with the multivocal and contradictory nature of most discourse, it is more fruitful to view these framing options as part of a continuum rather than as dichotomies. Both intentionally and unintentionally, for both affective and strategic reasons, activists often fashion variegated messages that appropriate materials from both the dominant symbolic repertoire and oppositional knowledge (Coy and Woehrle 1996). Indeed, in their analysis of the frames used by the women's suffrage movement in the United States, Hewitt and McCammon (2004) found that one of the key determinants of a frame's mobilizing capacity was the inclusion of both dominant and oppositional messages. In our data, this hybrid or combination approach is often taken by a PMO such that while one of its statements primarily (although seldom exclusively) challenges hegemony, another will primarily harness hegemony. Even more common are organizational statements that move back and forth between harnessing and challenging hegemony within the same statement, sometimes even within the same paragraph. Whether challenging hegemony, harnessing it, or combining the two approaches, social movement discourse and framing is partly a form of cognitive and affective praxis where movement actions, emotions, values, frames, and counterframes help to create dynamic, interactive spaces marked by interpretive tensions (Eyerman and Jamison 1991). As movements discursively interact with tradition, with opponents, with policymakers, and amongst themselves, they also create the four forms of "oppositional knowledge" described in chapter 1. This knowledge can then be applied in other—both current and future—arenas of framing politics.

In order to make the theoretical structure we have introduced in this chapter more concrete, we apply in the following section the challenging and harnessing hegemony framework to statements in our data having to do with one of the most ubiquitous and well-developed discourses associated with war and peace issues: the "support the troops" issue.

"Support the Troops" and Challenging Hegemony

During times of war, soldiers are deployed as weapons not only on the military battlefield, but also in the domestic policy arena and within the battle for public opinion. To mobilize support for war and to control dissent once soldiers have been deployed, U.S. political elites draw upon deeply engrained values, beliefs, and narratives regarding soldiering and the citizen's duty to support the troops. As mentioned earlier, military service has generally been valorized as the definitive demonstration of citizenship: the most heroic, the most dangerous, and the most selfless (Tickner 1992; Shapiro 1994; Snyder 1999; Coy, Woehrle, and Maney 2008a). Those serving in the U.S. armed forces are held in the highest regard and deemed to be deserving of uncritical respect. In such a context, challenging the dominant image of the good soldier—whose well-being ought to be uppermost in any patriot's mind—is a relatively dangerous discursive task for an oppositional group, particularly during war. That is why many peace groups consistently tried to make distinctions between the troops and those actually in charge of policy, as United States Labor Against the War promised to do on the eve of the Iraq War.

> As citizens and as trade unionists, we intend to participate vigorously in the debate about this war while also making a clear distinction between those policies and leaders who dragged us into it and the young men and women in our military who are being sent to do the fighting by those leaders. (United States Labor Against the War, March 19, 2003)

Even though it was more common for the groups in our study to harness the dominant discourse that soldiers should be viewed in a positive light or at least temper their statements with positive references, some groups offered a direct challenge to the image of the good soldier. This approach was most popular during the earliest days of the occupation of Iraq and also when the sexual torture of Iraqi prisoners at Abu Ghraib was revealed. The women's group CODEPINK clearly challenged hegemony in the passage below. In fact, they took the somewhat unusual approach of directly juxtaposing the lives of American soldiers with those of Iraqi civilians, pointedly telling the U.S. public what it is that they really ought to be concerned about: the lives of Iraqi civilians: "The Americans who are wondering how many Americans are being killed in Iraq, should be asking how many civilian Iraqis are being killed" (CODEPINK, November 19, 2003).

Another way that the PMOs challenged hegemony around the support the troops issue during the Iraq War had to do with criticizing how the troops interacted with Iraqi citizens, as in the passage below from the Fellowship of Reconciliation.

> Nermin tells of the neighbor who worked for the government. He thought he would be taken in for questioning so he packed a small bag that included some clothes and his medicine and sat and waited, the door unlocked. When the troops came they broke down the door (despite his calling out, "The door is unlocked, please come in."). He was roughed up, shackled, a sack tied over his head, and

led away. The family does not know where he is or how he is doing. (Fellowship of Reconciliation, November 21, 2003)

Support the Troops and Harnessing Hegemony

When it comes to discussing U.S. troops in times of war, the peace groups in our study overwhelmingly chose a less controversial and therefore less risky approach: that of harnessing hegemony rather than challenging it. In fact, the troops-related discourse of the peace movement organizations included in our analysis challenged hegemony only 6 percent of the time and harnessed hegemony 94 percent of the time! The two conflict periods where discourse about the troops was most prevalent were the Gulf War and the Iraq War. Five organizations issued statements in both of these conflict periods (AFSC, FOR, Pax Christi, Peace Action, and WILPF). We found three troops-related discursive practices. The first one, which we coded as troops-negative (i.e., passages that criticized soldiers), is associated with challenging hegemony. The second and third codes, troops-positive (i.e., passages that positively portrayed and supported soldiers) and troops-betrayed (i.e., passages that criticized the U.S. government for betraying the troops in various ways), are associated with harnessing hegemony.

The simplest way to harness hegemony within the confines of the support the troops discourse is for a peace group to say what New York City Labor Against the War (NYCLAW) said so directly here: "This antiwar movement offers the only way to support troops: bring them home! Right now!" (New York City Labor Against the War, March 17, 2003).

More often, the PMO harnessed the widespread sentiment for supporting the troops and coupled it to a more extended critique of government policies, as Peace Action did below. Here the group argued that the best way to support the troops is to cease fighting what they criticized as a war of aggression waged in a clearly illegal manner by the president.

> In committing our troops to fight a war of aggression, outside the rule of law, Bush has, in an act of malfeasance, put US troops at risk unnecessarily. We believe the best way to support our troops is to bring them home now and pursue the alternatives to war that other nations and world leaders still believe are possible. (Peace Action, March 20, 2003)

Peace groups also harnessed the power of widespread concern for U.S. troops to raise questions about continuing social inequalities, including the "poverty draft," as FOR did in this example:

> The Persian Gulf crisis impacts disproportionately on the poor, and on racial and ethnic minorities. In the Persian Gulf and here in the U.S., the poor and ethnic minorities are overrepresented in military forces. It is they who will suffer the greatest casualties and pay the greatest direct and indirect price. (Fellowship of Reconciliation, August 30, 1990)

Support the Troops and
Hybridized Approaches to Engaging Hegemony

Challenging and harnessing hegemony are not dichotomous choices. As PMOs respond to current political and cultural realities, and as they fashion messages accordingly, they move back and forth within these approaches, coupling them in various combinations and recombinations. The hegemonic power associated with concerns for the health and well-being of U.S. troops was even considered strong enough to overcome the traditional objectification of the enemy that occurs during war (Keen 1986). Thus a common approach by the peace groups in our data was to try to expand the web of concern beyond just the U.S. troops to include as well civilian casualties among the "enemy" population, as in this example from the Gulf War (Coy, Woehrle, and Maney 2008a).

> If the bellicose call for war is obeyed and only the echo remains, we will be left holding in our hand the mutilated bodies of Arab women and children, of teen-aged boys and girls from United States, of reservists who are fathers and mothers of young families. No amount of rhetoric and rationalizing will restore a single life or compensate for the agony of those left maimed, those left widowed and orphaned, homeless and destitute. (Pax Christi, November 29, 1990)

CONCLUSION

As peace movements attempt to mobilize their memberships and attract new participants during wars and political crises, they face formidable challenges. These obstacles push peace movement organizations to become more thoughtful, less impulsive, and more strategic while also adhering assiduously to long-standing ideologies. The interpretive frameworks we have presented in these first two chapters—the four forms of oppositional knowledge, and the harnessing and challenging hegemony continuum—prove helpful in sorting out and making analytical sense of the wide range of peace movement discourses developed across fifteen different organizations and five different conflict periods. In the next chapter, we pay further attention to the issues associated with nationalism and patriotism, two central concerns for the U.S. peace movement during times of war.

NOTES

1. Marc Steinberg (1999) also uses the concept of a repertoire. Like Steinberg, we believe that repertoires are developed through processes of discursive contention. The co-optation of oppositional knowledge by powerholders contributes to the wide and deep resonance of ideas within the dominant symbolic repertoire (Ku 2001). We also agree that this resonance encourages activists to draw upon the repertoire in their framing. Unlike Steinberg, however, we do not believe that

the concept of a repertoire should replace the concept of collective action frames (Ferree 2003; Maney, Woehrle, and Coy 2005). Rather we believe it more useful to recognize that the dominant symbolic repertoire provides familiar and authoritative reference points that those who are framing draw upon in various combinations. Both the usage and authority of ideas in a symbolic repertoire precede contemporary framing.

2. A compelling and disturbing cross-cultural documentation of how dominant symbolic repertoires become infused with interpretive and emotional intensity in times of war can be found in Sam Keen, *Faces of the Enemy: Reflections of the Hostile Imagination* (1986). Keen's visual sociological analysis is based on the propaganda posters and other visual images used by many different countries to foster enmity toward their respective "enemies."

3. Much of this paragraph and the next sentence is taken from Coy, Woehrle, and Maney 2008a.

4. The explanation of our theoretical framework for understanding how the dynamics of hegemony intersects with social movement discourse draws directly from and then builds upon some of our other publications, including Coy, Maney, and Woehrle 2003; Coy, Woehrle, and Maney 2008a; Maney, Woehrle, and Coy 2008; and especially Maney, Woehrle, and Coy 2005.

5. Of course, the discourse of social movements is no less multivocal and intersubjective in its meaning creation than is that of elites (Steinberg 1999). Although a social movement organization may strategically employ a discourse, its meanings cannot be completely scripted or contained by the organization, due to the situated, interactive nature of discourse.

3

Reconstructing Patriotism

> I should like to be able to love my country and still love justice. I don't want any greatness for it, particularly a greatness born of blood and falsehood. I want to keep it alive by keeping justice alive.
>
> —Albert Camus

Nations emerge due to the coalescing of a variety of forces and factors, ranging from the relatively concrete (e.g., a shared language; geographical features and constraints) to the more historically contingent and socially constructed (e.g., the antecedents of war; the formation of collective identity; the use of myths, memories, and symbols). When these factors are considered together we see that nations are "imagined" into existence in a variety of ways, including through discourse and narratives. As a "cultural artifact" the nation and the nationalisms associated with it elicit deep emotional responses, inspiring love and self-sacrifice in significant measures (Benedict Anderson 1991).

More broadly, nationalism is also a way of thinking, a kind of consciousness that perpetuates the notion that the nation-state is a normal, natural, and preferable way to order political and cultural affairs (Billig 1995). Five nationalist ideas within the dominant symbolic repertoire of the United States have aided powerholders in government and beyond not only in minimizing dissent to war, but also in generating high levels of popular opposition to peace movements: (1) the nation and the state are synonymous; (2) the state protects the nation from danger; (3) as "the greatest country on earth," the United States has a special responsibility to spread freedom, democracy, and prosperity throughout the world; (4) the loyalties of racial and ethnic minority groups to the nation are suspect; and (5) a patriot defends and does not question the state.

41

Taken together, these nationalist assumptions mean that precious little room exists for a calm discussion of the merits and costs of war. As a result, policy decisions that are very much matters of life, liberty, and death are not informed by the democratic debate that their significance warrants. This is the cultural and political context peace activists in the United States often face. This chapter examines the peace movement's engagement with the dominant nationalist discourse as part of its attempts to create dialogue and initiate policy change. At times the peace groups challenged dominant nationalist assumptions head-on. In other instances, they harnessed them. Reflecting both the depth of socialization into the dominant nationalist discourse as well as the strategic dilemmas that responding to hegemony presents, all groups both challenged and harnessed nationalism as a facet of hegemony (sometimes even within the same statement). Table 3.1 summarizes frequently recurring responses by the peace movement to the five assumptions mentioned above. In what follows, we will first explain each of these five nationalist assumptions, then describe the ways the peace movement challenged that assumption, followed by how they harnessed it.

PEACE MOVEMENT RESPONSES TO DOMINANT NATIONALIST ASSUMPTIONS

Nationalist Assumption #1:
The Nation and the State Are Synonymous

As the term "nation-state" suggests, the government is widely viewed as synonymous with the nation. The equating of nation and state is connected to the ideology of the Republic, where citizenship is defined through participation in public life (Flynn 2000). Since elected officials presumably make decisions that reflect their constituents' wishes, a belief in representative democracy adds legitimacy to the formulation. Because of the conflation of nation and

Table 3.1.   Peace Movement Response to Dominant Nationalist Assumptions

Dominant Assumptions	Challenging Assumptions	Harnessing Assumptions
The Nation is synonymous with the State	The State is *not* the Nation	Democratic accountability
The State protects the Nation	The State endangers the Nation	Measured response as test of a great Nation
A bastion of freedom	An oppressive empire	First among equals
The enemy within	Ethnic minorities are scapegoats	Defending the Nation's liberty
Love it or leave it	Americans should be ashamed	Promoting peace is patriotic

state, policies propagated by the state are viewed as the will of the people. Opposing the state's policies is tantamount to opposing the nation itself. On the other hand, when political powerholders discursively equate the nation with the state, their calls for war are likely to elicit a positive response from the general public. In fact, all five of the highest approval ratings ever received by a U.S. president in Gallup's polls were associated with the early stages of major wars. George W. Bush's approval rating shot up from 51 percent on September 11, 2001, to 89 percent on September 22, 2001, the second-highest approval rating in U.S. history. While the average bump in approval ratings from the "rally around the flag effect" is historically about 11 percent, in the immediate post-9/11 period President Bush enjoyed a whopping 38 percent increase. The belief that the nation and the state are synonymous is so pervasive in how Americans write, talk, and think about their national identity that even oppositional peace groups are no exception. All fifteen organizations at least once equated nation and state. Nonetheless, several of these same PMOs challenged this assumption by decoupling the nation from the state.

Challenging Nationalism: The State *is* Not *the Nation*

Due to its strategic focus upon electoral and legislative change, MoveOn frequently juxtaposed the Bush administration with a nation opposed to its policies: "President Bush believes he doesn't have to listen to the American public—which, even during war, has overwhelmingly been skeptical or strongly resistant to the idea of an American empire. . . . The election in 2004 is our chance to take our democracy back" (MoveOn, April 24, 2003).

Trying to protect civilians during war, Pax Christi delinked the nation from the state during two different conflict periods, including Kosova/o: "Just response to aggression must also be discriminate. It must be directed against unjust aggressors, not against innocent people. As the international community seeks to hold the Yugoslav government accountable, it must not hold the Serbian population hostage" (Pax Christi, July 30, 1999). Shortly after 9/11, Pax Christi also used a similar argument to narrow the scope of who is considered an enemy of the American nation, at the same time calling for protection of civilians in the Middle East:

> Right now across the Islamic world, innocent people are living in terror, wondering what President Bush may do to them. The President says, "We shall make no distinctions between the terrorist and countries that harbor them." Shall a whole country be condemned for the actions of its leaders? (Pax Christi, September 26, 2001).

In part because nationalist assumptions are so heavily reinforced during war, peace activists also chose to harness the assumptions instead of, or in combination with, challenging them.

Harnessing Nationalism: Democratic Accountability

The assumption that the state is synonymous with the nation is predicated upon another—that the United States is a representative democracy, where government officials are held accountable to the rule of law. If officials violate the law, mislead the people, or enact policies that contravene the people's will, they should be replaced. Violations of these tenets of representative democracy provide discursive opportunities for social movements to mobilize opposition.

The Fellowship of Reconciliation, Pax Christi, and Peace Action each insisted that the Bush administration receive congressional approval before using military force in the Persian Gulf. In a legislative alert, Peace Action stated: "Whether or not the U.S. goes to war in the Persian Gulf is not a decision to be left to one man. Our Constitution makes this the responsibility of Congress, not the President" (Peace Action, late 1990). By appealing to the U.S. Constitution—a sacred text and founding myth in the American civil religion—these statements harness a core assumption in the dominant nationalist discourse (for more on civil religion in the United States, see chapter 5). A decade later, Peace Action again demanded congressional oversight:

> The resolution authorizing the President to use force against those responsible for the September 11, 2001 attacks does not extend to a war on Iraq. Congress must hold hearings and vote on any potential war with Iraq or any other country. It's our job to hold Congress accountable to its own duties and to the growing voice of America's conscience. (Peace Action, "911 Growing Voice" n.d.)

By framing their opposition to war in terms of demanding adherence to the Constitution, peace activists presented themselves as citizen protectors of the democracy that empowers the nation (see also chapter 1). They also did this by highlighting government deception. After no weapons of mass destruction were discovered in Iraq, groups like MoveOn.org demanded a full investigation: "A President may make no more important decision than whether or not to take a country to war. If Bush and his officials deceived the American public to create support for the Iraq war, they need to be held accountable" (MoveOn, June 16, 2003). In addition to demanding Congressional hearings, MoveOn notified its virtual members of a "Claim vs. Fact database" created by the Center for American Progress. MoveOn reported that the database contains "statements from conservatives like President Bush, Vice President Cheney, members of Congress and Fox News personalities and compares those statements to the facts." MoveOn also placed a television ad that showed a polygraph blipping every time the president made a statement. The campaign culminated in a petition signed by more than 500,000 members calling upon Congress to "censure President Bush for misleading us into war" (MoveOn, February 18, 2004).

Peace groups also portrayed the decision to go to war as undermining democracy by contravening the expressed wishes of the American people. During the Iraq War build-up, Peace Action stated:

> In a country where only half of eligible citizens exercise their vote, the reluctance of Congress members to listen to their constituents will continue to disengage and disenfranchise potentially active citizens. This is Congress' opportunity to re-engage Americans by empowering our democratic system rather than neglecting it. (Peace Action, September 2002)

By equating their policy positions with the will of the people, peace groups presented themselves as defending the nation against the tyranny of the state.

Nationalism may even be harnessed to generate support for revolutionary change, as the War Resisters League did by referencing a core national myth:

> If we accept this analysis of the non-representative nature of our government, then our nation's own heritage tells us what we must do. We read in the Declaration of Independence of governments "deriving their just powers from the consent of the governed"; and "whenever any Form of Government becomes destructive of these ends, it is the Right of the People to alter or to abolish it, and to institute new Government" (War Resisters League, October 3, 2003).

By harnessing the assumption that the United States should be a representative democracy, WRL severed the cord between the nation and the state. In the process, defending the nation from tyranny logically requires withholding consent from an undemocratic state.

Nationalist Assumption #2: The State is the Defender of the Nation

Powerholders use the equating of the nation and state to legitimate both domestic and foreign policy agendas. Other aspects of the dominant symbolic repertoire make dissent against foreign policy decisions especially problematic. Within an anarchic international system, it is widely assumed that one of the primary roles of the state is to protect the nation and its citizens from external threats to their physical well-being (see chapter 7). From this perspective, war becomes a fight for the nation's very survival. Support for the state becomes the primary duty of every citizen who shares the fate of the nation. Conversely, by exposing the nation to harm and danger during its time of greatest need, resistance to war constitutes a grave betrayal of the nation and even suggests an abrogation of citizenship. Peace groups responded to this facet of the dominant nationalist discourse in two very different ways. We now offer examples of both approaches, starting with challenging responses.

Challenging Nationalism: The State Endangers the Nation

The realpolitik assumption that the State must use organized violence to protect its citizens often leads to the summary dismissal of peace activist claims as unrealistic. Peace groups challenged this assumption by arguing that State policies threaten the safety of the nation. This challenge was made repeatedly after September 11th in response to the "war on terrorism" discourse. Two weeks after 9/11, Pax Christi warned:

> In this climate of international disorder, where the most powerful can act with impunity, it should not surprise us that some among the disenfranchised will strike back in any way that is possible. . . . As long as the strong can lord their power over the weak, terrorism will continue to grow. (Pax Christi, September 25, 2001)

With the mainstream media presenting armed conflicts as if they occur in a historical and political vacuum, peace groups recognized that only through the production of *critical-interpretive* oppositional knowledge could they convince readers that the State's war fuels terrorism and endangers the nation. Black Voices for Peace provided a laundry list of foreign policies that endanger Americans:

> BVFP believes the domestic and foreign policies of the United States—U.S. military support for Israel's brutal, repressive and illegal occupation of Palestine; sanctions against Iraq, Cuba and Haiti; the bombing of Iraq; the reckless murder of innocent Afghan civilians; the denial of sufficient economic, developmental, trade and health assistance to Africa, the Caribbean, Asia and Latin America—contribute to international economic exploitation and oppression, political disenfranchisement, and environmental degradation, as well as hatred and attacks against the American government and people (Black Voices for Peace, January 2003).

This discourse presents the government's militaristic foreign policies as the root source of what threatens the nation. Supporting war, therefore, gives rise to the very conditions that powerholders insist require a military response.

Yet the deeply engrained assumption that the state protects the nation makes many in the general public summarily dismiss such challenges. The notion that "peace comes through strength" is oft repeated and widely accepted. Only superior military capacity and the occasional demonstration of a willingness to use force will keep the malevolent from dominating the nation. Since it is unlikely that challenging this assumption would resonate widely, another approach was often taken to convince the public of the inadvisability of war.

Harnessing Nationalism: Measured Response as Test of a Great Nation

Rather than asserting that the U.S. government was a threat to its own citizenry, some passages focused upon how the U.S. government could best use

Photo 3.1. Peace march in Syracuse, New York, links democracy with war resistance. (Photo by Patrick G. Coy)

its power to defend the nation. In particular, they argued that a state representing the American people uses its power judiciously and in adherence with the true character of the nation. In so doing, these statements harnessed a facet of the dominant nationalist discourse often referenced by powerholders to legitimate military intervention. For instance, during a December 9, 2001, speech appealing for international support for the war on terrorism, President George W. Bush stated, "Americans stand united with those who love democracy, justice, and individual liberty. We are committed to upholding these principles, embodied in our Constitution's Bill of Rights, that have safeguarded us throughout our history and that continue to provide the foundation of our strength and prosperity."

In contrast to the Bush administration's discourse, peace groups claimed that opposing war was more consistent with the true character of the United States.[1] Some peace movement organizations counseled that 9/11 and the national crises it unleashed should be understood as a testing period, a "crucial moment" that created an opportunity for the United States to rely on its true values and to uphold its most deeply held constitutional principles. They clearly saw that the definition of what it meant to be an "American" was being contested. For example, WILPF counseled: "Let us demonstrate that our strength is in our resolve to maintain a democratic and free society and break the cycle of violence and retribution" (Women's International League for Peace and Freedom, September 12, 2001). Similarly, Pax Christi issued statements designed to tap into reservoirs of national pride by consistently calling forth from fellow citizens "the best of [the] U.S. tradition" and the "best of who we are" (Pax Christi, September 25, 2001 and September 26, 2001).

Nationalist Assumption #3: A Light unto the Nations

A strong tradition of isolationism has sometimes undermined the legitimacy of U.S. military operations overseas. For example, the America First Committee argued that the United States could best defend itself by staying *out* of the Second World War. Prior to Pearl Harbor, opinion polls revealed that the majority of the public consistently agreed with this policy position (Gordon 2003). Something more than the immediate physical survival of the nation needed to be at stake to compel popular support for wars in distant lands. Enter nationalist mythmaking.

Mythmaking is part of nationmaking. It often involves such self-glorifying nationalistic myths as claiming unique skills and special virtues like good will and altruism toward others (Van Evera 1994). U.S. mythmaking includes the chauvinistic notion of manifest destiny, Theodore Roosevelt's reworking of the Monroe Doctrine, and Woodrow Wilson's use of democracy and self-determination to justify intervention in World War I. As the embodiment of enlightenment, the first among equals, and as the "shining beacon on the hill," the United States came to symbolize all that is best about nation-states.[2] And for many, this nationalist myth was strengthened further still by positing divine ordination upon it.

During the U.S. Senate's discussion of the Spanish-American War of 1898 and of U.S. expansionism in the Philippines, Senator Albert J. Beveridge articulated the myth rather plainly:

> God . . . has made us the master organizers of the world to establish system where chaos reigns. . . . He has made us adept in government that we may administer government among savage and senile peoples. . . . And of all our race He has marked the American people as His chosen nation. . . . This is the divine mission of America. . . . We are trustees of the world's progress, guardians of its righteous peace. (*Congressional Record* [56th Cong., 1st Session] Vol XXXIII, January 9, 1900)

Over time, the belief that the United States is the "greatest country on earth" became widespread; it is now taken for granted and is largely repeated unquestioned. It has become something like an unconscious national mantra. Many are also fond of adding a divine dimension to the myth as popular radio talk show host Michael Medved always does whenever he breaks for a commercial, saying that he is reporting from "the greatest country on God's green earth."

It is a truism to say that the nation has not only the right, but also the responsibility, to protect its way of life from enemies. In the run-up to war—when social mobilization and citizen sacrifices are most needed—nationalist myths always do the heavy lifting. The self-glorifying myth of the United States' unique role means that many believe that the United States has an additional responsibility: to project its power in the service of spreading liberty, democracy, and prosperity (Gamson 1992b). Self-glorifying nationalist myths largely emanate from political leaders who deploy them to encourage citizens to contribute to the nation by voting, by paying taxes, but especially by joining the military and fighting for the country (Van Evera 1994). Supporting the state during war not only ensures the nation's survival, but also reaffirms the shared ideals that unite citizens and make them proud to be members of the nation.

Challenging Nationalism: An Oppressive Empire

The assumption that the U.S. government spreads freedom, democracy, and prosperity was explicitly challenged by the AFSC in efforts to generate opposition to the U.S. occupation of Iraq:

> The ideological roots of this war continue to shape the debate. Some people believe this is a war of liberation that would bring democracy to Iraq and the Middle East, while others believe it is an imperial adventure, the extension of a modern empire and US domination. How people understand the war largely shapes their understanding of next steps. (American Friends Service Committee, "AFSC Maintains That the US Still Controls Iraq," n.d.)

Peace groups with identities rooted in awareness of class and racial inequalities were especially likely to portray the U.S. government as denying freedom both at home and abroad (Maney, Woehrle, and Coy 2005). Black Radical Congress stated: "The war against the innocent people of Iraq is also a war to intensify the war against the working people in the USA and against the oppressed of the world. This is a war to bring back old style colonialism where might makes right and militarism is substituted for negotiation and diplomacy" (Black Radical Congress, March 20, 2003). Black Voices for Peace asked if a colonizer and human rights violator could truly lead a war on terror:

> We believe the denial of human rights and human needs in this country are acts of terrorism. Historically and contemporarily, the slave trade, slavery, the massacre of the indigenous people of this hemisphere, lynching, the burning and bombing of Black churches, Jim Crow segregation and racial violence, the criminal justice system, the death penalty, police brutality, rape and sexual violence, and the pain,

suffering and deprivations of poverty and unemployment represent acts and systems of terrorism. (Black Voices for Peace, January 2003).

Rather than being driven by idealism, some PMOs argued that the Gulf War had to do with greed and the need for oil. Labor groups echoed this framing in their critique of the Iraq War: "Well, labor knows that this war is about oil profits and US empire; about distraction from corporate thievery and from a crumbling economy" (New York City Labor Against the War, March 17, 2003).

Occasionally, powerholders acknowledge these challenges. In his 2006 State of the Union address, President Bush stated that "America is addicted to oil, which is often imported from unstable parts of the world." Such attempts to appropriate oppositional symbols provide discursive opportunities for social movements to challenge hegemony. Trying to shore up his support among African Americans, President George W. Bush frequently spoke at events celebrating Martin Luther King Jr.'s legacy. For instance, on the January 18, 2002, federal holiday honoring King, he stated:

> It is with a great sense of pride and gratitude that we celebrate this 17th national holiday in honor of Dr. King's life and work. Let us take this opportunity to recall his vision and renew his call for equal justice for all. We enter this new year and this annual celebration with a revived national spirit. The events of September 11, 2001, have drawn us closer as a Nation and increased our resolve to protect the life and liberty we cherish. And while our patriotism and neighborly affections run high, these circumstances have given us renewed purpose in rededicating ourselves to Dr. King's "dream."

Here the administration's response to 9/11 was framed as consistent with a deeply revered national icon's efforts to liberate an oppressed people. The president emphasized King's views on racial equality while ignoring his views on poverty and militarism. The FOR and other peace groups seized the discursive opportunity and challenged the assumption that the United States spreads freedom and democracy abroad:

> President Bush defended the chaos and destruction brought down on the people of Iraq as "liberation," and promised to bring more "liberation" to the rest of the Middle East—or to any other region where he deems America's interests are being challenged. Dr. King, in his prescient essay on international affairs, The World House, warned that history was cluttered with the wreckage of nations who came killing in the name of liberation and peace. This month, as we celebrate the 75th anniversary of Dr. King's birth, we believe the great pacifist and civil rights leader would wince at Bush's words, and weep to see what America has become. (Fellowship of Reconciliation, January 22, 2004)

By invoking an essay seldom referenced by powerholders, FOR reclaimed on behalf of the peace movement the symbolic potency of Dr. King's broad critique of U.S. imperialism, otherwise ignored by President Bush.

Harnessing Nationalism: First among Equals

In order to anchor their policy critiques, peace groups also embraced the idea that the United States promotes freedom and democracy worldwide. They used the common claim that the U.S. government leads by example to argue that being the first among equals requires diplomacy, multilateral cooperation, and strict adherence to international laws.

> The mark of a truly great power is that it exhausts every opportunity of negotiation and diplomacy, bears even the most excessive frustrations and challenges, rather than resort to its military might. For the great power, war is the very last resort, not the exercise of a preemptive option. (American Friends Service Committee, September 20, 2002)

Shortly after September 11th, the FOR took an even more nuanced approach, arguing that relying on nonviolent solutions would actually reflect U.S. policy precedents:

> Terrorism feeds on human misery and hopelessness. Weapons of war do not nurture or house or educate people. What if the United States were to call on all nations of good will to undertake a bold plan to eradicate poverty and illiteracy in the world? The Marshall Plan in the aftermath of World War II helped a devastated Europe build a hopeful future. This is a precedent that draws upon the best of our humanitarian heritage; the times call for such idealism again. (Fellowship of Reconciliation, December 20, 2001)

Rather than challenging nationalism by introducing counter-informative knowledge, FOR appropriated and highlighted official knowledge that supported its policy recommendations. Embracing the assumption of U.S. world leadership enabled peace groups to articulate what this leadership should entail.

Nationalist Assumption #4: The Enemy Within

The influence of the ideology of the Republic on nationalist discourse in the United States suggests that individuals can become members of the nation simply by assuming the rights and the responsibilities of citizenship through naturalization. A historical analysis, however, suggests that the nation is often implicitly defined by ethnic, religious, and racial categorization. White Anglo-Saxon Protestant politicians and columnists lamented publicly that the Catholicism of Irish and Italian immigrants in the late nineteenth century would undermine the nation's commitment to liberty and democracy. Even culturally assimilated groups have found their national loyalty questioned because of the widespread but scientifically falsified and erroneous belief that differences in physical appearance are linked with other genetic differences that produce group-level variations in behaviors, abilities, and loyalties. During

World War II, Japanese Americans were interned in far greater numbers than Italian Americans, German Americans, or other U.S. citizens with ancestors born in "enemy states." As Lieutenant General John L. DeWitt, the architect of the internment policy, stated: "The Japanese race is an enemy race and, while many second and third generation of Japanese born on US soil, possessed the US citizenship, have become 'Americanized,' the racial strains are undiluted" (Meyers 2002, 419).

Survey evidence suggests the ongoing persistence of Eurocentric and racialized constructions of national loyalty in the United States. Data from the 1990 General Social Survey shows that Whites are rated most patriotic while Blacks, Asians, and Hispanics are put on the unpatriotic end of the scale. Reflecting the enduring nature of stigma, a multivariate regression revealed a significant relationship between not liking Japan and viewing Asians as unpatriotic (Tom Smith 1990).

These exclusivist strains of nationalist discourse in the United States place particular pressure upon ethnic and racial minority groups to distance themselves from the enemy Other as well as to faithfully reference dominant nationalist narratives. Expressing concern for the well-being of those of the same ethnic group residing in an enemy state runs the risk of having one's national allegiance questioned. To challenge domestic ethnic and racial inequalities is exposing the nation to danger by undermining the unity needed to respond effectively to a common threat.

Challenging Nationalism: Ethnic Minorities are Scapegoats

Peace groups devoted an extensive amount of text to challenging the assumption that racial minority groups are a threat to the nation. Scapegoating involves blaming the powerless for social problems in ways that serve the agendas of the powerful. During the build-up to the Gulf War, FOR chastised the government and the media for scapegoating:

> The administration and the press have also irresponsibly manipulated racial and ethnic stereotypes to build support for military actions. Racist and demonizing stereotypes of Arabs in general, and Iraqis in particular, have inflamed the language of debate and hampered efforts to look at the human dimensions of the crisis. There has been a dramatic increase in harassment and vilification of Arab and Muslim Americans. (Fellowship of Reconciliation, August 30, 1990)

As with several other PMOs during the Gulf War period and subsequently, FOR also appealed to readers to actively resist scapegoating: "Oppose demonization of 'the enemy' and actively reach out to Arab and Muslim Americans to counter a climate characterized by racism, xenophobia and hatred" (ibid).

During the Clinton administration's bombing of Northern Iraq in 1998, WILPF stated:

Anti-Arab racism is rampant in the US. Think about all the negative stereotypes of Arabs all around you. Do you really think all Muslims are violent terrorists? Islam is the fastest growing religion in the US. Who did they finger for the bombing in Oklahoma City? Who did it turn out to be? See? This anti-Arab racism makes it easy for the government/multinational corporations/media cartel to demonize Hussein, whip us into a frenzy about "Islamic Jihad terrorists," and get over with a war that doesn't benefit anyone. (Women's International League for Peace and Freedom, 1998)

BRC, CAIR, and WILPF all used the bombing of the Federal Building in Oklahoma City to caution against basing domestic and foreign policies upon racial stereotypes.

Harnessing Nationalism: Defending the Nation's Liberty

Americans are frequently told that they must sacrifice civil liberties to ensure national security during times of war. This belief is directly linked to the assumption that there are enemies living within the territory that present imminent threats. After 9/11, the U.S. peace movement faced a context where high levels of political repression were widely viewed as legitimate means of governance.

U.S. PMOs frequently responded to this legitimated political closure by framing war and political repression as grave threats to a core national value—civil liberties.[3] Davis and Silver's (2004) national Civil Liberties Survey, conducted in the months immediately following 9/11, found that while Americans were generally willing to trade off civil liberties for greater security, this willingness interacted with the degree of a sense of threat and with the degree of trust in government. Accordingly, PMOs argued that the ultimate threat to national security was not a terrorist attack, but the loss of civil liberties. PMOs anchored their framing squarely in the American tradition of constitutionalism and the importance of preserving civil liberties. They insisted that the job of the true patriot was to uphold the Bill of Rights. For instance, the American Friends Service Committee enumerated a long list of constitutional rights whose use would form a bulwark against the new dangers facing the country after 9/11. It concluded, "Working in your communities to use and protect these rights in the weeks ahead will guarantee that terrorism has not destroyed the fabric of liberty or undercut our Constitution" (American Friends Service Committee, December 19, 2001).

Nationalist Assumption #5: Love It or Leave It

Patriotism is defined by loyalty, support, service, and devotion to one's country. While patriotism is present in all nation-states, it is particularly strong in the United States (Pei 2003). There are at least three reasons for this. First, as discussed above, the idea that the United States promotes freedom, democracy, and prosperity worldwide makes it more difficult to critique foreign policy. Second, as a pluralist country fed by immigration, the loyalty to the nation that defines patriotism functions like a much-needed glue in the composite national fabric. Third, the strong strain of independent individualism that is repeatedly lionized in U.S. popular culture—think Horatio Alger, John Wayne, and Arnold Schwarzenegger—eventually retards the development of community and creates feelings of aloneness and isolation (Bellah et al. 1985). Some argue that these feelings may be assuaged by the expression of strong patriotic sentiments (Janowitz 1985).

Patriotism, however, is not a one-way street. Not only does it serve the belonging and meaning needs of the individual, but the group also depends in some measure on patriotism for its continued existence. Yet there exist obstacles to the development of patriotic feelings toward the broader collectivity. The members of large groups cannot directly experience anywhere near the full scope of the group's membership; the group as single unit escapes their physical perception. That is one reason why patriotism toward large entities like the United States and other nation-states has to be intentionally fostered and learned over time (Bar-Tal and Staub 1997). National political leaders exert considerable energies to impart patriotism to the nation's members and to solidify it as a required characteristic of group membership.

Frequently, these efforts lead to destructive forms of patriotism marked by an uncritical loyalty to the nation and intolerance of criticism. These iterations of patriotism also include a willingness to disregard the welfare of those who are not part of the nation (Schatz and Staub 1997; Staub 1997; Schatz, Staub, and Lavine 1999). Moreover, these forms of patriotism are related to political disengagement, militaristic nationalism, and a desire for cultural purity (Schatz and Staub 1997). The ideological assumptions that underline strident patriotism make opposition to the peace movement an important form of identity construction. To mobilize against peace movement challenges is to demonstrate one's commitment to the nation.

Challenging Nationalism: Americans Should Be Ashamed

The popular wartime phrase of "love it or leave it" promotes uncritical and destructive patriotism by attempting to silence criticism of the U.S. government or of prevailing social practices. Under this particular nationalist logic, it generally follows that opposing the war means to oppose the government, the American way of life, and the one nation, under God, indivisible, with liberty and justice for all. This is one reason why peace demonstrations frequently draw vociferous counterdemonstrations, particularly during war. When participants at an ongoing peace vigil in Colorado Springs decided during the Gulf War to fly a U.S. flag, they repeatedly suffered name-calling ("traitors"), spitting, intimidation, threats, harassment, and even physical violence from other residents who supported the war and who were outraged at the protesters' use of the flag—a nationalist symbol—to criticize government policy (Andrews 1997). By failing to support the U.S. state in the prosecution of its special mission, peace activists so dishonor the nation that they are considered treasonous.

In response to this uncritical patriotism, several peace groups challenged head-on the assumption that U.S. citizens should be uniformly proud of their country. Military conflicts in the Middle East were frequently framed as servicing Americans' addiction to oil, as typified by this Peace Action statement prior to the Gulf War:

> Now we are in a terrible mess. And the worst of it is, it's all for oil—to keep the supply plentiful and the cost of it low. We are prepared to shed blood not to further democracy and human rights in the area—few such rights exist; not to defend the independence of Saudi Arabia—were oranges the country's chief export, no American soldier would be there; not to defend the American way of life; but merely to support an American lifestyle where two percent of the world's population consumes 25 percent of its oil. If imposing suffering on behalf of greed is right, what's left to be called wrong? (Peace Action, August 24, 1990)

More than a decade later, CODEPINK used similar framing in describing the purpose of its citizens' tour of Iraq: "We will express our horror at the possibility of a war against the innocent Iraqi people because of our addiction to oil" (CODEPINK, January 2003).

Peace groups also argued that uncritical patriotism resulted in military intervention abroad and political repression at home becoming the American way of life. During the Gulf War, some groups created *radical-envisioning* oppositional knowledge by insisting that meeting domestic needs will make Americans truly proud.

> Our strength as a nation comes from providing equal opportunity for all our citizens to lead healthy and productive lives. . . . We need to invest in affordable housing, in alternative energy programs, in education and environmental protection. With the right investments we can create jobs and improve the strength of our economy. (Peace Action, late 1990)

Thirteen years later, during the Iraq War, the War Resisters League offered a similar vision:

> Hope of change, in the long term, requires a change in our own national values. We are in a country driven mad by fear, driven to spend obscene sums on the military at a time when the poor among us cannot find medical care or housing and when even those who are employed find themselves driven against the wall by cutbacks in social services. (War Resisters League, March 21, 2003)

Few like to hear that what they've been taught to believe in is a lie: that the U.S. government and the U.S. way of life actually threaten the American people and the rest of the world. In recognition of the limited ability of challenging hegemony to capture the hearts and minds of those who are intensely proud of being American, peace groups often pursued a quite different approach.

Harnessing Nationalism: Promoting Peace is Patriotic

Some U.S. peace groups promoted loyalty to the nation and embraced American identity while simultaneously arguing that this loyalty conflicts with unconditional support for the state. The usage of American identity themes was particularly strong in countering the war in Afghanistan. While there was broad popular support in the United States for bombing Afghanistan and the larger effort to hunt for Al Qaeda members, AFSC, FOR, WILPF, and Pax Christi each flatly rejected equating patriotic loyalty with support for U.S. policies in Afghanistan. NYCLAW explicitly harnessed American identity by proclaiming, "We are proud to be American trade unionists against the war," linking a traditionally pro-American image of the "trade unionist" to the anti-war movement (New York City Labor Against the War, November 18, 2001).

Harnessing "American identity" thus redefined patriotism to mean dissent, including dissenting from a War on Terrorism that, while it may have had a just cause, was nonetheless being waged in an unjust manner according to the PMOs.[4] Protest became defined as a legitimate means of showing love for one's country. Pax Christi turned the tables on those who used patriotism to silence policy critics when it claimed that the highest form of patriotism is criticism itself:

> There will be those who will try to tell us that criticizing our national policies in time of crisis is unpatriotic. But as William Fulbright, the former Senator from Arkansas reminds us, "Criticism is more than right; it is an act of patriotism, a higher form of patriotism, I believe, than the familiar ritual of national adulation. All of us have the responsibility to act upon the higher patriotism which is to love our country less for what it is than for what we would like it to be." (Pax Christi, September 26, 2001)

When the various ways that the PMOs both challenged and harnessed nationalism during these different conflicts are viewed together, it becomes apparent that the U.S. peace movement has developed a form of patriotism marked in varying degrees by the three central components of what Ervin Staub (1997) has termed "constructive patriotism": (1) a critical conscious-ness, which includes the ability to independently evaluate biased informa-tion on policy and national events; (2) critical loyalty, which includes dual commitments to the group's welfare and to universal ideals and values; and (3) a willingness to deviate from, resist, and challenge the current direction of the group. Here the nation's identity is not just defended, but positively and actively reconstructed on an ongoing basis, with the well-being of others also in mind. In addition, it is clear that the peace movement's challenging and harnessing of hegemonic notions of nationalism were not done in some willy-nilly fashion. Nor did they occur according to the whim or mood of the activists who drafted the organizational statements. On the contrary, the choice to challenge nationalism, to harness nationalism, or to blend the approaches appears to have been a considered one, as the longitudinal trends we highlight below indicate.

LONGITUDINAL TRENDS

Although this has rarely been demonstrated empirically, it has often been presumed that social movements are in a dynamic relationship with the social forces, institutions, and authority systems against which they are contending. This means that if social movements are to remain relevant and effective they must adjust their discourse, their actions, and their tactics in response to the shifting contexts, power differentials, and arguments of their opponents. Put another way, the relationship between structure and agency is dynamic: as political, discursive, and emotional opportunities shift, social movements face moments of decision about how best to act and react.

For example, when the Reagan administration dramatically increased military spending in the 1980s and coupled it to hard-line rhetoric suggesting that limited nuclear wars were feasible, a breakdown in elite consensus soon followed. Members of the U.S. foreign-policy establishment, emboldened by strong opposition from European allies to Reagan's discourse, spoke out against the policies of this popular president (Gamson and Meyer 1996). The nuclear weapons freeze movement (an offshoot of the U.S. peace movement) recognized and exploited this emergent political opportunity, fashioning a new set of arguments for disarmament that directly challenged dominant assumptions fueling the arms race. The movement focused on the simple idea of zero growth in nuclear weapons. It was an idea whose time had suddenly come as it resonated with the fears brought on by Reagan's radical rhetoric and perilous policies. The freeze movement grew with remarkable speed partly as a result.

Empirically capturing shifts like these requires a systematic approach to data analysis and presentation. In order to track whether and how the peace movement adjusted its discourse about nationalism across conflict periods, we created two groupings or bundles of codes that were strongly related to the dominant nationalist discourse (see appendix 2). One bundle includes codes that reflected movement attempts to challenge nationalist assumptions. The other bundle includes codes that reflected attempts to harness nationalist assumptions (see appendix 2 for details on all code bundles). Table 3.2 reveals significant variations in the frequencies of challenging and harnessing nationalism across conflict periods. Mean comparison tests indicate that the five

Table 3.2.   Responses to the Dominant Nationalist Discourse by Conflict Period

Conflict Period	Sum of Nationalism Code Bundles[a]		Challenging Nationalism Code Bundle[b]		Harnessing Nationalism Code Bundle[b]		Ratio of CN to HN[c]
	N	Col.%	N	Col.%	N	Col.%	
Gulf War	192.9	15.9	108.0	17.3	84.9	14.5	1.27
Iraq 1998	128.7*	10.6	86.9	13.9	41.8	7.1	2.08***
Kosova/o	186.9	15.4	120.0	19.2	66.9	11.4	1.79**
Sept. 11th	363.4	30.0	143.7	23.0	219.7*	37.5	0.65***
Iraq War	339.6*	28.0	167.5	26.8	172.1	29.4	0.97
Total	1211.6	100.0	626.1	100.0	585.5	100.0	
Mean	242.3		125.2		117.1		1.1
Std. Dev.	103.1		31.3		75.4		0.6

Notes: Analysis based on weighted data. For weights formula, see appendix 2. Only statements from the five PMOs issuing statements in all five conflict periods are included (American Friends Service Committee, Fellowship of Reconciliation, Pax Christi, Peace Action, Women's International League for Peace and Freedom). Includes only codes that are strongly related to the dominant nationalist discourse. See appendix 3 for specific codes in bundles. Table has rounding errors.

[a] * $p < .10$ of t-value for one-tailed difference of means test comparing the frequencies of codes in both the challenging bundle and the harnessing bundle during the conflict period to the frequencies for the other four conflict periods.

[b] * $p < .10$; ** $p < .01$ of the F statistic for a one-way analysis of variance comparing the frequencies of codes in the bundle during the conflict period to the frequencies for the other four conflict periods.

[c] * $p < .10$; ** $p < .01$, *** $p < .001$ of chi-square value for a 2x2 table comparing the aggregated frequencies of codes in the challenging bundle and in the harnessing bundle for the conflict period with the means of the aggregated code frequencies for the other four conflict periods.

PMOs included in the analysis engaged the dominant nationalist discourse significantly less during the Iraq 1998 period and significantly more during the 9/11 and Iraq War periods when compared to the overall mean for all codes for the other four conflict periods.

The peace movement challenged nationalism least during the Iraq 1998 conflict and most during the Iraq War. One-way analyses of variance indicate that, although variations in levels of challenging nationalism across periods were not statistically significant, variations in levels of harnessing nationalism were. Collectively, the groups were most likely to harness nationalism during the 9/11 period and least likely during the Iraq 1998 conflict.

In terms of the mixture of challenging and harnessing nationalism, PMOs challenged nationalism more than they harnessed it in three of the conflict periods (Gulf War, Iraq 1998, and Kosova/o), and harnessed nationalism more than they challenged it in the two most recent periods (9/11 and Iraq War). Chi-square tests reveal that the 9/11 period was significantly different from the other conflict periods in its relative emphasis upon harnessing nationalism.

Collectively, statistically significant variations across periods support the idea that the U.S. peace movement adapts its discursive response to nationalism to the particular conjunction of discursive, emotional, and political opportunities present within a given conflict period.[5] The field of framing analysis has rightly been criticized for emphasizing strategic considerations to the neglect of cultural aspects of discourse. However, our data suggest that Marc Steinberg (1999) and others go too far in the opposite direction by calling for a theoretical and methodological breach with framing analysis. Abandoning the argument is costly and premature. The findings suggest that U.S. peace movement organizations carefully crafted multivalent messages that seized upon context-specific opportunities to achieve resonance and potency with the public.

Adaptability in Framing

Peace groups adapted their framing to respond to the particular discursive, emotional, and political exigencies of the specific conflict. With regard to the below-average levels of challenging nationalism during the Gulf War, on average 71.8 percent of public opinion poll respondents supported the war.[6] International public opinion was also highly supportive with an average approval rating in five countries of 57.1 percent. This is the highest level of international public support for any of the five conflicts, including the war in Afghanistan.[7] Iraq's invasion of Kuwait was a blatant violation of the sovereignty of a U.S. ally. All of the PMOs thought it should be reversed; the question was how should it be accomplished and who should accomplish it. The blessing of the United Nations and the breadth of the international coalition involved in the retaking of Kuwait likely made it less relevant and more difficult for peace movement organizations to challenge U.S. nationalism during this period.

Peace groups devoted a significantly greater proportion of their text to nationalist themes after September 11, 2001.[8] Nationalist themes also prominently entered the discourse of political powerholders. In a televised speech to a Joint Session of Congress, President Bush stated, "Tonight we are a country awakened to danger and called to defend freedom. Our grief has turned to anger, and anger to resolution. Whether we bring our enemies to justice, or bring justice to our enemies, justice will be done." In the same speech, the president praised Republicans and Democrats alike for singing "God Bless America" on the steps of the Capitol along with approving $40 billion to "rebuild our communities and meet the needs of our military." In addition, the general public responded to the events of 9/11 with intense national pride. According to a study conducted after 9/11 by the National Opinion Research Center, 97 percent of respondents agreed "they would rather be Americans than citizens of any other country."

Peace groups responded to this political and cultural context by intensifying their harnessing of hegemony relative to their challenging of it. In fact, the only two conflict periods during which peace groups devoted more text to harnessing nationalism than to challenging nationalism occurred after 9/11.

The PMOs harnessed nationalism the least during the Iraq 1998 conflict. The 1998 crisis over enforcing the no-fly zone area in Iraq's north and Iraq's cooperation with the UN weapons inspection teams was relatively brief and did not garner significant popular interest. The day after the bombing, a CBS News/*New York Times* Poll found that only 39 percent of respondents had been following the situation in Iraq very closely, and 22 percent reported either not closely following the situation or not following it at all. Harnessing hegemonic concepts like nationalism means that a PMO must dance—and delicately—with more than one partner. When challenging movements harness hegemony to attract new members, they risk being perceived by longtime adherents as selling out, as being co-opted. Thus, during the short and relatively low-profile crisis with Iraq in 1998, the peace movement may have felt it had little to gain and more to lose by harnessing nationalism during this period. If anything, domestic conditions were ripe with disillusionment as President Clinton faced impeachment over the Monica Lewinsky affair. Taken together, these findings demonstrate, not only adaptability of framing practices in response to changing political contexts, but also learning over time by the five PMOs.

Fidelity in Framing

The U.S. peace movement is clearly strategic in its discursive choices; the PMOs actively managed the way they presented their views to the public in response to changing cultural and political conditions. Not to be lost in this finding, however, is the companion fact that these organizations were also true to their core assumptions and beliefs over time. A lack of significant variation in levels of challenging nationalism across periods suggests that the movement faithfully referenced ideas that stand in fundamental opposition to nationalist assumptions. In three out of five conflict periods the PMOs challenged nationalism more than they harnessed it. Even during the 9/11 and Iraq War periods, peace groups still challenged nationalist assumptions in substantial amounts of text. In fact, in terms of frequency, groups challenged nationalism to an even greater extent during 9/11 and the Iraq War than during any previous conflict included in our analysis. What does all this tell us about peace movement discourse over time?

The pronounced intensification of challenging nationalism during the Iraq War suggests that these PMOs strongly adhere over time to their core oppositional values and to the peace movement's historic tradition of resistance to war-making. The U.S. peace movement is ideologically driven and strongly values-based, with nationalism going against many of the movement's bedrock values and transnational ties. Indeed, two of the five PMOs in the longitudinal data are pacifist. Across the twentieth century, the U.S. peace movement has been primarily a movement that challenged from the margins or the outside, articulating a truly alternative set of values and beliefs from the dominant nationalist discourse, including, for example, a rejection of nationalism and a deep commitment to supporting conscientious objectors (Chatfield 1971; Wittner 1984).

Insofar as strongly nationalist sentiments are not widely and warmly welcomed in much of the U.S. peace movement, harnessing nationalism does not come easily. After all, activists' belief systems do have a constraining influence on the production of meaning (Benford and Snow 2000). In this context, the unparalleled increase in harnessing nationalism by the peace movement during the 9/11 period gains added significance. Perhaps the period demonstrated to movement strategists that it was possible to talk positively and effectively about nationalist identity and to harness nationalist ideas and assumptions without betraying the movement's core principles and foundational beliefs. This would explain the fact that although there is a steep increase in challenging nationalism from 9/11 to the Iraq War, during the Iraq War the U.S. peace movement still continued to harness nationalism to a significant degree (more so than in any other period outside of 9/11). In addition, despite the steep increase in challenging nationalism from 9/11 to the Iraq War, there is only a very modest increase in the use of American identity-negative discourse from 9/11 to the Iraq War. This suggests that the experience of effectively harnessing nationalism during 9/11 included the peace movement overcoming a conceptual hurdle of sorts in affirming and harnessing basic American principles.

These findings of continuity and fidelity by the peace movement to its core values and beliefs are strengthened further by our longitudinal analysis of the movement's use of nationalist and oppositional identities. Figure 3.1 shows a spiked increase in the peace movement's use of nationalist identities during 9/11, when such identities presumably had wide resonance with a U.S. public

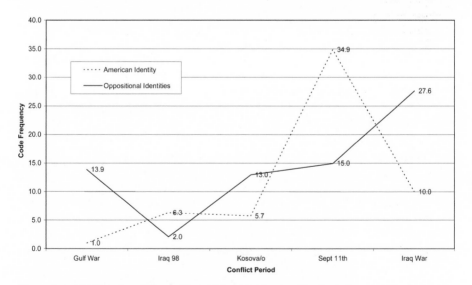

Figure 3.1. National and Oppositional Identities by Conflict Period
Notes: Analysis based on weighted data. For weights formula, see appendix 2. Only data from the five PMOs issuing statements in all five contact periods are included (American Friends Service Committee, Fellowship of Reconciliation, Pax Christi, Peace Action, Women's International League for Peace and Freedom). Oppositional identities include identities based upon class, gender, race, and sexual orientation.

under unprecedented attack by outside terrorist forces. However, this spike in the use of nationalist identities by the peace movement was followed by a steep drop-off during the Iraq War, when the PMOs argued that Bush administration policies and the behavior of U.S. troops on the ground in Iraq were badly besmirching U.S. identity worldwide.

At the same time, figure 3.1 also shows a steady increase in the movement's use of oppositional identities from Iraq 1998 onward, despite the spike in the use of nationalist identity during 9/11. This steadily increasing referencing of oppositional identities suggests fidelity to the movement's historic oppositional identities. The movement's harnessing of nationalist identity clearly supplements but does not replace its appeals to gender, class, racial, and religious identities (see chapter 6). The trend also reflects the emergence of flexible, multifaceted movement identities in the age of Internet mobilizations (della Porta 2005; Bennett 2005). The Internet facilitates the diffusion of organizing styles and approaches, making it possible to reach a broad and diverse bystander public relatively quickly and easily. In addition, the forces of corporate globalization made it more essential to make these broad appeals to many identity groupings, as all are impacted by globalization forces (see chapter 8). Overall, figure 3.1 illustrates well that the U.S. peace movement found itself caught at the crossroads between periods of resurgent nationalism in the context of globalization.

ON THE EDGE OF THE NATION: ETHNIC MINORITY PMOS

The stigmatizing of minority groups perceived to share ancestral origin and cultural practices with enemy combatants presented discursive dilemmas, not only for the U.S. peace movement as a whole, but in particular for peace movement organizations mobilizing on the basis of self-identification with a targeted ethnic group. These organizations are disproportionately likely to be targeted for exclusion, detention, and violence. The stronger the identity boundaries that powerholders draw with the enemy, the more likely it is that the minority group will be widely viewed as not belonging to the nation.

This facet of hegemony presents a major discursive dilemma for PMOs with minority-based identities. On the one hand, rejecting patriotism runs the risk of intensifying attacks on the group by strengthening national identity boundaries. Moreover, minority group members strongly identifying themselves as Americans may be incapable of challenging core assumptions of the dominant discourse. On the other hand, asserting uncritical loyalty to the American nation risks reinforcing a set of assumptions that contributes to the oppression of members of the group both inside and outside of the United States.

To ascertain how some minority-identified peace movement organizations have responded to this dilemma, we compared weighted frequencies

Table 3.3. Comparison of Minority Identified Discourses to Other PMOs: Iraq War Period

Organizations	CAIR[a] (N)	BRC[b] (N)	Other PMOs (Mean N)
Civil liberties	28.4*	13.1	8.9
Scapegoating	15.8*	4.4	1.5
Religion	20.5	0.0	16.6[c]
American identity-positive	20.5*	0.0	3.8
American identity-negative	0.0	2.2	1.2
Paramilitary terror-condemned	14.2*	0.0	0.8
State terror-condemned	1.6	2.2	0.3
US troops-positive	1.6	8.8	12.1
US troops-negative	30.0*	0.0	0.8

Notes: Analysis based on data weighted for fourteen PMOs issuing statements during the Iraq War period. BVFP is excluded due to insufficient number of words of text. For weights formula, see appendix 2.
* Identified as outlier value using the Hamilton's Interquartile Range formula. The formula defines a value x as an outlier if $x < Q(25) - 1.5IQR$ or $Q(75) + 1.5IQR < x$ where Q is the quartile and IQR is the interquartile range. The interquartile range is the difference between the 75th and 25th percentile.
[a] Council on American-Islamic Relations
[b] Black Radical Congress
[c] Mean for all religious-based PMOs except for CAIR (i.e., AFSC; FOR; Pax Christi)

for selected codes in statements by the Council on American-Islamic Relations (CAIR) and the Black Radical Congress (BRC) to the mean of weighted code frequencies in statements by twelve other PMOs issued during the Iraq War period. Table 3.3 presents the findings. Reflecting its status as the only organization in our study identified primarily with the ethnic group most stigmatized during the Iraq War (i.e., Muslims), CAIR, more than any other peace movement organization: (1) negotiated the stigmatized identity; (2) attempted to blur identity boundaries by condemning attacks on the nation and asserting their loyalty to the nation; and (3) used discursive opportunities to criticize the government for oppressing those identified as belonging to the group and living in other societies.

Negotiating Stigma

Negotiation constitutes an important form of collective identity construction. Verta Taylor and Nancy Whittier (1992, 118) define negotiation as "ways that activists work to resist negative social definitions and demand that others value and treat oppositional groups differently." Both BRC and especially CAIR were more likely than other PMOs to challenge negative stereotypes of Arabs and Muslims by portraying the group as convenient scapegoats for the powerful. The BRC drew parallels between the racial profiling of African Americans and Arabs and Muslims:

In the name of fighting terrorism, there is a sharp rise in racist repression. African Americans and other people of color are facing a new level of racial profiling and violence. . . . Arabs, Muslims, immigrants, and people resembling those of Middle Eastern/North African/Central Asian descent are special targets of racist violence and government repression. (Black Radical Congress, June 2003)

By constructing a collective identity inclusive of Arab Muslims as people of color, BRC statements encouraged identity-based resistance to political repression.

Reflecting its religious-based identity, CAIR also addressed misconceptions of Islam. In response to the Bush administration's raising the terror alert on the day of the Muslim religious observance of Hajj, CAIR not only rejected "any suggestion that Islam and terrorism are inextricably linked," but also tried to explain the meaning of Hajj: "Hajj, or pilgrimage to the city of Mecca, is a once-in-a-lifetime journey of spiritual purification, repentance and renewal, not an excuse for killing innocent people" (Council on American-Islamic Relations, February 8, 2003). In the process, the organization sought to effect changes in how the general public viewed their religion and the people who practice it.

Recognizing the negative consequences of scapegoating for the rights of their members, both groups were more likely to use civil liberties discourse in their statements when compared to other PMOs. Here they asserted their citizenship rights to equal treatment under the law. When Hamilton's Inter-quartile Range formula was used as a measure of statistical significance, the data supported the finding that CAIR devoted significantly more text to scape-goating and civil liberties than any other group in the data set, including the BRC. This finding suggests that organizations identified with a minority group directly targeted as part of nationalist mobilization in the United States will devote the most attention to negotiating stigma.

Blurring Boundaries

Table 3.3 supports the idea that a PMO representing an ethnic group heav-ily stigmatized as the enemy Other during a conflict will devote substantially more of its text towards trying to shift the construction of the ethnic group from being categorized as the enemy Other to being viewed as belonging to the nation. CAIR was significantly more likely to condemn terrorism by paramilitary groups during the Iraq War. CAIR also assiduously avoided mak-ing any negative reference to being American. Beyond distancing themselves, and by proxy, Muslim Americans from the enemy Other, CAIR also actively asserted their American identity to a far greater extent than any other PMO in our data set. In its statements, the group repeatedly referred to "American Muslims." In opposing the USA PATRIOT Act, the group declared, "We stand firmly in support of our nation's security" (Council on American-Islamic Rela-tions, July 30, 2003).

In contrast, the BRC made greater-than-average negative references to being American, thereby strengthening identity boundaries. The organization was also less likely than average to make positive references to being American or to condemn terrorism by paramilitary groups. The contrasting discourses reflect not only the anti-imperialist, pan-African nationalist ideology of the BRC, but also the greater extent of stigmatization of Arabs and Muslims in the war on terror discourse.

Transnational Allegiances

BRC and CAIR were two of only five PMOs to condemn terrorism by the state. In addition, the types of condemnation issued reflected a deep identification with those being targeted. In response to the start of the Iraq War in March of 2003, BRC stated: "Above all, this war continues the traditions of racial genocide of the US military. Black people have seen the real effects of racial terror and violence. All freedom-loving persons reject terrorism as a form of political intervention" (Black Radical Congress, March 20, 2003). Violations of the human rights of those constructed as belonging to the ethnic or racial group created strong identity boundaries that encouraged these groups to define the U.S. government as the enemy.

Far more than any other group, the Council on American-Islamic Relations criticized U.S. soldiers for human rights violations in Iraq. Challenging one of the most revered symbols of the nation is incongruent with CAIR's careful efforts to blur identity boundaries and assert nationalist membership. These challenges, however, took place in the context of extensive media coverage of U.S. troops killing unarmed civilians and torturing prisoners in Abu Ghraib. The images of fellow Muslims having their basic human rights violated likely triggered identity commitments that made CAIR willing to run the risk of being defined as an enemy sympathizer. At the same time, the overwhelming evidence of human rights violations presented a discursive opportunity for challenging frames to achieve empirical credibility with an otherwise skeptical U.S. public.

CONCLUSIONS

Like Albert Camus and his quote that opened this chapter, U.S. peace movement organizations wanted to find ways to love their country while still loving justice. But they had an added burden in that they wanted their arguments to appeal to the general public during wartime. Consequently, they had to critically engage deeply engrained nationalist assumptions that encourage popular support for military intervention abroad and political repression at home. Insofar as nationalism is a way of thinking, the strength and vitality of the assumptions underlying the dominant nationalist discourse presented both obstacles and opportunities to the U.S. peace movement. These obstacles and opportunities were conditioned by the particular political and cultural contexts facing the peace movement in each conflict period. The changing contexts created discursive opportunities that were more or less promising, depending on the intensity of the shifts and on the ability of peace movement activists to recognize the changes and to respond constructively to them. Our longitudinal analysis across the five conflict periods empirically demonstrates that the United States peace movement—represented by five major organizations—evidenced adaptability in fashioning messages to take advantage of discursive opportunities as well as fidelity to its core assumptions and beliefs. Moreover, we've shown that while the peace movement both challenged and harnessed hegemonic notions of nationalism, it nonetheless primarily focused upon one approach or the other during one specific conflict. Our analysis has also shown, however, that this patently strategic approach was also infused with deeply cultural considerations, as illustrated by the movement's fidelity to its historic messages and by the examples provided by CAIR and BRC.

Directly engaging the dominant assumptions undergirding nationalism, as the PMOs did, means that they were also indirectly expressing an alternative understanding of patriotism. Earlier in this chapter we suggested that the peace movement evinced forms of patriotism that Staub (1997) defined as constructive. Our detailed analysis of how the movement discursively both challenged and harnessed the five dominant assumptions of nationalism over a fifteen-year period demonstrates the many forms of constructive patriotism put forward by the movement. On the one hand, by challenging nationalist assumptions, the peace movement demonstrated critical and evaluative consciousness. On the other hand, by harnessing these same nationalist assumptions, the PMOs evinced critical loyalty to the nation, to movement traditions as well as to broader values. Even pacifist groups embraced nationalist values, especially immediately following 9/11. Finally, peace movement discourse on nationalism was often designed not only to differentiate between the nation and the state, but also to expand the boundaries of who is considered as part of the nation.

NOTES

1. Much of this paragraph is taken from Coy, Maney, and Woehrle (2003).

2. Although it may have originated with the Puritan leader John Winthrop, President Ronald Reagan was particularly adroit at articulating and manipulating this trope (Ramsey 2004). In his February 2, 1988, "Address to the Nation" urging support for the U.S.-funded war against the Nicaraguan government, he reminded the country that "I've often expressed my belief that the Almighty had a reason for placing this great and good land, the New World, here between two vast oceans. Protected by the seas, we have enjoyed the blessings of peace—free for almost two centuries now from the tragedy of foreign aggression on our mainland. Help us to keep that precious gift secure. Help us to win support for those who struggle for the same freedoms we hold dear. In doing so, we will not just be helping them, we will be helping ourselves, our children, and all the peoples of the world. We'll be demonstrating that America is still a beacon of hope, still a light unto the nations" (Reagan 1988, Ramsey 2004).

3. Much of this paragraph is taken from Maney, Woehrle, and Coy (2005).

4. This paragraph is taken from Coy, Maney, and Woehrle (2003).

5. By highlighting the movement's discursive trends that occur in response to the changing cultural and political contexts facing the peace movement, we do not mean to imply that the peace movement exclusively relies upon one approach during any conflict period. In fact, the two approaches clearly coexist and are even blended at times within the same statement.

6. As a measure of trends in how the mass public reacted to dominant policy discourses, we took the mean of monthly averages of several major public opinion polls in which respondents answered favorably to questions regarding the advisability of military intervention in each of the five conflict periods included in the study.

7. For international public opinion, we used the mean of the average approval rating in five countries (Canada, France, Germany, Great Britain, Italy, and Russia) for each military intervention. These polls were available less frequently than domestic polls. As a result, differences in international opinion across conflict periods could be an artifact of the timing of the polls included in the data set.

8. Much of this paragraph is taken from Coy, Maney, and Woehrle (2003).

II

CONTESTING EMOTIONS AND IDENTITIES IN WAR AND PEACE

4

Capturing Hearts and Minds

Emotions and Peace Appeals

If I can't dance, I don't want to be in your revolution.

—Attributed to Emma Goldman

People organize around and contest what they feel strongly about, including identities, resources, values, lifestyles, justice, their jobs, and their neighborhoods (Cress and Myers 2004). Consequently, social movement activities are often rich with emotion. Whether the occasion is a spirited picket of striking workers, a solemn memorial service for fallen comrades, a joyous celebration of a hard-fought campaign, an identity-affirming action like a gay pride rally, a censuring of a college dean, or the delivery of an oppositional statement to a congressional office, oppositional activities can be emotional affairs.

This has not always worked in favor of social movements, given the largely pejorative connotations associated with the public expression of emotions in the political arena. Insofar as women are often stereotyped as emotional while men are stereotyped as rational, emotion expression is also a highly gendered activity The animal rights movement—originally made up primarily of women—was often framed or perceived as emotional and therefore as less politically credible (Einwohner 1999; Groves 2001). A challenger's concerns can be more easily dismissed if they can be painted as largely emotional reactions and counterposed to the rationality and clear thinking attributed to men (Einwohner, Hollander, and Olson 2000). This dualism is so deeply rooted in U.S. public life that men are seldom permitted to express even the "manly" emotion of anger in conventional politics, an arena often restricted to men. For example, when former National Security Agency official Richard Clarke went public in 2004 with his withering critiques of the Bush-Cheney

71

administration's responses to 9/11 and their invasion of Iraq, he was painted publicly as a bitter, emotional man, blinded by his anger, and therefore untrustworthy. This occurred despite his long and distinguished career in the intelligence services under both Republican and Democratic presidents. As the passage below shows, MoveOn.org quickly went to bat for Clarke and his views, organizing television ads to counteract this smear campaign, and to reinforce Clarke's message.

> Already, the White House spin machine is in overdrive. Since they can't rebut Clark's [sic] facts—which independent witnesses have confirmed—they're trying to paint him as an angry partisan, even though he's a Republican. But Clark's words remain a searing indictment of the Bush administration's campaign against terrorism. Together, if we act today, we can beat back the spin by widely airing a TV ad which gets these uniquely credible comments directly to TV viewers. (MoveOn.org, March 26, 2004)

Similarly, Howard Dean's bid for the 2004 Democratic Party presidential nomination was derailed in part because of the intensity of his expression of enthusiasm, what became known as his "scream." Emotion expression in the political arena is clearly governed by norms which regulate which emotions can be appropriately expressed by whom, in what context, and at what intensity levels. Since even established political insiders like Clarke and Dean are held to account by these emotion expression norms, even more so must challengers like social movements attend to them. These norms can present a formidable obstacle and a set of tensions which must be continuously negotiated if the social movement's alternative message is going to be given credence.

SOCIAL MOVEMENTS SCHOLARSHIP AND EMOTIONS

Given the important role that emotions have played in social movement organizing, it is reasonable to expect that social movement scholarship would have differentiated itself from the dominant negative perception of emotions in politics and instead give a prominent place to the study of emotions. Not so, for the sociological study of emotions in collective action has been rather slow to develop, thanks in part to a misguided and overly pejorative view of emotions by social movement scholars in the 1950s. The characterization of social movement actors as irrational and maladapted stemmed from three literatures: (1) early studies of riots using concepts like contagion and mass hysteria (e.g., Le Bon 1897/2002); (2) studies of the Nazi movement using concepts like authoritarian personality and charismatic leadership (e.g., Weber 1947/1997; Adorno, Frenkel-Brunswik, Levinson, and Sanford 1950/1993; Arendt 1951); and (3) functionalist studies portraying social movements as the irrational actions of socially isolated and maladapted individuals responding to structural shifts beyond their comprehension and understanding (e.g.,

Kornhauser 1959; Davies 1962; Johnson 1964; Huntington 1969). It was particularly this third literature that social movement scholars in the 1970s rebelled against. Their solution was to theorize that activists were in fact rational actors who, structurally disadvantaged and marginalized from politics, sought redress of their grievances through the primary means available to them: collective action (e.g., Eisinger 1973; Tilly 1978; McAdam 1982). Protesters were portrayed not as angry people, but instead as rational participants seeking beneficial social changes.

As a result, the question of emotions was largely left out of the social movements literature. More recently, however, this neglectful approach to emotions and social movements has been corrected. Feminist scholars have described how emotions like grief and rage in women's protest have led to empowered action (Harris and King 1989) while other social movement scholars have helped make the deeply cultural aspects of the emotional dimensions of activism a central line of inquiry (Burkitt 1997; Goodwin, Jasper, and Polletta 2000; Aminzade and McAdam 2001).

All of this also required that an even more basic problem be overcome: the dichotomous view of emotions and cognitions. René Descartes' aphorism *cogito ergo sum*—I think therefore I am—captures in one pithy proclamation the privileged nature of rationality in much Western thought. Much else in human experience, and especially emotions, were pushed aside and marginalized in favor of dispassionate thought (Barbalet 1998). We now know, however, that emotions and thoughts are not so much separate strands of human experience as they are blended and woven together in a manner that is difficult to disentangle. They are each, after all, constitutive dimensions of our interpretive processes. Just as we make sense of our social and political situations by thinking about them, we also pay attention to our emotions and what they tell us about the events we experience. Indeed, what we choose to think about and how we think about it are inherently emotion-informed processes. Although emotions are present in all forms of collective behavior, they are particularly salient with regard to motivations for action. When PMOs communicate with the public about the issues that deeply animate their group, they include references to the emotions that motivate their activism. In fact, emotions are crucial components to the social processes that people use to adopt and subsequently to nurture oppositional values and lifestyles (Aminzade and McAdam 2001).

Like so much else in human experience, emotions have a social context; they are not simply an individual experience. They possess at least three socially interactive dimensions that are part of the emotion itself (Leach and Tiedens 2004). First, a person's emotional state of being is responsive in that it is achieved partly in response to a social event or experience. Second, emotions are regulated by values, norms and social practices. Finally, emotions are socially constituted in that they are defined by social relationships even as they give meaning to those relationships. As we show below with regard to the Bush administration's cultivation of a climate or culture of fear, this deeply cultural understanding of emotion is particularly relevant for social movement scholarship.

Many of the causal factors identified by social movement scholars (i.e., collective identities, social networks, collective action frames, moral shocks) gain their potency through the emotions they induce in movement actors (Goodwin and Pfaff 2001). The emotional dimensions of human experience are important enough to social movement organizing that emotions may take center stage in movement narratives (Polletta 2006), in identity construction (Yang 2000), and in mobilization efforts (Robnett 1997). Although they have been too little studied by social movement scholars, emotions themselves even become the object of movement framing processes, as we've shown they were for the U.S. peace movement in the period immediately following 9/11 (Maney, Woehrle, and Coy 2005; Maney, Woehrle, and Coy forthcoming). More important, and as we will demonstrate in this chapter, analysis of discourses about emotions is essential because talking and writing give not only expression but also form to emotions. Emotions are constructed through language (Gould 2004) and they are also restructured in the process of being communicated discursively (Jackson 1993; Burkitt 2002). Discursive expression can also lay bare the responses pursued in emotional reactions to particular events.

In summary, the official statements of U.S. peace movement organizations provide a rich opportunity for the study of emotions. Peace movement organizations care passionately about peace and war. And while emotions may at times be rather opaque during movement activities and events (one cannot always be certain what other persons are feeling simply by how they appear to be acting), the emotion expression contained in the peace movement organization's written statements are relatively explicit.

This chapter will proceed along three lines of analysis. First, we present and briefly discuss the broad trends in the emotions discourse of the PMOs across different conflict periods. This first section will focus on the presence or absence of emotional opportunities and how the U.S. peace movement's emotional work responded to those shifting cultural conditions. Second, we will provide a detailed analysis of the ways that the PMOs constructed their discourse around the emotions of fear during the 9/11 and Iraq War periods. We show that the U.S. peace movement responded to the emotional opportunities presented by the exacerbated climate of fear present in these two conflict periods. The organizations actually made emotions into a site for contentious politics, an arena where challenging groups battled to influence the feelings and the emotional state of the U.S. public. They did this by engaging the fear emotion on multiple levels. First, on the societal or macro level, the PMOs directly challenged the climate of fear. Second, on the individual or micro level, they engaged the fear emotion by promoting what we've termed the faculty of "critical feeling," counseling their members and the public on the importance of overcoming fear, and providing advice and resources on how to free the individual human heart from the tight grip of fear. Third, we analyze a cyber-project, called the Iraq Photo Project, aimed at publicly expressing emotions other than fear that was promoted by a number of the PMOs. We argue that it was designed to enable Americans to break through the culture of fear by reclaiming individual moral agency during war. Citizens expressed their strong feelings about the War on Terrorism and the Iraq War through the posting of photographs of themselves on the Internet, photos wherein they were expressing emotions to the people of Iraq. Finally, our research shows that emotions are not expressed and discussed within the peace movement solely for strategic reasons, but also to enable members and others to honor their emotional states and to reclaim moral agency during times of high conflict.

LONGITUDINAL TRENDS

Scarcity of Emotion Expression: The Gulf War and Iraq 1998

Since the Gulf War was not a long-running conflict, opportunities for emotional work by the PMOs that focused on mounting troop and civilian casualties or on human rights abuses were limited. Emotional opportunities are defined as those time periods or moments when the public expression of particularly potent emotions is widely regarded as socially or politically appropriate (Maney, Woehrle, and Coy 2005). A lack of emotional opportunities inhibits challenging groups from directly expressing strong emotions about government policies they oppose. For example, there were few emotional opportunities present during the Gulf War. The striking lack of emotional work done by the peace movement during that conflict reflects this, and suggests a close relationship between emotional opportunities and the expression and use of emotions in peace movement organizing.

For the U.S. peace movement, degrees of public emotion expression varied considerably across our five conflict periods. As figure 4.1 shows, emotions were not much of an issue during the first two conflict periods. This is explained by a number of factors. Iraq violated international law and norms by invading the sovereign country of Kuwait in 1990. There was a long run-up period of nearly six months to the actual war (arguably not a very emotion-rich stage). Armed conflict then commenced with a multiweek bombing campaign followed by a relatively brief invasion of Kuwait to dispel Iraq by a U.S.-led coalition of UN-sanctioned ground forces. It is likely that the first Bush administration's multilateralism, its willingness to work through the United Nations, and its decision not to carry on to Baghdad and attempt to topple the Hussein government all coalesced to dampen emotional responses or emotion-rich opposition to U.S. policies. After all, our data also show that the U.S. peace movement places a high premium on international cooperation and multilateralism in U.S. foreign policy and consistently argues—including

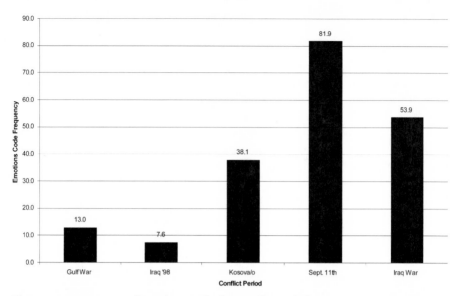

Figure 4.1.   Frequency of Emotions Codes by Conflict Period
Notes: Analysis based on weighted data. For weights formula, see appendix 2. Only data from the five PMOs
  issuing statements in all five conflict periods are included (American Friends Service Committee, Fellowship
  of Reconciliation, Pax Christi, Peace Action, Women's International League for Peace and Freedom).

across different conflict periods—for placing the United Nations at the center
of international affairs. Moreover, since this conflict was about turning back
an invasion of a sovereign country—something the U.S. peace movement also
supported in principle—their emotional reactions were no doubt rather tempered and their use of emotion expression also moderated.

Similarly, there was relatively little emotion expression or discussion of
emotions in peace movement discourse around the 1998–1999 crises over
militarily enforcing the UN weapons inspections and the no-fly zone in Iraq.
With a few exceptions, the documents issued during this period by the U.S.
PMOs in our analysis were marked by tempered and diplomatic language.
One such exception were those statements that were clearly aimed at peace
movement members. These statements tended to contain more emotion
expression, presumably resonating with the emotional states of many peace
movement members and spurring them to increased activism. In the following example of this genre, WILPF did all this, first setting the emotional stage
and then concluding with a motivational pitch about meaningful and efficacious activism:

We are all in such a state of outrage about our government's actions and intentions with regard to Iraq. We hear "war" and "bombings" and our stomachs all
begin to churn. We look for an avenue to express ourselves, and our ardent desire that these things not happen. We look for effective strategies to change our
government's position and to move public opinion away from the vengeful and

bloodthirsty, bottom line—"Just bomb them. And get it over with." I trust that many of you are already active in this area, and we must trust that everything that we do somehow contributes to the effort that makes a difference. (Women's International League for Peace and Freedom, 1998, "Dear Friend Letter")

On the whole, however, the groups tended to speak only of being "troubled" or "deeply concerned" that after nine years of sanctions and almost eight years of bombing by the United States in the so-called no-fly zones following the Gulf War, the United States was embarking in 1998 on an even more sustained bombing campaign to enforce the weapons inspections. The lack of public interest in the issue made it unlikely that the general citizenry would respond to any appeal, even an emotional one. In addition, Saddam Hussein's hot-and-cold, back-and-forth cooperation with the UN weapons inspectors made it doubly difficult for the U.S. peace movement to fashion an emotional appeal to the broader public. As a result, PMOs generally chose to adopt measured tones as they abided by the emotional norms of powerholders and others whom they hoped to influence.

Many of the peace movement groups chose to capitalize on the weapons inspections issue by broadening its scope considerably. They essentially argued that what is good for the goose is good for the gander; that is, weapons inspections ought to be universal, including in the United States. Some groups even took the opportunity to argue for the abolition of all weapons of mass destruction, including any covertly developed by Iraq and overtly by the United States. Articulating these quite unpopular positions was not conducive to using emotional language. With little chance of generating mass opposition, PMOs resigned themselves to bearing witness not only against the impending bombing campaign, but also against the inequities and injustices that they perceived were inherent in the international political system.

Kosova/o: Anger at the NATO Bombings

There was a sizeable increase in emotion expression by the peace movement during the Kosova/o period. We found there were multiple reasons for emotion work by the peace movement, including the fulfillment that comes from emotional expression along with tactical concerns having to do with constructing effective discursive messages. All of the PMOs in our Kosova/o data are deeply committed to the nonviolent resolution of conflicts, and they appeared frustrated by the unproductive positions taken by the United States and NATO during negotiations to end the ethnic wars. The PMOs (and many other commentators) were convinced that a negotiated solution was not only desirable but entirely within reach at the peace talks at Rambouillet. The NATO bombing campaign that followed the failed negotiations was well publicized, lasted for seventy-eight intense days, and included such tactics proscribed by international law as the dropping of cluster bombs in civilian areas. Civilians were being killed by NATO bombing to save still other civilians from ethnic cleansing, the latter of which had been widely reported in the U.S. press. In addition, it was the first aggressive military campaign mounted by NATO. Like others, the peace movement saw it as a dangerous precedent, undermining international law and the role of the UN. These issues are very dear to the hearts of U.S. peace movement organizations, likely occasioning their increased use of emotion expressions in their official statements.

Much of the increase in emotion expression during the Kosova/o period had to do with the peace movement's anger over the NATO bombing. Even while strongly condemning the ethnic cleansing tactics of the Serbians, without exception the peace movement organizations nonetheless saw the NATO bombing as unnecessary and deeply counterproductive, further endangering civilian life in the region. As the WRL put it, civilians now had to deal with dual terrors: escaping the Serb paramilitaries while also avoiding the NATO bombing. Civilian immunity is a treasured precept that carries considerable emotional resonance in the United States. Its resonance with the public is partly why both the Pentagon and the peace movement refer to it so frequently. The Pentagon claims to do everything possible to protect civilians, and uses sanitizing language to quell any emotional responses to its actions. Thus "collateral damage," "surgical strikes," and "smart bombs" have entered the vernacular, serving to obscure the human reality on the ground. For their part, the PMOs highlight the inevitable civilian casualties in war both to appeal to the general public but also to be true to their emotions, identities and values. The peace groups were particularly piqued at the bombing's destruction of a long-running and multiethnic prodemocracy and reform movement in Serbia and Kosova/o. Many in the Western peace movement had been promoting and advising that movement, which they saw as an important ingredient in a viable long-term regional solution (Clark 2000). Anger was also frequently expressed at the violations of international law and at NATO's usurping of the role the PMOs felt belonged to the United Nations. In summary, the increase in emotional work done by the peace movement during the Kosova/o period reflected both more emotional opportunities arising from the peculiarities of the conflict, and a set of issues that were also emotionally salient and less internally conflictive within the peace movement.

9/11: Emotional Opportunities and Emotional Norms

The 9/11 attacks were clearly a "moral shock" for many U.S. citizens. A moral shock occurs when an event (usually public) instills enough of a sense of outrage in people that it moves them toward mobilization (Jasper and Poulsen 1995). The torrent of emotional responses caused by 9/11 therefore created a variety of emotional opportunities for challenging movements to organize around. The AFSC approached this emotional moment directly by asking a series of poignant questions, strongly emotional and motivational in tone.

Now that the initial shock of the September 11 terrorist attacks have passed, deep grief and profound anger have set in for many of us. Now the critical questions that confront us all are several: How can we best comfort those who mourn? How can we begin to heal some of the wounds to all of our souls as well as our bodies? How can we see that justice is really done? How can we build bridges of understanding and reconciliation among all people so that there is no more harm done and no more hatred sown? (American Friends Service Committee, September 26, 2001)

The widespread expression of strong emotions by the public in a period such as 9/11 provides a platform for challengers to create critical interpretive knowledge. In the passage below, the Fellowship of Reconciliation suggested what kinds of public policies are likely to result if strongly felt emotional experiences and expressions are not subjected to critical evaluation.

The United States is awash in patriotism. It is a natural impulse to look for support in the wider community when there is widespread grief, morning [*sic*], fear, and rage in the face of the heinous events of September 11. . . . But there is great danger when these appropriate feelings and actions get channeled into an uncritical call to arms, massive military appropriations, and a jingoism that harms the safety and well-being of our Muslim and Middle Eastern neighbors here at home, and wages war abroad. (Fellowship of Reconciliation, November/December, 2001)

Certainly an emotion commonly experienced across the country following the attacks of 9/11 was the desire for revenge. In a Pew poll of U.S. citizens released on September 21, 2001, 79 percent thought that "punishing terrorists is an important reason for using military force" (Pew Research Center 2001). This widespread embracing of retribution and revenge clearly concerned the peace movement. In fact, revenge was by far the emotion that most often appeared in the PMO statements in the immediate post-9/11 period. For example, while revenge accounted for 78.5 percent of the emotions discourse during 9/11, it made up only 16.4 percent during Iraq 1998, and only 5.1 percent during the Iraq War. It was missing entirely from the Gulf War and Kosova/o. This intensive focus by the peace movement on revenge during the 9/11 period occurred for at least two reasons.

First, the PMOs were not expressing a desire for revenge, but were responding to political realities and emotional opportunities. Their statements reveal that they wanted to help the public think more deeply and critically about an emotion that had broad public appeal at that moment in U.S. history. We suggest that in the same way that the faculties of critical thinking need to be developed for responsible citizenship, so too do the skills associated with what we call "critical feeling." Here the critical interpretations and meanings of emotions are understood to fall within the legitimate purview of a peace movement. Second, the extensive public discourse about retaliation, justice, and revenge after 9/11 created an emotional opportunity for the peace movement to critically assess not only the meanings and appropriateness of these emotions, but also any foreign or domestic policies that might be connected to them. In the example that follows, Peace Action's discourse around revenge created oppositional knowledge of the *critical-interpretive* type with regard to the war on terrorism.

> War, however, is not the best response to the attacks on the Pentagon and the World Trade Center. When political leaders turned the people's feelings of anger, injustice, and helplessness into a call for revenge and retribution, the cycle of violence was accelerated rather than stopped. The war on terrorism is not an effective way to make the world, or America, safer. (Peace Action, "9/11 Justice")

Our coding of presidential statements following the attacks of 9/11 indicates that President Bush spoke frequently about his resolve to militarily pursue and defeat terrorists and terrorism all across the globe. He largely abided by U.S. norms regarding emotion expression, avoiding expressing feelings of revenge and retaliation while highlighting the construct of justice. Here are two representative examples.

> The fight we have begun will not be quickly or easily finished. Our enemies hide and plot in many nations. They are devious and ruthless. Yet we are confident in the justice of our cause. We will fight for as long as it takes, and we will prevail. (President Bush, November 24, 2001)
>
> After September the 11th, I vowed to the world that we would bring to justice those who killed innocent women and children and men here in America. I also said that any nation that harbored a terrorist, that aided a terrorist, that abetted a terrorist would be held accountable. And that's exactly what's taking place today. Thanks to our military, thanks to friends and allies, we are destroying the Taliban military and we're destroying the camps that terrorists use to plan attacks on nations such as America. (President Bush, November 28, 2001)

The president framed his ambitious global policy as a military quest for justice. He honored strong emotional norms that proscribe the seeking of vengeance, even for such contemptible acts as the 9/11 attacks. Although they were equally interested in the norm of justice, many in the peace movement nonetheless took the president directly to task for equating justice with military intervention. Declaring "justice, not vengeance," New York City Labor Against the War created *transformative* oppositional knowledge by insisting that the proper way to seek justice was through "an independent international tribunal to impartially investigate, apprehend and try those responsible for the September 11 attack" (New York City Labor Against the War, September 27, 2001). The American Friends Service Committee also used the emotional norm of not seeking revenge to put forward an alternative conception of justice. The example below demonstrates the dynamic interplay involved in harnessing—at the same time—both a hegemonic concept like justice and an emotional norm against seeking revenge. In so doing justice was once again redefined: justice cannot include the creation of more victims.

We encourage like-minded groups and supporters of peace throughout the U.S. and the world to organize candlelight vigils, marches and other gatherings in showing our call for peace and Justice—not war, revenge or retaliation. . . . Let there be no more victims, either in the U.S. or abroad. (American Friends Service Committee, October 2, 2001)

Grief was the second most recurring emotion during 9/11. Given the historic emphases in the peace movement on solidarity, empathy, and humanitarian- ism (Chatfield 1971; Wittner 1984), this was likely the fruit of the genuine experience of grief within the organizations. It was also an attempt to heighten the potency of their critical discourses on governmental policies by honoring the hard-to-ignore emotional norm to grieve the loss of innocent life. We have empirically shown elsewhere (Maney, Woehrle, and Coy forthcoming) that during the 9/11 period peace movement organizations overwhelmingly chose to honor and appropriate emotional norms, as opposed to rejecting them (84 percent vs. 16 percent of emotion-related codes). Revenge is mostly proscribed from both experience and expression in the United States, channeled instead into the broad but badly defined construct of justice. Grief, meanwhile, is well defined and expected to be expressed, and it was widely experienced and shared after the 9/11 attacks. The PMOs followed this framework in their statements without exception. We argue that this also allowed the PMOs to use these emotions as "carriers" (Maney, Woehrle, and Coy 2005) linking the movement's unpopular policy critiques to emotional norms and to those emotions that were extensively shared, thereby granting the critiques more legitimacy.

The 9/11 period demonstrates the dynamic, interactive relationship be- tween emotional opportunities, emotional norms, and the emotional work of the peace movement. Seizing emotional opportunities by conforming to emotional norms allowed the peace movement to create much-needed oppo- sitional knowledge in a particularly critical, fast-paced cultural moment. We turn now to a brief consideration of the longitudinal trends contained within the Iraq War data.

Iraq War: Using Emotions to Challenge Policies

As figure 4.1 demonstrates, although there was some overall drop-off from the 9/11 period, the peace movement's emotion expression and discussion of emotion remained markedly pronounced during the Iraq War. This, too, was an emotion-rich time following so closely on the heels of 9/11. The peace movement learned from and built on the emotional labor it performed in the earlier period. Fear was by far the predominant emotion, followed by grief, hope, anger, empathy, and pain in descending order. Revenge barely ap- peared. What accounts for the quite high level of emotion work done by the peace movement during the Iraq War?

The invasion and occupation of Iraq by the United States moved the world's sole superpower into uncharted territories, creating emotional opportunities specific to the conflict. Different types of emotional opportunities will lead to different types of emotion work by social movements. For example, the war on Iraq was a preemptive attack on a sovereign country posing no real threat to the United States. It was conducted under a cloud of obfuscation and misrepresentation. The invasion and occupation lacked UN support, wasn't nearly as multilateral as the Gulf War coalition, and wasn't supported by domestic or international public opinion (see chapter 8). It occasioned high levels of civilian casualties and was marked by flagrant violations of Iraqi human rights at Abu Ghraib and elsewhere. The occupation failed to reconstruct the infrastructure destroyed by the invasion, and terrorism found a firm foothold in the country where there had been little previously. On July 11, 2003, when the invasion and occupation was less than six months old and civil war had not yet even engulfed Iraq, 64 percent of Americans surveyed in an ABC News/*Washington Post* poll felt that the war had already damaged the United States' image in the rest of the world either a great deal or somewhat. Obviously this broad list of issues and concerns gave occasion for many Americans to react emotionally, not just in the peace movement proper. The presence of strong emotions like anger, grief, indignation, and others arising from a sense of injustice are clearly important, if not critical, for mobilizing opposition (Aminzade and McAdam 2001; Gamson 1992a). These emotions must be acknowledged, highlighted, and used as a springboard to sustained and hope-filled mobilization, as the women's group CODEPINK did below.

> So as women from every part of the country converge on Washington to march for women's lives, we do it with indignation, but we also do it with hope. . . . The media and fearful Bush administration can tell us differently, but we know better. We feel the groundswell and we hear the drum beat. We know the world will continue to rise up, speak out, and say enough is enough. (CODEPINK, April 19, 2004)

The deeply felt concerns throughout the country over the Iraq War created distinctive emotional opportunities for the peace movement. During 9/11, in the midst of a period of political closure, the PMOs largely abided by emotional norms while attempting to defuse emotions hyped up by powerholders and by many others throughout society. They also engaged in significant amounts of harnessing of dominant emotions. In contrast, the Iraq War period was marked by dissensus among both the governing elite and the public, not only in the United States but also internationally (see table 8.2 in chapter 8).

As the CODEPINK example above demonstrates, and as the next section shows in greater detail, this much more open political context during the Iraq War meant that PMOs felt increasingly able to engage in emotional work that directly challenged the full range of Bush administration policies on Iraq. In what follows, we will document and analyze in much greater detail the many ways that the peace movement engaged the culture of fear propagated by the Bush administration during the 9/11 and Iraq War periods.

CONTENDING OVER A CLIMATE OF FEAR

Discursive contention over emotions themselves and over emotional climates are actually a site for contentious politics, broadly conceived. While contention over emotions is evident in our data for a number of emotions during specific conflict periods, in what follows we will focus on the emotion of fear during two related conflict periods: 9/11 and the Iraq War. The emotional labor performed by the peace movement around fear was sustained and complex enough to provide rich potential for analysis.

Fear is a potent and complex emotion, worthy of our detailed attention here. Some evolutionary psychologists argue that it is the oldest and most influential human emotion (Walton 2004). It is impossible to understand the emotion expression of the U.S. peace movement during the 9/11 and Iraq War periods without taking into account the fact that emotions like fear are multidimensional, intertwined, and more important, usually have a history. The anger and fear felt in the post-9/11 period (including during the first two years of the Iraq War) is intimately connected to a long strand of U.S. cultural history wherein generations of Americans felt extremely safe, secure, and protected while on U.S. soil. This was largely thanks to geographical location, wide-ranging cross-cutting national ties, and U.S. global dominance in military matters. The shockingly sudden severing of those feelings of physical security by the 9/11 attackers gave added lift to the widespread feelings of anger and fear. This is an example of J. M. Barbalet's (1998) concept of emotional climate. Emotions aren't only individualized experiences; they also possess collective aspects that are related to shared memberships in particular groups. Emotional climates are socially constructed by group members through the ways that they interact with one another on important issues with affective dimensions (de Rivera, Kurrien, and Olsen 2007).

President Bush assiduously stoked the fires that fueled a climate of fear. For instance, early on following 9/11 he tended to paint stark, dark, and evocative pictures, designed to instill fear and vigilance in the public.

> The great threat to civilization is not that the terrorists will inspire millions. Only the terrorists themselves would want to live in their brutal and joyless world. The great threat to civilization is that a few evil men will multiply their murders, and gain the means to kill on a scale equal to their hatred. We know they have this mad intent, and we're determined to stop them. (George W. Bush, December 11, 2001)

One common way that the PMOs addressed the emotional climate of fear following 9/11 and the first two years of the Iraq War was to first affirm fear as an entirely appropriate emotion. But the issue for the peace movement ran deeper: to what ends was this emotion being put? The PMOs turned the government's exploitation of legitimate fear into a struggle over the emotional mood and the policy direction of the country, that is, into a site of cultural and political contention. Consequently, the PMOs wrote about fear often and extensively, highlighting its potential to be manipulated by a government at war. In fact, during the Iraq War, fear was by far the single emotion most often discussed by the PMOs. Our analysis shows that the peace groups made two quite different approaches to discursively engaging this cultural climate of fear.

First, virtually all of the groups named and then directly challenged on the societal, macro level the administration's propagating of fear. Here they wrote about the short- and long-term costs to the nation and to the body politic if fear were the driving force in U.S. domestic and foreign policy. Second, many of the groups also attempted to address this issue by challenging its influential grip on the personal, micro level. They cajoled and counseled their members and citizens on how to recognize the many manifestations of the climate of fear in their personal lives, and also on how not to fall under its sway in the first place. They attempted to develop the faculties of "critical feeling" among their members and the broader public that we referred to above. In what follows below, we will discuss each of these two approaches in turn.

Macro-level Contention over the Climate of Fear

With regard to the first approach, at the beginning of the Iraq War, Pax Christi employed medical imagery as it "grieved" over the fact that government "lies" were creating a "contagion of fear and distrust" that was sweeping the country to war. Similarly, the Black Radical Congress warned of a "bankrupt and disingenuous administration committed to promoting domestic fear" in order to justify its policies. CODEPINK, whose very name challenges and rejects—through a play on words—the administration's color-coded security alerts "that are based on fear," claimed that the administration "lied" about the alleged Iraqi threat in order to "scare people into backing their war." TrueMajority and many other groups claimed that the president used Americans' fears after 9/11 to restrict civil liberties at home and human rights abroad. Some groups created critical interpretive knowledge by linking this current culture of fear with that of the Cold War. For example, on one hand the FOR affirmed the emotional state of many Americans by acknowledging that they should be "justifiably anxious" about terrorist threats. Yet on the other hand they nonetheless charged that President Bush had created a "terrorist bogeyman—much like the Communist bogeyman of the Cold War." USLAW delivered a sweeping critique and direct challenge to the emotional work of the administration and the hegemonic climate of fear, laying a host of social problems at its doorstep:

We are living in an era in which the government has manipulated our nation's fear of terrorism to launch wars, destroy our economic security, undermine government services, erode our democratic rights and intensify racism, sexism, religious discrimination and divisions among working people. (United States Labor Against the War, December 2003)

Eight months into the Iraq War, fear discourse still dominated President Bush's speeches. The president was on somewhat of the defensive in his State of the Union address of January 2004 since the much-touted weapons of mass destruction in Iraq had not been found, and U.S. soldiers were clearly not being welcomed as the liberators that Vice President Cheney had insisted they would be. In this context the president's speech emphasized why his administration and all Americans needed to be continually fearful of terrorist threats and concerned about security. Our coding of that speech indicates that over half of the paragraphs (thirty-seven of seventy) were about perceived terrorism threats to the United States and the Bush administration's responses. Suffused with evocative emotional imagery, the speech left the impression that the United States faced only one major problem: a sustained and insidious threat of terrorism, one that could only be successfully resisted through a continuation of Bush-Cheney's hard-nosed foreign and domestic policies. As the president put it,

I know that some people question if America is really in a war at all. They view terrorism more as a crime, a problem to be solved mainly with law enforcement and indictments. . . . After the chaos and carnage of September the 11th, it is not enough to serve our enemies with legal papers. The terrorists and their supporters declared war on United States, and war is what they got. (Applause) (George W. Bush, State of the Union Speech, January 20, 2004)

Although it was dressed up some for the formalized occasion of the State of the Union address, the speech nonetheless contained the classic elements of simple "fear-mongering" tactics: repetition, depicting isolated incidents as trends, and misdirection (Glassner 2004; Maney, Woehrle, and Coy forthcoming). The president was frequently interrupted by applause from the Republican-dominated Congress. However, the very next day the American Friends Service Committee not only refused to applaud, but directly challenged the emotional work of the president in the chambers of Congress. AFSC issued a lengthy press release that was a detailed rebuttal of the address. Among much else, AFSC also said that the "President's emotional imagery exploits a culture of fear and creates the economy fueled by a perpetual multibillion-dollar war" (American Friends Service Committee, January 21, 2004). The rebuttal focused on redefining notions of security and detailed the complex of human costs associated with the war on terrorism and the occupation of Iraq.[1]

When citizens are fearful and insecure, other emotions such as revenge, anger, love, and empathy are most likely to be transposed into political action

(Berezin 2002). Considered collectively, all the examples presented above about how the PMOs contended over the climate of fear suggest that they recognized the political potency of the fear emotion. The question for the peace movement was, what kind of political action and for what purposes? To address this dimension of the problem, the PMOs turned to the micro level, a turn we document and analyze in what follows.

Micro-level Contention over the Climate of Fear

The other dominant approach was not simply to challenge on the macro level the Bush administration's cultivation of a climate of fear, but to redirect attention to the personally destructive dynamics of fear on the individual, micro level. It was here—on the level of the individual citizen—that some of the groups felt that the negative effects of a burgeoning climate of fear could best be mitigated. They identified the individual human heart as a promising arena for them to engage the politics of contentious emotions. We see this as an example of oppositional knowledge that transforms the ways that individuals feel about war and the fears that drive it.

This approach was primarily employed by some of the spiritually based organizations (AFSC, FOR, Pax Christi), but not exclusively, for the secular War Resisters League also utilized it. AFSC often presented fear as an emotion that must be "owned" on a deeply personal level so that it won't paralyze the individual but can be overcome. These Quakers said that the Christian scriptures teach that fear and greed are the root causes of war and strife; therefore, fear must be "overcome" on the individual level so the cycle of violence will be derailed and people can act for peace. Here fearful individual citizens are seen as important contributors to a spiraling cycle of violence resulting in an ill-defined war on terror and an invasion and occupation of a sovereign Iraq. Similarly, the interfaith Fellowship of Reconciliation advised that fear is part of the human condition and can only be addressed through an individual's faith since God is the source of true security. The Catholic group Pax Christi organized the "Iraq Peace Journey," a delegation of religious leaders to Iraq in December 2002 on the date of the UN deadline for Iraq to disclose its weapons of mass destruction. The delegates' statement below supported a nonviolent solution to the crisis and named fear as a powerful distorting force in human affairs, but one that must be overcome on the level of the individual heart:

> Our world today is scarred by fear: fear of war, terrorism, weapons of mass destruction. Our government's pervasive rhetoric of fear distorts our vision, divides the human family, and ultimately creates the very violence we dread. We need to deal with terrorism, but we in the United States cannot allow fear to rule our hearts. (Pax Christi, December 4, 2002, in Iraq)

These responses, and others like them in the data, are marked by their close associations between collective identities, such as pacifist Quaker (AFSC), progressive Catholic (Pax Christi), or interfaith pacifist (FOR), with the emotional labor involved in "overcoming" on the individual level the effects of a broader climate of fear. While the president sought to increase fear in order to justify foreign and domestic policies that many citizens were uneasy about, the PMOs refused to cede this emotional turf. In their battle for the both the minds and the hearts of their members, the peace organizations appealed to the spiritual identities of their members. They drew directly from shared religious traditions for resources that their members could use in order to triumph over a fear that would otherwise paralyze them politically while leading to yet more violence. By confronting fear and its political consequences, these peace movement organizations traveled down a well-worn social movement pathway. Decades earlier, activists in the U.S. civil rights movement were also beset by fears—of imprisonment, violence, and death. Identification and a sense of belonging to a larger movement that was making history helped many overcome those fears and remain politically active (Goodwin and Pfaff 2001).

One of the many reasons why emotions are so sociologically interesting is because power relations are often embedded in emotional exchanges. This is true on multiple levels, including between individuals, between groups, and in relations between individuals and groups and their governments. Governments employ emotions to influence the way that people think, feel, and ultimately behave politically. For instance, during the 1999 NATO bombing of Serbia, the AFSC said Milosevic came to power and maintained control by appealing to nationalist feelings and by manipulating emotions about other Balkan peoples that ran back decades or longer. As we've just seen above, the U.S. government also engaged in emotional work designed to support its power and maintain its control by nurturing political acquiescence based on fear. Emotions then are an integral dimension of political relations, if not the root of political relations (Burkitt 2005). Consequently, it is not only religious groups that challenged the climate of fear on the individual level. In the passage below, the secular War Resisters League advised Americans that the individual's fear of death is a potent mechanism of social control, and they cited Gandhi on the need to conquer it.

> We must use whatever internal and external resources we have to overcome our fear of death and to help others to do the same. Fear of death remains the ultimate means by which the government and its corporate media control the people. We cannot "protect" ourselves by greater death dealing. Gandhi said that he became nonviolent the moment he conquered fear. (War Resisters League, March 21, 2003)

FEAR OVERCOME: THE IRAQ PHOTO PROJECT

The high numbers of civilian casualties in the Iraq War, and the widespread distribution of photographs depicting torture of Iraqi prisoners at the hands of U.S. servicemen and servicewomen, revealed a side of the U.S. invasion and occupation with which many Americans were not comfortable. These events were emotionally upsetting and did not square with a common image of the United States as a protector of human rights and as a benign and benevolent superpower. In this political and cultural context, the FOR wished to reclaim the power of photography for the communication of compassionate and conciliatory emotions. As they put it, "The power of visual images has brought us many gruesome and shameful messages from Iraq: Let's use the same visual tool to send back messages of compassion, shared grief and a sense of our oneness as human beings" (Fellowship of Reconciliation, Iraq Photo Project, n.d.).

In the context of war, fear has a human face. We fear the enemy, the Other, and the dangerous belief systems that they supposedly embody (Keen 1985). One way to actively overcome the propagation of fear that occurs during wartime is to reach out to the enemy Other, to reject the emotional dualism at the core of warfare and to treat the Other with respect and dignity. To do so is always an intensely emotional process. Some PMOs overtly rejected that emotional dualism, reaching out through the Internet in an emotion-rich photographic campaign, which we describe below.

The Iraq Photo Project was launched by the Fellowship of Reconciliation in the summer of 2004, and also promoted by Pax Christi, AFSC, and other organizations.[2] It was a concrete demonstration of a creative cyberprotest mechanism through which U.S. citizens could reject the culture of fear and overcome their fears to act politically through structured, collective expressions of emotions. The focus of the project was people-to-people communication of emotions, thereby helping participants feel emotionally fulfilled even while granting those emotions both a deeper moral meaning and enhanced political potency. The project encouraged U.S. citizens and activists to gather in groups of three or more to make a large three-by-five-foot sign with their own hand-written message to the Iraqi people and others in the Arab and Muslim world regarding their feelings toward the war and occupation. They then had themselves photographed holding that sign, and sent the photographs to the FOR for posting to the Internet and for coordinated distribution to Arab and Muslim media outlets worldwide. In language that was heavily emotion laden, Iraq Photo Project promotional literature encouraged sign makers to "speak from the heart."

> Many of us feel distraught over the war in Iraq . . . our hearts heavy with grief and shame. We cry over the news and experience profound despair. We don't feel that the explanations and declarations of our government represent us. We search for ways to express our feelings. We wish we could communicate our anguish directly to the people who are suffering so much. . . . The power of visual images has brought us many gruesome and shameful messages from Iraq: Let's use the same visual tool to send back messages of compassion, shared grief and a sense of our oneness as human beings.

We hope the messages will convey our profound sense of grief and shame, as well as our heartfelt apology for what has been done in our name. We hope for messages of peace, friendship and common humanity. Above all, we hope individuals and groups, small and large, will write original messages, expressing their own feelings "in their own words." (Fellowship of Reconciliation, "Iraq Photo Project," n.d.)

The organization included sample messages in the Photo Project literature, and posted examples of photographed messages on their website. They were full of rich and evocative feeling words and phrases like "we weep," "we are mortified," "we apologize from our hearts," "we are profoundly ashamed," "our hearts overflow with tears," and "our hearts ache." In addition, participants were advised, "When it is time to take the photograph, please stand seriously and solemnly. Photos of laughing, grinning, waving people, and flippant messages or gestures are not appropriate and will not be included."[3] Clearly, this mobilization of emotion expression was carefully thought out, managed, and overtly orchestrated to various degrees. Both societal emotion norms as well as movement emotion norms were articulated and enforced. A unified public face of the movement was presented, so that the mobilization of strong emotions in a coordinated fashion might gain greater political power. The staged and photographed emotion expressions were used strategically in the battle for the hearts and minds of the U.S. public, of the Iraqi people, and of Internet viewers worldwide. We hasten to observe that this social construction of emotions does not necessarily mean that those feelings were any less genuine or any less meaningful, either for those in the photographs, or for those viewing them.

Photo 4.1. An example of the emotionally expressive photos sent to Iraq and posted online through FOR's Iraq Photo Project. (Photo courtesy of Bob Wallace. Used with permission)

Photo 4.2. Iraq Photo Project entry from Gainesville, Florida. (Photo courtesy of Fellowship of Reconcilation. Used with permission.)

At a Washington, DC, news conference on October 20, 2004, the FOR announced that the project was ready for distribution to Arab and international media, for Internet posting, and for distribution to domestic media outlets. The organization hoped that Iraqis and others across the world would see in the photo message another face of the United States—not of bombardiers, occupiers, or torturers—but of decent compassionate Americans who were not just concerned, but deeply ashamed of what was being done in their name. During the presidential inauguration week a few months later, the FOR also exhibited the photos at a Washington, DC, church as part of a broader counterinaugural mobilization. In midsummer 2005, one year after its launch, when they stopped promoting and adding to the project, FOR had received over 400 photos involving more than 2,000 people.[4] They put 200 photos on their website and on CDs for distribution to the media. Photographs posted on the Iraq Photo Project web site came from thirty-four states, the District of Columbia, and other territories.

The Iraq Photo Project appears to have had multiple goals, including building bridges of emotional solidarity with Iraqi victims of the war, providing emotional expression for U.S. citizens frustrated and angered by the administration's war policies, and instilling a sense of meaning for stalwart peace activists who had seen their activism bring precious few tangible results. It was also about challenging and rejecting the climate of fear associated with the enemy Other. This creative grassroots cybercampaign helped ordinary citizens create and distribute *transformative* oppositional knowledge by demonstrating how the emotional dualisms at the core of war-making could be overcome. In addition, it recognized that emotions provided opportunities; they were creatively deployed to reclaim moral ground lost through such events as the torture of Iraqi prisoners at Abu Ghraib.

Finally, the Iraq Photo Project demonstrates that emotions are complex phenomena in that they have a fundamentally ambivalent dimension to them. In the face of grief or shame, for instance, a cause for that emotion is searched out and, when found, the grief or shame may change, to be experienced and even expressed as anger (Nussbaum 2001). In the late 1980s, for example, ACT UP successfully moved many gays and lesbians from grief and anger to militant activism (Gould 2004). Similarly, thousands of Americans got in touch with their emotional feelings about the war by taking part in the Iraq Photo Project. They carefully considered what they felt about the war, wrote it on a placard, had themselves photographed, and sent the photographs to the FOR to be sent to the media and posted to the Internet as a collective exercise in emotion mobilization. In the process, many also identified the cause of their shame, their frustration, and their anger about U.S. government policies in Iraq, and included that in their messages.

CONCLUSION

Our analysis of the shifting levels of emotion expression by peace movement organizations across five conflict periods suggests how changing emotional opportunities impact the emotion work of social movements. This examination also demonstrates that emotions are intentionally made a site for contentious politics in multiple ways, and under varying political and cultural conditions. It is true that social movement organizations do this when they and their supporters are themselves experiencing and expressing strong emotions. But that is only part of the story. Movement organizations also make emotions a site of contention in response to the use of emotions by their opponents, as in the case of PMOs' challenges to the Bush administration's cultivation of a climate of fear to justify repression of civil liberties at home and the prosecution of preemptive and aggressive wars abroad. Equally important, by demonstrating that this contention over emotions was discursively conducted in a sustained way by the movement on both the macro level and on the micro level, this analysis begins to fill a lacuna in the theoretical literature.

The emotional labor of the peace movement that we have described suggests that social movement organizations play important cultural roles in their communities and in the lives of individual citizens. The emotion work of helping citizens to develop the faculty of "critical feeling" to complement the critical thinking skills associated with oppositional knowledge creation is an example of the important cultural roles played by movement organizations.

As we have also demonstrated above, many of the mechanisms that facilitate social movement mobilization do so in significant part via the emotional dynamics that they engage (Aminzade and McAdam 2001). But equally key is that our analysis suggests that the emotion work of the organizations is critical to mobilization and also to sustaining participation under varying emotional conditions. Specifically in that regard, our analysis of the Iraq Photo Project shows how the peace movement read the emotional landscape and created vehicles that activists used to express their feelings. On the one hand, emotions were wielded in the Iraq Photo Project as a tactical tool against a war that caused many Americans shame and anger. On the other hand, emotions were also used as a bridge-building mechanism to connect with victimized citizens on the other side of the emotional and of the conflict divide. We argue that in both of these instances, the Iraq Photo Project assisted U.S. citizens in reclaiming not only their emotional agency but also their moral agency in a time of war.

NOTES

1. For a full analysis of how the PMOs redefined security, see the discussion in chapter 6.

2. The Fellowship of Reconciliation (FOR) engaged in more emotion expression during the Iraq War than any of the other fifteen groups. Also, the FOR, the AFSC, and CODEPINK collectively accounted for 47 percent of emotion expression by our PMOs during the Iraq War.

3. www.forusa.org/programs/iraq/iraqphotoproject/iraq-photoproject-statement.html, accessed February 26, 2007.

4. Phone interview by Patrick Coy with Ethan Vesely-Flad, editor of FOR's *Fellowship* magazine, February 26, 2007.

5

Gods of War, Gods of Peace

The country was up in arms, the war was on, in every breast burned the
holy fire of patriotism; the drums were beating, the bands playing, the toy
pistols popping . . . while in the churches the pastors preached devotion
to flag and country and invoked the God of Battles, beseeching His aid
in our good cause in outpouring of fervid eloquence which moved every
listener.

—Mark Twain, "The War Prayer," 1905

The anthropologist Clifford Geertz (1973) developed an influential understanding of religion as a "cultural system" of symbols that provide understandings, motivations, and meanings regarding many dimensions of human
experience, from the special and the peculiar to the common and everyday.
This meaning-making both shapes and is shaped by social relations. "Religious symbols form a basic congruence between a particular style of life and
a specific (if, most often, implicit) metaphysic, and in so doing sustain each
with the borrowed authority of the other" (Geertz 1973, 90).

Few political issues cut closer to the heart of religious sensibilities—and
are, therefore, more ripe for religious discourse and activism—than choices
associated with a country's decision to wage war or make peace. This is not
fully explained by the religious dimensions present in some conflicts, nor
is it because some wars have religious differences at their core. Rather it is
connected to the value that most religions place on love, peace, charity, and
justice, and to the fact that most teach some version of the golden rule with
its basic ethic of reciprocity. In short, religions have a lot to say about violent
conflicts and war, religious people often care intensely about those issues, and

Religion = War

93

Religious discourse [handwritten margin note]

religious discourse frequently figures prominently in the civic debates about waging wars. Religion is also important for challenging movements because of the legitimacy it provides for certain policies through a process of ideational affiliation. That is, if believers are convinced that their gods demand certain actions, they are more likely to support policies that are in line with those demands and actions. Political leaders frequently rely on this very process to mobilize support for far-reaching and costly policies.

For example, President George W. Bush gave a speech during a religious service at the National Cathedral a few days following the 9/11 attacks, on what was called the "National Day of Prayer and Remembrance." The cathedral swelled with a crowd that included his cabinet, former presidents, large contingents from both the Senate and House, ministers, rabbis, Catholic cardinals, Muslim clerics, and many other top public and private officials. He framed his mission and that of a mourning country in what Bob Woodward called a "grand vision of God's master plan" (Woodward 2002, 66–67). The president spoke forcefully and plainly: "Just three days removed from these events, Americans do not yet have the distance of history. But our responsibility to history is already clear: to answer these attacks and rid the world of evil" (Bush, September 14, 2001). As the service ended, the entire gathering in the National Cathedral stood and sang the righteous patriotic anthem "The Battle Hymn of the Republic."

Religious discourse is a many-headed Hydra. In the same way that President Bush relied on it at the National Cathedral, religion's cultural dominance helps ensure that a significant percentage of the U.S. population will be discursively attuned to and cognitively open to messages that reference common religious beliefs, even when they are oppositional. Thus religious discourse provides opportunities for movements trying to fashion oppositional cultures of counterhegemonic resistance (Billings 1990). Moreover, religion provides a host of other assets for challenger movements, many of which are rich with meaning and resonance. They include challenges that are complimented by divine legitimation for protest activities as well as moral imperatives associated with justice, peace, charity, and equality. Religion also provides sacred rituals that uphold political engagement, and values that foster self-sacrifice and sustained activism on behalf of others. As a social institution, religion offers movements experienced and respected leadership, financial and material resources, familiar and authoritative discourses, and even safe political or civic spaces. Last but certainly not least, religion provides movements with preexisting solidarity networks, communication systems, and those cross-cutting collective identities that are so important to mobilization (Christian Smith 1996). Some of these religious riches have been hard-won in the U.S. tradition of ideological struggle, while others have gradually and almost imperceptibly accumulated over time given the prominent place religion holds in the country's history.

CHAPTER OVERVIEW

We begin this chapter with a historically informed discussion of the influential role civil religion has played in the United States and the concomitant influence which that history imparts to religious discourse. Given the prominent role of religion in his campaigns and presidency, we have focused this chapter on the two conflict periods in our data associated with President George W. Bush: the 9/11 period and the first two years of the Iraq War. We provide a brief overview of Bush's religiosity and follow that with a detailed analysis of his religious discourse. Here we show that George W. Bush's religious discourse was marked by extensive use of binary thinking and the repeated construction and demonization of a largely religious enemy. Having set the table in this way, we then turn to our analysis of the religious discourse of the U.S. peace movement during these same two conflict periods. Our qualitative analysis reveals that the U.S. peace movement had three primary responses to Bush's religiously based discourse. First, they directly challenged his reliance on binaries and his demonization of a broadly-defined enemy. Second, they harnessed the president's overt religiosity and his religious discourse and turned the power of these symbols against him and his policies. Third, many of the PMOs constructed oppositional knowledge by focusing their statements on providing remedial education about Islam. Our quantitative analysis further reveals a close relationship between the peace movement's use of religious discourse and its identity-based talk. In addition, we also found a close relationship between the movement's religious discourse and advocating for extra-institutional, protest-based politics.

U.S. CIVIL RELIGION

The Puritans believed that God had assigned a uniquely divine mission to the nation that they were creating. Massachusetts Governor John Winthrop confidently proclaimed as early as 1630 that "The God of Israel is among us. . . . We shall be as a city upon a hill" (Ahlstrom 1975, 464). Notwithstanding this early ardor for joining God and state in the American experiment, the separation of church and state through the disestablishment clause of the Constitution is commonly hailed as the central and greatest political innovation of the United States (Fowler, Hertzke and Olson 1999). Somewhat paradoxically, this separation, when combined with the constitutional guarantees of free speech and assembly, has helped make it possible for religion to be an influential force in U.S. political and social history, profoundly shaping the national experience (Wills 1990; Heyer 2003). Religion has played two powerful roles: one largely a supportive, maintaining role for a government that grants it free exercise; the other a visionary corrective to a state whose policies violate various religions' often professed commitments to peace, justice, and equality. While religion has helped to maintain and serve the status quo throughout U.S. history, it has also often been a prickly thorn in the side of a sleeping public conscience through moral judgments, protests, and political mobilizations of the faithful. These dual roles are often conceived of as competing—or complimentary—manifestations of the country's "civil religion." In the analysis that follows of White House and peace movement discourses, both of these traditions will be amply represented.

Nearly forty years ago, sociologist Robert Bellah argued that the United States is marked by a civil religion, "a collection of beliefs, symbols, and rituals with respect to sacred things and institutionalized in a collectivity" (1967/2005, 46). While many of these beliefs and symbols are culturally associated with the Christian tradition in particular and a transcendent dimension more generally, others are also intimately connected to the country's political history and the values of freedom, liberty, and democracy associated therein. Many scholars have used Max Weber's basic distinctions between the priestly and prophetic leadership types played by religion to identify not a single unified American civil religion, but two primary strains (Williams and Alexander 1994; Fairbanks 1981). The first strain is state centered and priestly with its focus on the United States as a chosen nation with exceptional responsibilities to do God's will on earth; this is often associated with the doctrine of the United States' "manifest destiny." This doctrine has fueled U.S. neoimperial interventions from Mexico to the Philippines to Chile and, arguably, to Iraq. The second strain includes a prophetic vision that not only cares about justice at home but also turns outward to globally promote cooperation, disarmament, internationalism, and equality (Wuthnow 1988; Billings and Scott 1994; Kent and Spickard 1994).

Civil religion in the United States is remarkably strong, especially from a comparative perspective. Following his tour of the young United States in 1831, Alexis de Tocqueville reported that "There is no country in the world where the Christian religion retains a greater influence over the souls of men than in America" (Lipset 1996, 62). It is well known that the United States is a predominantly Protestant country. What is less often realized is that national opinion polls by Gallup and others indicate that Americans are not only the most churchgoing in Protestantism but are also the most fundamentalist in all of Christendom (Lipset 1996). Meanwhile, according to the most recent World Values Survey (2005), fully 81% of those U.S. citizens surveyed report that they describe themselves as a religious person—independently of whether or not they go to church. In comparison, for selected European countries (Austria, East Germany, West Germany, France, Italy, Netherlands), the percentage was on average significantly lower (55%).[1]

THE RICHES OF RELIGIOUS DISCOURSE

Given the strengths of the religious tradition in the United States, religious discourse itself may be the most valuable aspect of what religion has to offer to social movements (Billings 1990). This is at least partly because it is widely available and easily understood across the U.S. population, including as a framework for thinking about and interpreting public life (Rhys Williams 2004). How else to make sense of the contradictory public policies that Reverend Pat Robertson and Reverend Jesse Jackson manage to advocate while relying upon strikingly similar religious symbols and language? Civil religion is, at base, a public religious discourse: that is, a complex of cultural practices and religiously infused traditions deployed by groups on behalf of their own interests and agendas (Williams and Demerath 1991). We think it best to conceive of this U.S. civil religious discourse as the distinctly religious dimension of the dominant symbolic repertoire—the vast stock of durable images, ideas, and beliefs whose frequent use by authority figures (both secular and religious) over time infuses it with more resonant and more potent meanings. Consequently, it is not just presidents or pastors who can make use of the images associated with civil religion, as this example from Pax Christi from the first weeks following 9/11 clearly demonstrates.

> We need to honor those impulses as a nation and in our faith. Our call to be the peace of Christ will take the same courage and creativity, strength and honesty to live out the best of U.S. traditions—those which reflect Christ's discipline of love: affirming the human dignity in ourselves, our neighbor (especially the vulnerable), and our enemy alike. These "better angels of our nature," as Abraham Lincoln called them, are embodied in a vision that presents an alternative to war—neither excusing nor fueling acts of terror. (Pax Christi, September 25, 2001)

Here the peace group extolled the moral teachings not only of Jesus Christ but also of Abraham Lincoln, a venerable U.S. figure, and fused their teachings tightly to a national identity that is said to eschew war.

When religious discourse is further wrapped in a package of nationalist symbols and myths of origin, not only is it widely available for appropriation, but its resonance and its potency is multiplied. Just as the singing of "The Battle Hymn of the Republic" in the National Cathedral helped give President Bush religious legitimacy for war abroad and repression at home, oppositional groups may achieve similar effects from their use of other nationalist hymns. In the example below from a public letter to President Bush during the run-up to the Iraq War, the American Friends Service Committee harnessed elements from the dominant symbolic repertoire in the form of a beloved and often-sung national hymn. A prayerful yet substantive plea to President Bush was wrapped in the deeply religious lyrics of a national song in order to cajole, inspire, and plead with the president to enact policies that live up to the lofty promises and national symbols in the hymn. In the process, what it means for a country to be a "great power" was redefined as the peace group created oppositional knowledge of the *radical-envisioning* type:

> Each stanza of our great national hymn, "America the Beautiful," turns from celebration of the bounty and strength which God has granted us to a prayer of

thanksgiving and petition. In that hymn we pray: "America, America, God mend thy every flaw, confirm thy soul in self-control, thy liberty in law." That prayer is the burden of this letter.

The mark of a truly great power is that it exhausts every opportunity of negotiation and diplomacy, bears even the most excessive frustrations and challenges, rather than resort to its military might. For the great power, war is the very last resort, not the exercise of a preemptive option. We urge you, Mr. President, to show us the self-control, patience and long-suffering appropriate to a great power. Use the good instruments of international law, international institutions such as the United Nations, World Court and International Court of Justice to resolve our conflict with Iraq. (American Friends Service Committee, September 20, 2002)

In order to adequately demonstrate how the United States peace movement responded to the dominant religious discourse as a component of hegemony, we will focus in the next section on the religious discourses of President George W. Bush and those of the peace movement during his presidency. He was in office for two of our conflict periods, and he is the most overtly religious of the White House occupants during the fifteen years of our study period; here was a president who made so-called "faith-based" initiatives a centerpiece of his policy agenda. In addition, the religious discourse of the PMOs is comparatively frequent during the 9/11 and Iraq War periods. We begin with a profile of Bush's religiosity and his discourse, focusing on his construction of a religious enemy, followed by analysis of the peace movement's religious statements in response.

Bush's Religiosity

When Texas Governor George W. Bush was just beginning his presidential push, he called influential religious leaders from the region to the governor's mansion. They then carried out a ritualized "laying on of hands" on the soon-to-be candidate that served to religiously validate for evangelical Christians his "calling" to the presidency. Not long after, in December 1999, Republican candidates in a presidential primary debate were asked which political philosopher had the most impact on their political beliefs. George W. Bush stunned many by promptly and boldly replying, "Christ, because he changed my heart." The candidate's spiritual autobiography, *A Charge to Keep*, which also appeared in 1999, recounts a series of conversion experiences and religious "testimonies" cast in traditional terms and apparently meant to define his born-again religiosity to the country. Therein Bush constructs a compelling narrative in which he has other figures suggesting to him that he is called to be today's Moses, chosen by God to courageously lead the United States in its presumed mission to spread freedom, democracy, and moral values (Bush 1999). Bush's national prominence increased significantly as he highlighted his conversion experiences and increased his devotion to the evangelical Christian agenda (Gurtov 2006).

Some have claimed that no modern White House occupant has ever cast his presidency in such deeply spiritual terms as George W. Bush (Urban 2006).

Empirical evidence suggests this is true, with the possible exception of Ronald Reagan. Analysis of State of the Union addresses from Franklin Roosevelt in 1933 to George W. Bush in 2005 shows that Bush engaged in more "God talk" than any other president, with Reagan running a close second. More important, Reagan and Bush were also much more likely to posture as "prophets." That is, they linked their discourse about God and about freedom and liberty with suggestions that they had personal knowledge of God's desires, wishes, or intentions in these matters (Coe and Domke 2006), as in the example below, which we've taken from a Bob Woodward interview with Bush.

> I say that freedom is not America's gift to the world. Freedom is God's gift to everybody in the world. I believe that. As a matter of fact, I was the person that wrote that line, or said it. . . . And it became part of the jargon. And I believe that. And I believe we have a duty to free people. I would hope we wouldn't have to do it militarily, but we have a duty (Woodward 2004, 88–89).

This sort of discourse from the president of a military superpower is rather sobering. When the commander in chief of the U.S. military conflates his mind with the mind of God, debate is stifled, alternatives go unexamined, and the divine mission may become one with the national mission, all as defined by the president himself.

Even more challenging for oppositional social movements, however, may be the fact that for many Christians in the U.S., so little of this was problematic. Reverend Pat Robertson resigned as president of the Christian Coalition in December 2001 after Bush had ramped up his religious rhetoric in response to 9/11. As influential Christian conservative Gary Bauer put it, "I think Robertson stepped down because the position has already been filled. There was already a great deal of identification with the president before 9–11 in the world of the Christian right, and the nature of this war is such that it's heightened the sense that a man of God is in the White House." A former Christian Coalition head, Ralph Reed, commented on the new role of the evangelical movement in national politics by saying that it had succeeded in electing Bush: "You're no longer throwing rocks at the building; you're in the building" (Milbank 2001, 2). Actually, the Christian right went far beyond throwing rocks at the White House, or even just getting in the door. The fusing of Christian fundamentalism with White House policies under George W. Bush was coupled with the centralizing of authority and increased levels of secrecy within the executive branch of government. The constricting of policymaking dialogues that resulted created grave dangers for the future of democracy in the United States (Hedges 2006).

Bush's Binaries

In keeping with some traditions of religious fundamentalism, George W. Bush's presidency was marked by an absence of doubt, an unwavering certitude even with regard to quite complex and complicated foreign policy issues (Woodward 2004). Bush has employed a consistent dichotomy between the forces of good (the United States) and the forces of evil (terrorists, Islamic fundamentalists, and all those who "hate America"). One of the more famous examples of this type of dichotomous thinking infused with religious power occurred during his address to a joint session of Congress on September 20, 2001.

> Every nation, in every region, now has a decision to make. Either you are with us, or you are with the terrorists (Applause). . . . Freedom and fear, justice and cruelty, have always been at war, and we know that God is not neutral between them (Applause). Fellow citizens, we'll meet violence with patient justice—assured of the rightness of our cause, and confident of the victories to come. In all that lies before us, may God grant us wisdom, and may He watch over the United States of America. (George W. Bush, September 20, 2001)

David Domke's (2004) comparative analysis of Bush's discourse both before and after 9/11 revealed that the president's usage of the good/evil binary nearly tripled in the period immediately following the attacks and up to his "mission accomplished" speech when he prematurely claimed from the flight deck of an aircraft carrier that major combat operations in Iraq were over. In our own research, we collected and coded a total of seventy-five statements from President Bush during the 9/11 period. Forty-six (61.3 percent) of those presidential statements included binary thinking of the "good versus evil" variety. Clearly, this rhetorical device (and way of interpreting the world) was repeated frequently by the president of the United States, including in many different ways and in scores of different contexts.

From the point of view of discursive politics, we argue that binaries advance the agendas of powerholders in three ways. First, they discount and in many ways serve to reject certain ways of thinking and being. In so doing, they also create an authoritative interpretive hierarchy where one way of viewing the world soundly trumps the other one. Second, insofar as they are often rooted in fundamentalism, they carry a moral and even religious power that can strongly influence popular opinion. For example, empirical research shows that during the Iraq War the potential influence of presidential moralizing was magnified further still thanks to a subservient mainstream media whose editorial pages largely excluded criticisms of the invasion on moral grounds (Nikolaev and Porpora 2007). Third, binaries are easily understood, all the more so if they have a religious hue. They take little ink and, therefore, promptly become a favored device in both the mass media and in the popular mind. For example, David Domke also compared the presence of the good/evil binary in newspaper editorials in twenty major newspapers published in the two days following each presidential address. They increased by nearly sixfold relative to newspaper editorials appearing in the two days following each presidential address in the pre-9/11 period (Domke 2004). This substantial "echo effect" granted to moralizing presidential discourse by the mainstream media con-

tributes to political closure and has powerful implications for shaping political discourse, including that of the U.S. peace movement.

From Binaries to Enemies

One of the binary-based discursive approaches taken by President Bush was to engage in a significant amount of enemy construction within the context of his religious discourse. Constructing a loathsome enemy who represents (at best) the worst of humanity is a common, perhaps even universal, accompaniment to armed hostilities (Keen 1986). The us vs. them thinking inherent in enemy images produces a kind of "group think" that focuses attention and constricts other formulations (Merskin 2004). As a hegemonic device, well-defined enemy images divert awareness from potentially problematic domestic policies (e.g., civil liberties repression) outwards toward a shared enemy instead—all the more so if the enemy constructions can be given a religious or, at least, a moralized overlay. Of the sixty paragraphs we coded for religion in statements by President Bush during the 9/11 period, nearly a quarter of them (23%) are focused on the president's constructions of a religious enemy. Collectively, he paints a stark and forbidding portrait of terrorists, the Taliban, Al Qaeda, Osama bin Laden, and generic Islamic extremists. The quotes below from President Bush are a partial listing of the enemy images constructed by him. They all occurred within the context of his religious discourse in the post-9/11 period.

According to the President, the Islamic extremists whom he defines as the country's enemy:

- have tried to hijack a great religion
- hate Christians and Jews
- love only one thing—they love power
- celebrate death
- despise creative societies and individual choice
- have no home in any faith
- have a special hatred for America
- are heirs to fascism
- want to force every life into grim and joyless conformity
- encourage murder and suicide
- are isolated by their own hatred and extremism
- destroy religious symbols of other religions
- are drug dealers
- are murderers
- are barbaric in their meting out of justice
- dare to ask God's blessings as they set out to kill innocents
- have no place in any culture
- resent and resist freedom

- are the likes of which we have never seen before
- are incredibly ruthless
- gloat over killing fellow Muslims
- can't stand what America stands for
- hate women
- disrupt humanitarian supplies
- have no conscience
- don't educate children
- forbid children to fly kites, or sing songs or build snowmen
- imprison women in their homes
- dictate how to think and how to worship
- deny women basic health care and education
- steal food from starving people
- beat girls for wearing white shoes
- are evil and determined
- commit mass murder against innocents
- destroy great monuments of human culture

And finally, the president claims they

- are so evil that those of us in America can't possibly comprehend why they do what they do

President Bush clearly evinced a propensity to address important and complex policy choices through the extensive use of simple binaries that are embedded within religious discourse. When this is combined with his repetitive and stark constructions of a religious enemy, we would expect the U.S. peace movement to take note of this context in its own discourse. As we show in what follows, they most certainly did.

THE PEACE MOVEMENT'S RELIGIOUS DISCOURSES

The peace movement's religious discourses have at least two origins, not mutually exclusive. First, for at least some of the organizations, it emanates from a set of deeply held values that are associated with religious identity. That is why the American Friends Service Committee would so often preface their religious discourse with the phrase "as Quakers," while the Fellowship of Reconciliation would say "as faith-based pacifists," while Pax Christi would say "as Catholics" or "as followers of the nonviolent Jesus."

Following these identity-based introductions, the groups would go on to make spirited, religiously based critiques of U.S. policy. Second, peace movement organizations are also strategic as they talk back to powerholders in a

Photo 5.1.   Religion as identity-based introduction (poster in red, white, and blue displayed at a Peace Action–sponsored rally in Wisconsin). (Photo by Lynne M. Woehrle)

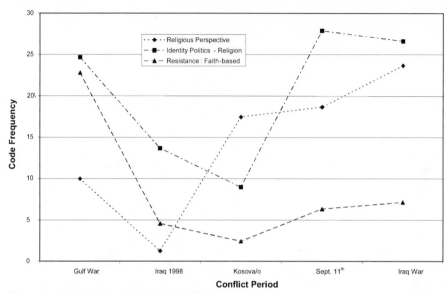

Figure 5.1.   Code Frequencies by Conflict Period

Notes: Analysis based on weighted data. For weights formula, see appendix 2. Only data from the five PMOs issuing statements in all five conflict periods are included (American Friends Service Committee, Fellowship of Reconciliation, Pax Christi, Peace Action, Women's International League for Peace and Freedom).

dialogical fashion (Steinberg 1999). Here they appropriate and attempt to undermine the religious dimensions of the dominant discourse that serve to legitimate power and lend religious credibility to presidential policies. Both of these approaches are well represented across our data set. As our longitudinal analysis across the five conflict period shows (see figure 5.1), the peace movement responded to the religious discourse of George W. Bush with extensive religious rhetoric of their own. Our identity politics: religion code is defined as "spiritual beliefs and/or religion as a means of organizing people to resist, including appeals to a person's religious identity." The movement's use of an identity politics–based religious discourse was higher during the two periods associated with George W. Bush's presidency (9/11 and the Iraq War) than any of the other three periods (see chapter 6 for more details on religious identity talk). In addition, our religious perspectives code is defined as "articulation of a religious tradition and/or what its teachings say." As figure 5.1 also shows, the movement's use of a more generalized religious perspective discourse was highest during the Iraq War period, and comparatively high during the 9/11 period as well.

There were three primary ways that the peace movement responded to Bush's religious discourse and his enemy constructions during 9/11 and the Iraq War: 1) by challenging what was seen as divisive demonizing; 2) by harnessing the president's self-presentation as a man of faith; and lastly, 3) by doing remedial education on Islam. We will treat these three approaches in turn in what follows below.

Debunking the Demonizing

A few days after the beginning of the Iraq War, Mary Ellen McNish, the general secretary of the American Friends Service Committee, responded on behalf of the organization to an invasion that it was unalterably opposed to on religious grounds. She put the Iraq War in the context of contemporary U.S. political history by noting that the primary proponents of the war within the George W. Bush administration were hard-line neoconservatives who had been deeply disappointed by the first Bush administration's failure to depose Saddam Hussein during the Gulf War.[2] Their subsequent blueprint for U.S. global military dominance, dubbed "The Project for a New American Century," favored unilateralism over cooperation and partly tied the United States' greatness to the degree to which others held it in awe and fear.[3] These neoconservatives and President Bush utilized the moral shock of the 9/11 attacks to justify a newly aggressive, preemptive set of foreign policies in Afghanistan, Iraq, and elsewhere. The president's much-used terminology of an "axis of evil" is discursively emblematic of these developments.[4] The AFSC chief harnessed the axis of evil discourse by dipping deeply into the historic well of Quaker humanitarian service to redefine the nature of evil and the country's true enemies. Here poverty, militarism and environmental decay are labeled the true axis of evil about which all good-thinking Americans ought to be concerned.

> When Americans cried Why? in the face of 3,000 dead at the World Trade Center, they were offered a list of scapegoats, an Axis of Evil. They [the Bush administration neoconservatives] offered America their vision of what true safety required. They knew what they believed, and they spoke with great confidence. In opposition to this vision, Quakers and the other peace churches had another vision to offer. We saw the same facts, but the eyes of our historic witness made us see those facts very differently. Our experience tells us, and you may have heard me say this before, that the true axis of evil is pandemic poverty, environmental degradation, and a world awash in weapons. (American Friends Service Committee, March 27, 2003)

Shortly after 9/11, when President Bush's rhetoric was most fulsome, some groups named and then directly challenged the president's lack of distinctions and his ready reliance on binaries, as Pax Christi does here.

> Right now across the Islamic world, innocent people are living in terror, wondering what President Bush may do to them. The President says, "We shall make no distinctions between the terrorist and countries that harbor them." Shall a whole country be condemned for the actions of its leaders? (Pax Christi, September 26, 2001)

During the Iraq War, the Fellowship of Reconciliation also took a challenging approach to the demonizing issue. In a statement titled "Torture in Iraq: No Monopoly on Capacity for Evil," the interfaith group addressed the root causes of the abuse of Iraqi prisoners by U.S. troops at Abu Ghraib. The FOR laid responsibility for the abuse at the feet of the president due to what the organization called his "cavalier" attitude and because of his "ongoing demonization of the Arab and Muslim world." The FOR used the reality of the abuse to argue that facile distinctions between the enemy and U.S. citizenry are fundamentally false and morally bankrupt.

> The violence of the last few weeks [at Abu Ghraib by the United States and in Fallujah by insurgents] throws light on an essential truth: The "enemy" holds no monopoly on evil and "our side" no monopoly on good. All humankind has the capacity to perpetrate evil and violence upon its fellows. All violence, whether depicted graphically in photographs and videos, or taking place anonymously, out of the camera's range, is an affront to the God-given humanity of all. Americans now face the humbling task of asking themselves and their government how it could possibly have been in any nation's interests to provoke such violence by invading and occupying a nation that never attacked us. (Fellowship of Reconciliation, May 14, 2004)

The U.S. peace movement engaged the president's demonizing language in other ways, too, including by challenging it directly from a variety of approaches. The Islamic group, CAIR, took their challenge into the Washington, DC, marketplace by hosting an interfaith memorial at the Capitol Reflecting Pool to mark the second anniversary of the 9/11 attacks. They labeled their action as a direct "challenge [to] those who seek to divide America along religious or ethnic lines" (Council on American-Islamic Relations, August 23, 2003). In the passage below, the Black Radical Congress rejects the president's divisive approach not only on religious grounds, but also quite overtly on racial identity grounds. Note, too, how religious faiths of all persuasions are presumed to lead each believer to oppose the Iraq War.

> The Black Radical Congress opposes the war against the Iraqi people and call on all black, brown, red, yellow, and white people (in short, the majority of the peoples of the world) to oppose this war. The attempts to use religion to divide the non Islamic peoples of the U.S.A. from the peoples of the Islamic faith must be opposed. Peoples of all religious faith and all spiritual orientation must call on their innermost powers to oppose the war. (Black Radical Congress, March 20, 2003)

Harnessing a Religious President's Discourse

When powerholders utilize elements of the dominant symbolic repertoire, including religious language and images, they open themselves to counter-challenges that harness the same language and images. In the example below, the FOR accused the president not only of exploiting religion but also of engaging in an "extremist rhetoric" that was akin to none other than Osama bin Laden's. Here the peace group turns the rhetorical tables on the president via their labeling of him with the same language and enemy image that he has so painstakingly constructed in his own religious discourse.

> The religious language used by the President (evil, God, U.S. as the agent of God to give freedom to the world, and faith-based initiatives) attempts to claim righteousness for policies that disregard the public opinion of the world and the substantial moral objections of many Americans. This obvious manipulation of religion for political ends comes at a time when the overwhelming majority of U.S. religious leaders have spoken out against the Administration's war in Iraq and have questioned the morality of such an aggressive policy. It is a direct parallel of the extremist rhetoric of Osama bin Laden, and is leading us in a very similar direction. (Fellowship of Reconciliation, January 30, 2003)

There is no question that George W. Bush's courting of the evangelical Christian vote through his overt expressions of religiosity—first on the campaign trail and later during his first term in the White House—reaped significant electoral dividends for him. What is too often overlooked, however, is the other half of this equation. Just as the president used religious discourse to his advantage and to promote his policy agendas, so too did his extensive use of religious language make him and his policies vulnerable precisely on those same religious grounds. As the AFSC plainly put it at the beginning of the Iraq War, "It is surprising that a man who says he is guided by faith has ignored the council [*sic*] of major religious leaders in this country and internationally, who condemn this action as an unjust war" (American Friends Service Committee, March 21, 2003). As the example below shows, this put the president at risk to critiques from the religious community.

About two weeks following the invasion of Iraq, a coalition of religious groups including Pax Christi and the Fellowship of Reconciliation organized a demonstration at the White House that featured the arrest of sixty-eight prominent religious leaders. Pax Christi's press release announcing the arrests is rich with examples of the harnessing hegemony dynamic as the religious PMOs turned the moral demands of Christianity squarely back on to the Bush administration. For example, although President Bush has frequently emphasized the "born-again" nature of his Christianity, he is actually a member of the United Methodist Church. Thus, Pax Christi strategically highlighted the words of United Methodist Bishop C. Joseph Sprague at a press conference just prior to the action, where the bishop explained why he felt compelled to commit nonviolent civil disobedience at the White House.

Pax Christi's statement also included Catholic Bishop Thomas Gumbleton's withering moral condemnation of Bush's war policies in explaining why he, too, was arrested, along with a group of Nobel Peace Prize laureates.

Photo 5.2. U.S. religious leaders demonstrate in Lafayette Park across from the White House before being arrested, March 27, 2003. From left to right: Front row: Catholic priest Fr. Roy Bourgeois, Catholic bishop Thomas Gumbleton, Nobel Peace Prize winner Mairead Corrigan, Mary Robinson, FOR executive director Patricia Clark. Back row: the Reverend Roger Gench, Methodist bishop C. Joseph Sprague, author and activist Daniel Ellsberg. (Photo courtesy of Pax Christi. Used with permission)

"The United Methodist bishops have sent four letters to the president and vice president, whom many of you know are both Methodists, seeking a meeting to discuss this war," stated Sprague. He went on to say that that they only received "one terse reply" from the Bush administration and no meeting. . . . [Catholic] Bishop Gumbleton of Detroit, who traveled to Iraq in January, was among those arrested in Wednesday's action. "As people of faith and conscience, we proclaim that it is a grave sin to support this war," said Gumbleton. "We cannot stand silent while the Bush administration murders innocent men, women and children." (Pax Christi, March 27, 2003)

When President Bush scheduled an audience with the Pope during his 2004 reelection campaign, Pax Christi took him to task for ignoring the counsel about the war provided by religious leaders even while he exploited his connections to those same religious leaders. As the president's visit to the Vatican approached during the summer of 2004, Pax Christi released a statement that focused on the fact that Catholic religious figures around the globe were using the president's appearance with Pope John Paul II to ramp up their moral critiques of Bush's war. In their statement, Pax Christi quoted far-flung bishops and cardinals who were each criticizing the invasion and occupation of Iraq from a religious perspective. They also called the president out for his selective use of religious teaching to further his own electoral needs.

President Bush should have used today's meeting [with the Pope] to offer explanations why the opinions of the world's religious leaders are ignored by himself and others in his administration. . . . Instead, what we see is blatant political opportunism, orchestrated to confuse U.S. Catholics into thinking that President Bush is in tune with the principles of their faith. (Pax Christi, June 4, 2004)

In the U.S. context, religious discourse is so deeply a part of the culture that it is democratically available (Rhys Williams 2002), at least in the sense that one need not be a believer in order to use religious discourse and the powerful symbolic riches associated with it. While we think there are issues associated with credibility—in that some are more able to use religious discourse effectively than others—the point still holds generally true, as it also does when historic religious figures and leaders are quoted. In fact, we found that secular groups also used religious discourse, especially by quoting historic religious figures like Reverend Martin Luther King Jr. When PMOs challenge the state as it goes to war, the political deck is heavily stacked against them thanks to the legitimated political closure that follows the decision to wage war. Rallying around the flag in the moment trumps attempts to discuss the long-range consequences of war. In such a game, activists find they are dealt a rather hapless hand, with few cards to play of consequence. But religious discourse—and the moral authority and political legitimation that accompanies it—can help to level the playing field. And when the discourse is harnessed to especially hallowed and resonant figures like Rev. King, even quite radical critiques can be proffered.

In a statement focused on the domestic needs going unmet due to the costs of the Gulf War, the secular group Peace Action used King's words to raise the issue of the spiritual health of the national soul: "A nation that continues year after year to spend more money on military defense than on programs of social uplift is approaching spiritual death." When President Bush laid a wreath at King's tomb on the national holiday devoted to him, the FOR called it a "cynical gesture" insofar as his preemptive war to bring "liberation" to Iraq is contrary to what Rev. King taught. The FOR quoted King to the effect that history was cluttered with the wreckage of nations who came killing in the name of liberation and peace. This is an especially effective case in point of our argument that when powerholders use elements of the dominant symbolic repertoire it actually provides opportunities to legitimate oppositional claims by holding powerholders accountable to the same standards that they appealed to in their own discourses.

And in the passage below, the secular War Resisters League reports on the arrest of forty-six of its members at the U.S. mission to the UN during the Afghanistan war, following a four-day series of presentations and training reflecting on the life of the religious leader.

Dr. King's dream of a just society has yet to be realized. As King said, "The greatest purveyor of violence is my own country." . . . This is still true, and our collective conscience calls us to confront not only the violence committed on behalf of Americans, but also the institutions committing those acts.

Most Americans will always be rather resistant to the notion that the United States is the greatest user of violence around the world; it doesn't square with prevailing versions of national identity. Thus this is never an easy argument to make at any time. For the WRL to make this point only four short months following the attacks of 9/11 was a particularly bold move insofar as it risked easy rejection and self-righteous ridicule. The political maelstrom in the spring of 2008 over very similar remarks made by presidential candidate Barack Obama's former pastor indicates the dangers inherent in making such an argument. But the WRL's tactic of standing behind the frock of the widely respected Rev. Dr. King presumably helped some bystanders to not immediately and reflexively reject the peace group's argument.

Remedial Education on Islam

The third primary way that PMOs responded to the administration's rhetoric and to events on the ground in Iraq and the United States was to create oppositional knowledge by disseminating alternative information about religion in general and about Islam in particular. In addition, many groups emphasized constructive commonalities that they insisted existed between religions, as CAIR did below.

> Over the last few weeks, Americans of all faiths have been horrified by images of violence in the Middle East. The Iraqi prisoner abuse scandal does not represent America or Christianity. The Israeli missile that killed innocent Palestinian children in Gaza does not represent Judaism. And the beheading of an innocent American man, Nicholas Berg, does not represent Islam. Islam, Christianity and Judaism share the basic values necessary to create a world in which tolerance and peace prevail. We have an opportunity to build bridges between our faiths and to challenge those who attempt to divide humanity along religious and ethnic lines. (Council on American-Islamic Relations, May 26, 2004)

Already faced with the scapegoating of American Muslims five days after 9/11, CAIR offered the country *counter-informative* oppositional knowledge about American Muslims by reminding the country of the many august contributions made by Muslims to the United States.

> It was a Muslim who was the architect for the Sears Tower. Islam is the fastest growing religion in America and in the world. We are doctors, lawyers, engineers, mechanics, teachers, and store owners. We are your neighbors. (Council on American-Islamic Relations, September 16, 2001)

It was not just the Islamic group in our study that attempted to stem the tide of religious intolerance that intensified after 9/11 by creating oppositional knowledge about Islam. The AFSC, BRC, NYCLAW, FOR, and Pax Christi also built *counter-informative* oppositional knowledge about Islam, as in the example below from the FOR.

> The religion of Islam, which claims more than one billion global adherents including eight to nine million within the USA alone, cannot be characterized as being "extreme" or "violent." Individuals who engage in acts of war against civilians violate the most sacred tenets of Islam. Muslims of all nationalities who reside in the United States vigorously condemned the events of September 11 and are actively involved in all aspects of humanitarian relief and recovery following this tragedy. (Fellowship of Reconciliation, September 19, 2001)

The taking of civilian hostages became widespread in Iraq in the summer of 2004, including some high-profile U.S. hostages. In this shifting political context, the Council on American-Islamic Relations used its standing in the religious community to organize U.S. imams to issue a declaration, released at a Capitol Hill press conference, which condemned hostage-taking as a violation of Islamic beliefs and called for the release of all hostages in Iraq, no matter their faith or nationality. CAIR also launched an online petition drive called "Not in the Name of Islam" that was designed to disassociate Islam from the violent acts of some Muslims. CAIR hoped that Muslims around the world would sign the ad and work to correct misperceptions of Islam and the Islamic stance on religiously motivated terror. Over 50,000 Muslims signed the petition within the first two weeks of its posting. As the excerpt below demonstrates, the strongly worded petition is a good example of a social movement group creating *critical-interpretive* oppositional knowledge, in this case about the nature of the Islamic faith. *alternative interpretation*

> We, the undersigned Muslims, wish to state clearly that those who commit acts of terror, murder and cruelty in the name of Islam are not only destroying innocent lives, but are also betraying the values of the faith they claim to represent. No injustice done to Muslims can ever justify the massacre of innocent people, and no act of terror will ever serve the cause of Islam. We repudiate and dissociate ourselves from any Muslim group or individual who commits such brutal and un-Islamic acts. We refuse to allow our faith to be held hostage by the criminal actions of a tiny minority acting outside the teachings of both the Quran and the Prophet Muhammad, peace be upon him. (Council on American-Islamic Relations, August 31, 2004)

The final way that the PMOs built bridges across faith traditions, did remedial education on Islam, and challenged the president's dichotomous discourse was by organizing concrete actions of solidarity with the Islamic community. The religious groups in particular (AFSC, FOR, Pax Christi) made extensive use of this approach, recommending their membership and bystanders to study Islam, to visit mosques, and to reach out in many different ways to American Arabs and to Muslims. We present only one example below—Pax

Christi's call for acts of spiritual solidarity during the month of Ramadan. Note the subtle ways that the PMO tries to lead its readers into creating *transformative* oppositional knowledge by advising them on how to dive deeply into the spiritual riches of Islam. Here is a view of Islam that is radically different from the dominant one in the United States.

→How to apply the new knowledge

> During the upcoming season of Ramadan, we want to show a gesture of respect and appreciation for Muslim brothers and sisters and to learn from them. We welcome an opportunity to be in solidarity with Muslims who rely on the month of Ramadan to help inculcate values of simplicity, service, sharing, compassion and mercy. We recognize the need for these virtues in our own lives. We invite you to join us in this effort of solidarity with our Muslim brothers and sisters, as a shared prayer and action for peace that depends on conversion from ways of injustice and reliance on war. . . . The intent of this call is to urge people to grow closer to our Muslim brothers and sisters through whatever gesture of solidarity they can make beginning October 26 and continuing through the following four weeks. (Pax Christi, October 11, 2003)

Since war and peace concerns are oftentimes paramount for religious believers, we were also interested in understanding the relationships between the religious discourse of the U.S. peace movement during wartime and identity talk. Offering a corrective to dominant understandings of Islam was only one way that some movement organizations developed their religiously infused oppositional politics. We also investigated possible associations between religious discourse and the actual political tactics promoted by the peace movement. We turn to this more quantitative analysis in what follows.

RELIGIOUS IDENTITIES AND TACTICAL TENDENCIES

Rory McVeigh and Christian Smith's (1999) U.S.-focused survey research found that compared to the nonreligious, Christians were at least two times more likely to have engaged in institutional politics rather than taking no political action. In addition, frequent church attendance was found to significantly increase the likelihood that individuals would engage in protest relative to institutional forms of politics. More specifically with regard to social movement organizations, some studies have found empirical evidence that religious and faith-based peace movement organizations tend to support and engage in "unruly," noninstitutional forms of political engagement—including nonviolent forms of protest and civil disobedience (Epstein 1990; Pagnucco 1996; Nepstad 2004). Finally, religion is frequently a highly salient factor in the development and refinement of a movement organization's identity (Coy and Woehrle 1996; Christian Smith 1996a). Our analysis of the discourse of the U.S. peace movement from 1990 through 2005 as contained in our data set tends to support these findings.

Table 5.1. Frequency of Religious Code Concurrence in Same Passage

Coupling Codes	N of Base Code Passages	% of Base Code Passages	N of Base Code Documents	% of Base Code Documents
Base Code—Religious Perspectives				
Identity Politics: Religion	30	16.7%	18	17.8%
Organizational Identity	22	12.2%	20	19.8%
Violence Condemned: Costs	17	9.4%	15	14.9%
Nonviolence Supported	16	8.9%	15	14.9%
Civil Liberties	16	8.9%	11	10.9%
Resistance: Faith-based	11	6.1%	8	7.9%
Base Code—Identity Politics: Religion				
Resistance: Faith-based	65	26.1%	38	32.5%
Nonviolence Supported	48	19.3%	36	30.8%
Organizational Identity	37	14.9%	33	28.2%
Religious Perspectives	30	12.0%	18	15.4%

Notes: Base codes are religious perspectives and identity politics: religion. For each of the base codes, eighty-three code couplings were examined. Includes documents from all five conflict periods. Only the five PMOs for which there is data for all five conflict periods are included (American Friends Service Committee, Fellowship of Reconciliation, Pax Christi, Peace Action, Women's International League for Peace and Freedom). Analysis based on weighted data. For weights formula, see appendix 2.

Table 5.1 shows those codes that most frequently appeared within the same paragraph, with our two primary religion-related codes: "religious perspectives" and "identity politics: religion." As explained earlier, religious perspectives are defined as "articulation of a religious tradition and/or what its teachings say." The identity politics: religion code is defined as "spiritual beliefs and/or religion as a means of organizing people to resist, including appeals to a person's religious identity." The first finding to take note of is the high concurrence of the organizational identity code with these two religion codes. This suggests that religious discourse is critical to identity construction.

The code most associated with our "identity politics: religion" code across the five conflict periods (i.e., the code that most often appears in the paragraphs also coded as identity politics: religion) was "resistance: faith-based." The latter code has to do with PMO calls for resistance to war activities, specifically resistance work that includes a religious faith basis or component. The concurrence within the same paragraph between these codes was quite substantial, over 26 percent. The code that appears second most often with identity politics: religion across the five conflict periods is "nonviolence supported," which is defined as explicitly advocating for nonviolent action and conscientious objection. The concurrence within the same paragraph here was also substantial, over 19%. If we look at concurrence within the same document, it is over 30% in both cases. The nonviolence supported code is also associated with the more generalized "religious perspective" code across the five conflict periods; in fact, it is tied for the fourth highest concurrence among eighty-three possible couplings. The resistance: faith-based and the nonviolence supported codes each has to do with mobilization, more particularly with encouraging engagement in potentially costly, extra-institutional politics, as in the civil disobedience at the White House profiled earlier in the chapter. Consequently, these findings demonstrate the important role that a religiously based identity politics plays in such mobilization efforts for the U.S. peace movement.

The PMOs' general discourse (religious and secular) around nonviolent action and costly forms of resistance was wide ranging. The tactical repertoire promoted by the peace movement to directly challenge hegemony across the conflict periods included calls for and reports on demonstrations, pickets, pray-ins, various kinds of civil disobedience, breaking the embargo on Iraq by shipping humanitarian and medical supplies there, engaging in citizen diplomacy by traveling to Iraq, fasting and donating money saved to humanitarian needs, disruptions of events where high-level Bush administration figures would be appearing, boycotts, work stoppages, labor union refusals to transport war-related materials, women shaving off their hair in front of the Liberty Bell, vigils, war-tax resistance, conscientious objection, providing sanctuary for objectors and military resisters, die-ins, burning of tax forms, sit-ins and obstructions at military recruitment centers and congressional offices, delivering the names of those killed in war to the White House and to Dover Air Force Base, holding nonviolent action trainings, and much more.

As the above list implies, engaging in nonviolent action may entail high risks for its practitioners. These risks can be wide ranging and include the affective, political, social, and financial dimensions of an activist's life. For example, social stigmatization and political ridicule can combine with imprisonment and lost wages for practitioners of nonviolent civil disobedience in ways that seriously dampen mobilization efforts. Identity construction, validation, and appeals can help overcome these obstacles to mobilization. Strategically highlighting religious commitments and moral values to boost positive identification with being a nonviolent resister to the hegemony of violence was a common tactic for the faith-based groups, and was even used by some secular groups as well.

The religious PMOs for whom we have data for all five conflict periods (i.e., AFSC, FOR, Pax Christi)[5] often tied their nonviolent action mobilization efforts directly to their religious identities, to those of their members, and even to the wider American public. In other words, they highlighted and appealed to religious identities and sensibilities while trying to mobilize extra-institutional forms of resistance to war and militarism. Pax Christi did this more often than any other group, and frequently fashioned its identity appeals to match the target audience and forms of contention requested. They were strategic about when they would use sectarian appeals and highlight themselves as "Catholics," as "Catholic Christians," or as "followers of the nonviolent

Jesus," versus when they spoke more generally as "people of faith," or even more generically simply as "citizens," or as "people of good will."

Finally, it is useful to note that violence functions in a hegemonic way in U.S. society. It is featured if not lionized in a majority of media formats from children's cartoons to video games to Hollywood movies to nightly TV news programs. With regard to international affairs in particular it is commonly presumed that the United States has a wide-ranging right to use its violent might. When presidents wrap their calls for war, a militarized economy, and civil liberties repression at home in religious garments, the hegemony of violence is strengthened further still. In short, violence is culturally routinized and normalized, and therefore difficult to directly challenge in an effective manner. Equally important is the fact that violence is also normalized through its coupling with religious discourses that legitimate it. In the context of what is generally presumed to be a "Christian country," where Christian broadcasting on television and radio is ubiquitous and where the foreign policy utterances by Christian leaders like Reverend Pat Robertson and others are commonplace, it may become even more important for oppositional voices to respond to these religiously based calls to arms. Peace activists must contest and redefine the meaning of religious identities much in the same way they contested nationalist identities as we showed in chapter 3. Those who want to mobilize others must utilize cultural materials, themes, and collective identities—including religious identities—that have enough potency and resonance to stand against the powerful position of violence in the U.S. culture. In this regard, and as our final example, below Pax Christi attempted to harness none other than the symbol of Jesus Christ on the first day following September 11.

> As people of faith and disciples of the nonviolent Jesus, we must be willing, even now in this darkest moment, to commit ourselves and urge our sisters and brothers, to resist the impulse to vengeance. We must resist the urge to demonize and dehumanize any ethnic group as "enemy." We must find the courage to break the spiral of violence that so many in our nation, we fear, will be quick to embrace.
>
> We therefore call for restraint on the part of our nation's civilian and military leaders. The appropriate response to this despicable act is not a despicable act of violence in kind. Vengeance is not justice. The only kind of justice that will honor the memory of all those who lost their lives is a justice based on international law, not reckless retribution.
>
> To follow the nonviolent Jesus in the midst of unimaginable violence is the call and the challenge to which we remain committed. (Pax Christi, September 12, 2001)

CONCLUSION

Religion and religious discourse are important dimensions of U.S. cultural life. As the passage from Mark Twain's "War Prayer" that opens this chapter suggests, religion is often put to work on behalf of the nation and the state's war policies. Yet our findings clearly demonstrate that religious discourse is also widely available and that it was used in interesting, creative, and at times passionate ways by the U.S. peace movement from 1990 to 2005.

The political closure always associated with presidential and congressional decisions to go to war makes added demands on oppositional groups like peace movement organizations. Political legitimacy becomes an even more precious commodity. During war, it is hard for oppositional groups to get a hearing, much less to have their alternative perspectives taken seriously and given credence. The roles that civil religion has historically played in the United States show that religion is an interpretive framework that is broadly familiar across the American social landscape, and the familiar is always hard to reject outright. In such a context, the rich and malleable qualities of religious discourse were strategically used to confront the hegemony of violence in U.S. foreign policy, to appeal to members and bystanders, and to provide a sense of meaning, purpose, and legitimacy marked by transcendent dimensions. In addition, our analysis of George W. Bush's presidency clearly showed his overt religiosity, his reliance on binary thinking, and his propensity to demonize a religious enemy. In turn, our analysis of movement discourse revealed how its organizations harnessed religious discourse to talk back to President Bush and to undercut his policies and positions from a religious perspective.

Peace movement organizations challenged Bush's reliance on binaries and the demonization of a broadly defined enemy. This is particularly significant insofar as the moral certainty and religiously informed devotion to his and to the country's "calling" that so marked President Bush was a potentially perilous combination for the country, and even the world. After all, such a combination residing in the hands of the leader of the world's sole "super-power" may easily change an already problematic U.S. exceptionalism into an even more problematic U.S. adventurism in foreign affairs (Gurtov 2006). We have also shown that peace movement organizations harnessed the president's overt religiosity and his religious discourse and turned the power of these symbols against the president and his policies.

In addition, we found that many of the PMOs constructed oppositional knowledge by focusing their statements on providing remedial education about Islam. This was done as a bulwark against both the real and the potential scapegoating of Muslims in the United States and elsewhere. Equally important are our findings that by quoting familiar and authoritative religious leaders to bolster movement positions, the PMOs helped ensure that the more radical of their critiques may enjoy some resonance among the general public.

We must also remember, however, that the movement's religious discourse was not simply strategic; it was often rooted in deeply held beliefs and principles that even defined some of the organizations and their members. Our findings of the close association of identity talk with religious discourses in the peace movement statements support this interpretation. Moreover, religious values and discourse were strongly associated with support for engaging in extra-institutional politics like nonviolent action, offering not only inspiration and motivation, but the potential of individually validated rationales. In this way, religious PMOs appeared to put the agency of the individual activist in the political foreground, fostering an activism that might be uncommonly genuine and authentic in its meaning-making, and therefore have longer staying power as well.

Finally, we believe our research further suggests that peace movement discourse may, over time, influence civil religion itself. One way this influence will likely take shape is by transforming civil religion in ways that constrain powerholders rather than facilitating their agendas. Thus the dominant priestly strain of U.S. civil religion may be undermined while its dissenting prophetic strain would be strengthened. This would be a cultural shift of significant proportions.

NOTES

1. Ronald Inglehart's World Values Survey data is available online at www.worldvaluessurvey.org/.

2. For an insider's view of the significant influence of the neoconservatives on George W. Bush's policies, see former treasury secretary Paul O'Neill's account of Bush's candidacy and the early years of his presidency (Susskind 2004, 80–82).

3. This helps explain why the invasion of Iraq was dubbed by these same neoconservatives with the widely publicized codename "Shock and Awe."

4. One revealing account of how the "axis of evil" terminology emerged within the Bush White House in the post-9/11 period attributes it to Michael Gerson, the Bush speechwriter primarily responsible for the president's State of the Union address four months after the attacks. Gerson, a theology graduate from religiously conservative Wheaton College, was a self-described evangelical Christian who Bob Woodward reports found a way to fuse "biblical high-mindedness and the folksy" in many speeches he drafted for Bush throughout the months following the attacks (Woodward 2004, 86–87).

5. The Muslim group, the Council on American-Islamic Relations (CAIR), was included in our data for the last two conflict periods: 9/11 and the Iraq War. Interestingly, CAIR made no mention of nonviolence whatsoever during either of the two periods, and there was only one instance of "resistance-costly" in both periods combined. This is likely due to two factors. First, among all the organizations in our data set, CAIR is among the least oriented toward peace as a descriptor of its fundamental organizational identity, being somewhat more of a civil rights–oriented organization. Second, CAIR's use of religious discourse was overwhelmingly (ten of twelve passages in six documents) associated with teaching the U.S. media and public about Islam generally, and protecting Islam by correcting misperceptions about it more specifically (e.g., seven of the ten religious discourse–related passages had to do with disassociating Islam from terrorism). Since Islam is not part of the dominant symbolic repertoire and is widely disparaged by powerholders, CAIR had to be on the discursive defensive rather than the discursive offensive like Christian groups. Their statements are an instance of articulated assimilation, highlighting facets of Islam compatible with religious elements of powerholder discourse.

6

Mobilizing the Margins

Race, Class, Gender, and Religion

An identity would seem to be arrived at by the way in which the person faces and uses his experience.

—James Baldwin

You manifest based on who you are already—so you must own the identity of the dream in order to manifest it.

—Joy Page

COLLECTIVE IDENTITY AND DISCOURSE

Among social movement theorists there is longstanding debate about how influential the development of collective identity is as a means to motivate group participation (Friedman and McAdam 1992; Taylor and Whittier 1992). Are movement joiners motivated by opportunity, by macro social forces, by rational self-interest, or by a sense of belonging?

Strategies such as "identity politics" or "separatism" have at times been critiqued for causing subdivisions within movements, or accused of taking away from the "real" political issues (Armstrong and Bernstein 2008). Meanwhile, occasions of superordinate identity formation, such as happened when oppositional politics confronted the World Trade Organization at the "battle for Seattle," are lauded as important for their construction of unity among diverse groups.[1] Actually, each of these approaches attracts members by making people aware of their shared connections to issues and to each other, in other words, their collective identity (Melucci 1989). Appealing to identity appears to offer a constructive option for social movement development through the achievement of resonance and the mobilization of constituents.

Identity emerges from two places, how we see ourselves and how others see us. It is useful to think of our identities as constructed within the context of the society to which we belong. Some aspects of our identity attach to us at our birth while others develop through the life course, and some we even choose ourselves. At any time, we carry multiple identities; these are our social identities. When a particular identity is strong and persuasive we talk about it as being salient. Collective identity comes out of a group of people believing that they can work together because they share a characteristic, belief, or goal. In other words, our social identities can be the basis for us feeling connected to a group. Collective identity can be based on many shared identities, including, among others, categories of people with similar individual characteristics, such as race[2], ethnicity, class, gender, and religion.

In this chapter we consider some of the social bases for identity and how the organizations studied utilized collective identities to appeal to the public, to express their own forms of oppositional knowledge, and to challenge or harness the dominant symbolic repertoire. We are interested in the link between subgroup identity and peace movement organization (PMO) discourse. These identities emerge as important to PMOs in two ways. Some organizations such as CODEPINK, United States Labor Against the War, and the Black Radical Congress (among others) use social identities as central to their organizational definition (i.e., gender, class, race). Other organizations refer to social identities as part of their framing of the issues, for example, when the Fellowship of Reconciliation organized a tour of Iraqi women to visit the United States. In the documents we studied, organizations included references to religion, race/ethnicity, class, gender, and sexual orientation. We find they employ collective identity discourses for a variety of reasons. As Mary Bernstein (1997) argued, there are both strategic and culturally based reasons for these appeals.

The work of PMOs to construct the link between social identities and opposition to war has another layer of resistance attached to it. Already existing in the broader culture are identity definitions prioritized by powerholders. These identity constructions shape the dominant discourses about identity. For example, there are well-established gender scripts attached to the categories of male and female. From infancy we are inundated with the "caring female" and the "heroic male" identities. Such identities are used to circumscribe what roles (and thus behaviors) are available to the members of each category. To challenge these socially constructed and arguably false divisions, activists point to the overarching similarities regardless of sex category. In much the same way, the veracity of racial categories is questioned as false separations introduced to shore up systems of stratification. These efforts of feminist, civil rights, and humanist movements move away from using salient collective identities to define social structures. Consequently, the strategy of calling upon social identities with the intent of increasing issue resonance and emotional potency must be handled carefully if it is to truly challenge the dominant discourse without reifying and reinforcing part of the discourse. Social identities have strong potential to increase the resonance of a movement's message.

Appealing to women, people of color, and working-class people to join the peace movement provides an identity-based pathway into the movement and a way of helping people to answer the question, Why is peace making relevant to me? More than just a point of entry, such solid collective identities can provide the foundation for long-term commitment to the movement. In addition, participation in the movement can become one way to express commitment to the group identity. A firm foundation for identity is important to sustaining the movement's oppositional culture. A movement also needs to provide the basis for alternative formations of identity and community. This can be done through identity politics—politicizing existing identities and developing alternative frameworks that deviate from the hegemonic norms organizing society (Carroll and Ratner 2001). Discourse about identity can be done to draw in people who share the identity but are new to the issue, or to strengthen the commitment of those who support the issue but feel only a loose connection to the movement.

COMPLEXITIES IN USING IDENTITY DISCOURSES

It is not always easy to appeal to identity without creating a new set of problems around exclusion and stereotypes. One of the challenges of SMOs is to wean people from their attachments to hegemonic construction of their identities and move them into oppositional constructions (Carroll and Ratner 2001). That it takes effort to argue that certain social identities fit well with opposing war is evidenced in the following examples:

> Under the mantle of National Security, the present Administration seeks to reverse decades of victories won by working people to regulate corporate conduct, protect the environment, strengthen the rights of workers, defend civil liberties and end racism, sexism and discrimination and provide an adequate social safety net. (United States Labor Against the War, October 25, 2003)

> If ever there was a time for lesbian, gay, bisexual and transgender (LGBT) people to broaden the framework of our anti-violence work to oppose racism, abuses of law enforcement authority, militarism, and war, that time is now. (American Friends Service Committee, November 8, 2002)

In each case the organization is extending identity-related commitments to connect concerns it has acted on before to the present concern: in these cases, civil liberties and militarism. Thus social identities can be constructed as relevant to participating in an oppositional peace culture. Social identities are a very rich tool for movements to achieve resonance with particular, targeted audiences (e.g., women, Catholics, trade unionists). However, while a social identity is put forward as salient to the peace movement, those who do not self-identify with that category may be left out by such a targeted appeal.

Groups that work on women's rights, civil rights, and labor rights are not necessarily part of the peace movement. Nonetheless, groups involved in those challenges may at times choose to overlap with the policy perspectives and agendas of the peace movement. Identity discourse can be used to empower people self-identified with those groups, or as an end in itself (to strengthen that particular identity), or as a tool to raise awareness and offer alternatives on some issue (Bernstein 1997). Risks in using identity discourse are present, as Deana Rohlinger points out, because establishing a core organizational identity leads to establishing boundaries that influence actions and messages that are acceptable to the group (Rohlinger 2002).

An additional complexity of using salient identities to draw people into the movement is that the identity base itself might need challenging within the broader culture (e.g., the stereotype that women are naturally peaceful, or that Arab people are raised to be violent). This means that in the statements we studied, identity work was multilayered. For example, CODEPINK—an organization describing itself as "women-initiated" and formed to highlight women's issues and involvement in the peace movement—critiqued increasingly sexist social structures in the United States and Iraq by arguing as follows:

> Just as Bush is working hard to drag U.S. women back to pre-1973 status, the Bush administration-appointed Interim Governing Council and its supporters threaten to drag Iraqi women back to pre-1959 status with Code 137. This resolution would relegate women to a time when they were not permitted to travel freely, a time of forced marriages and no education . . . it threatens to wrench the legal status of Iraqi women back to the dark ages. (CODEPINK, April 19, 2004)

This issue put women's rights front and center in the work of war resistance. So did a statement by the Women's International League for Peace and Freedom, responding to a claim by the Bush Administration that the wars in Iraq and Afghanistan were to secure women's equality: "We . . . call on our elected officials to remedy the policies of the current U.S. Administration which also seek 'to oppress and persecute' women" (April 14, 2004).

Moreover, the motivation for emphasizing collective identity in discourse is not purely strategic. While it may be a good way to create a resonant appeal, there can also be values-based motivations (Taylor and Whittier 1992; Armstrong and Bernstein 2008). There is meaning and even satisfaction in honoring one's values and sticking to one's principles, even if doing so may actually narrow the group's appeal. Offering a values-based cultural critique that also empowers members of their identity group may at times rival in importance the goal of appealing to an ever-widening audience. Consider, for example, the following statement that the Women's International League for Peace and Freedom aimed at gathering opposition to the 1998 bombing of Iraq:

> **It's a testosterone thing** (bold in original)
> Even though all the military types admit that bombing Iraq and even ground troops haven't and won't get rid of Saddam Hussein or prevent Iraq from producing weapons if they want to, they still claim "We said we were gonna do it and by God we're gonna!" They're all puffed up, and say bombing is the only choice because they can't lose face. Just ask for directions, guys! (Women's International League for Peace and Freedom, "Stop, Look and Listen" 1998)

Since the groups have commitments to multiple issues, they may at times forgo the pressures of popular opinion and utilize possibly unpopular discourses in order to construct, express, and shore up subgroup identity (Ferree 2003).

Yet another complexity in the use of identity-based discourse is that not all categories carry the same ideas for all people. Not everyone using the same label defines who can be part of the group and what it means to be part of the group in the same way. Identities are contested even among the affiliated. Cultural contexts and life-course changes shape thinking about identity. For example, feminist identity, including its definition and use, have changed, especially among those born after 1966 compared to those born from 1936 to 1965 (Davis 1991; Evans 2003; Baumgardner and Richards 2000; Kutz-Flamenbaum 2007). Many "feminist" values have gained wider acceptance while, at the same time, there is less agreement in the young generations about what it means to be a feminist. While many of the values (e.g., women's equality) remain central, they are not consistent predictors of whether a person calls herself or himself a "feminist" (Schnittker, Freese, and Powell 2003). For these reasons, groups may be better off delineating packages of specific values and goals being sought after rather than relying on general terminology such as "the feminist perspective" or "the protestant perspective" (Oliver and Johnston 2000; Rohlinger 2002).

Yael Azmon (1997) found that PMOs used "motherhood" instead of "woman" as an identity that legitimated their participation in the public discourse on peace and security. The groups avoided connecting their opposition to war to being women as it brought ridicule and closed access to participation in the discursive events, since discussion of foreign policy traditionally falls outside of the purview of women. However, they found that the mother discourse around children and security and well-being expanded women's discursive opportunities with regard to war and peace. Mothers have a role in war as they are the source of soldiers. The "motherly language" of words like "child," "responsibility," "enemy child," and "soldier child" helped to transform the view of the conflict among Israelis and Palestinians. The motherly language served as a way to increase sensitivity about the experience of the enemy. It also provided a way to describe a form of parenting (nurturance) that could be accessed by both men and women (Azmon 1997). Similarly, in her comparative study of Germany and the United States, Myra Ferree (2003) found that cultural context shaped the discursive opportunities and thus the particular symbolic repertoire chosen from among possible feminist framings.

DISCOURSE AND RAISING CULTURAL CONSCIOUSNESS

Do peace movement organizations invoke discussions of identity merely to build membership? Probably not, because invoking those identities runs the strong risk of losing potential constituents for whom the particular identity referenced does not resonate. Moreover, a successful use of identity discourse is not achieved by a single mention of a category. The organizations using identity discourse to appeal to members or potential members need to pass the "test" of consistent narrative fidelity (see chapter 3 for another example of this idea). Narrative fidelity means that frames resonate with stories, myths, and folktales held dearly by members or potential members (Snow and Benford 1988). These are typically oppositional narratives that unite the minority groups against powerholders (Armstrong and Bernstein 2008). Such unity can form around creating oppositional knowledge and engaging in resistance activities. Often there are deeply held oppositional narratives that are called on consistently to create that consonance. For example, in our data there were multiple references to paying reparations to African Americans for slavery and its legacies instead of spending money on war. And there were repeated discussions linking U.S. foreign policy around war to job loss and trade policies seen as deleterious for working classes. In January 2003, during the run-up to the Iraq war, Black Voices for Peace (BVFP) urged that commemorations of the Martin Luther King Jr. holiday should focus on several points, one of which was the following:

> Promoting a national people's agenda for affordable housing, accessible and affordable health care, education, jobs at livable wages and job training, income security and food safety net, environmental protection and other human needs—linking opposition to militarism as part of this effort. (Black Voices for Peace, January 9, 2003)

Resonance was sought by linking antiwar activism to improving the quality of life at home. These appeals were at times made utilizing identity references. They were framed as "because of who you are . . . you should be opposed to this war."

Discourses of Identity as Strategy

Identity speaks to people by appealing to what seems commonsensical from their standpoint. For example, United States Labor Against the War spent considerable energy informing the public on how post–U.S. invasion

Iraqi workers are actually worse off than they were before the intervention. A very concrete and data-driven analysis gave USLAW the opportunity to stress that workers' rights are an integral part of democratization. It pressed their organizational agenda and allowed them to link home and abroad while also appealing to humanitarian concerns for the victims of the war. In discussing their organizing plans, USLAW writes:

> One task force will coordinate closely with veterans organizations and Military Families Speak Out in trying to reach veterans who are union members. The Education task force will help get a labor audience for a popular education workshop developed by United for a Fair Economy that focuses on teaching people on how to effectively talk with co-workers on the war and the economy. A third will take up international solidarity and defense of Iraqi labor rights. (United States Labor Against the War, December, 2003)

The strategic use of identity is not disconnected from the cultural context, however. Such discourse expects an audience that has sensitivity to and concern for issues associated with racism, ethnocentrism, economic injustice, religious intolerance, and sexism. In the following example, WILPF used *counter-informative* oppositional knowledge and depended on the reader's sympathy to women's rights in shaping their criticism of existing policies:

> [WILPF] is outraged at the notion that this unjustified war was fought for women's rights. Not only has this Administration pursued an agenda which puts women at risk around the world, but grassroots movements for women's rights already exist throughout the Arab world. To declare that the total destruction of both Afghanistan and Iraq was a necessary step in securing women's equality is as patronizing as it is dangerous. (Women's International League for Peace and Freedom, April 14, 2004)

Creating oppositional knowledge that shows what is missing, ignored, or misdirected challenges the public to think critically and perhaps even imaginatively; it also suggests ways to resist reinforcing social inequalities.

CODING IDENTITY

In order to map the use of identities, we coded for two types of passages. First, our family of codes labeled "identity politics" marked passages where the organization was framing its appeal toward specific social identities (i.e., race, gender, class, religion) with the explicit or heavily implied goal of expanding the movement and heightening a feeling of resonance with the messages of the group. For example:

> Identity Politics-Religion: "The policies of this [Bush] administration stand in stark contrast to the values we hold as Catholics." (Pax Christi, March 18, 2003)

Identity Politics-Race: "We know that presently about 30% of those deployed in the Gulf are African American." (American Friends Service Committee, Third World Coalition Gulf Statement)

Identity Politics-Gender: "Women all over the world oppose the bombing of Afghanistan started on October 7, 2001." (Women's International League for Peace and Freedom, 911 Housework)

Identity Politics-Class: "The U.S. occupation of Iraq is in crisis. As any sensible union member knows, the first thing to do when you find you've dug yourself into a hole is to STOP DIGGING." (USLAW, April 30, 2004)

A second type of identity-related passage was those that discussed the particular costs of going to war. Among the range of subcodes regarding costs of war were those referring to gender, race/ethnicity, and class. At times these passages co-occurred with the material coded as identity politics, so only the latter is included in our statistical analysis to prevent double-counting particular passages. However, including passages about costs of war in our qualitative analysis and broad picture of coding practices helps to show that many of the pragmatic arguments against the conflicts were targeted to specific groups in society. For example, by invoking a "rich vs. poor" paradigm, the BRC sketched the costs of war as deeply relevant to the working class: "Money for education, health care and to rebuild our cities is being diverted to pay for a vast increase in military spending and another round of proposed trillion dollar tax cuts for the wealthy" (Black Radical Congress, June 2003).

PRACTICING IDENTITY POLITICS: MAJOR THEMES IN THE DATA

Race and Ethnicity

There were six major themes in the overall data set related to questions of race and ethnicity:

1. Concern about the unfair burden shouldered by minorities who serve in the military
2. Xenophobia
3. Unity in shared oppression against the forces of "divide and rule"
4. Why being Black should lead a person to oppose war
5. Repression at home is linked to war abroad (civil liberties/state terrorism and spending priorities)
6. Global racism

In response to conflicts connected to the Middle East (Gulf War, 9/11, Iraq War), peace movement discourse included concerns about anti-Arab sentiments. Disproportional military service of Blacks, repression of Blacks in the United States (prisons and civil rights), and militaristic spending priorities which hurt the poor in the United States and globally (disproportionately people of color) are the balance of the concerns discussed around this social identity. A strong theme in the data is similar to one voiced historically: why are those who carry the burden of war not the powerholders in society? The groups appealed to the sentiment that Blacks are treated as second-class citizens when it comes to distribution of power and wealth in U.S. society, but are called on to pay the costs for the collective whole. The themes of racism and ethnocentrism were connected to militarism, at times subtly and at other times blatantly.

Gender

Not only is U.S. society structured around norms and assumptions related to gender, but the topic of violence has long carried significant links to societal ideas about being male and female. Wartime is typically rife with gender-related scripts and tends to be a time of heightened divisions between male and female social roles. The image of the tearful mother and the proud father waving goodbye to their deployed son charts gender roles related to war. Increasingly common is the image of the woman soldier, but it is often softened by the stuffed teddy bear clasped in her arms. These images remind us that the dominant culture embraces competing values: killing is wrong and violence protects the peace. The dualism of female/male is called on to represent contradictory attachments to both peace and war. These discourses that the dominant gender scripts embrace are directly challenged by CODEPINK in their "Call to Action" statement:

> We call on women around the world to rise up and oppose the war in Iraq. We call on mothers, grandmothers, sisters and daughters, on workers, students, teachers, healers, artists, writers, singers, poets, and every ordinary outraged woman willing to be outrageous for peace. Women have been the guardians of life—not because we are better or purer or more innately nurturing than men, but because the men have busied themselves making war. (CODEPINK, About Code Pink)

Our data shows that the peace movement's gender analysis can be usefully grouped into five areas:

1. The importance of solidarity as women (e.g., International Women's Day, cultural exchanges, concern for victims, Mother's Day as a call for peace)
2. The links between masculinity and sexual violence
3. The "testosterone thing"—linking masculinity with oppressive power

Photo 6.1. WAND t-shirt worn at peace rally in the Midwest. (Photo by Lynne M. Woehrle)

4. Women's relationship to war and peace (e.g., mothering and the military, "preemptive strike for peace," women as victims of war, gender divide in support for war)
5. Women's policymaking as being different from men's

The overall theme in the data is that women act on behalf of peace. Sometimes this was presented as regaining peace in response to war. Other times it was discussed as preempting the tendency of the patriarchal power structures to assume war is the answer. Some PMOs claimed this preemption is accomplished by advocating peace and pointing out when political leaders are moving the state to war so peace-loving activists can get in the way. While women increasingly participate directly in the military system, a strong attachment to women as peacemakers remains in U.S. society. The gender analysis offered by the groups sought both to challenge traditional stereotypes of women's social roles and to further construct women as offering an approach to foreign policy that highlights dialogue and diplomacy rather than violent responses to conflict. The movement's aim appears to promote the idea that women lead us towards peace, not because they are weak, but because they are insightful and politically adept.

Class

Likewise there were major themes around how social class impacts the experience of war and responses to war. The class-related themes in our data included the following:

1. Workers should be opposed to war
2. In war, the wealthy win and the poor lose (e.g., taxes, corporate malfeasance, spending priorities)
3. War is a forum for restricting the rights of "the working people" (e.g., union busting, civil rights, working mothers' issues)
4. The costs of war are borne by the working people (e.g., military service, job losses from 9/11, social services cuts)
5. War opposition is a source for worker empowerment and solidarity

Class-based arguments paralleled in some ways the arguments around race: namely, those who gain from war do not pay the costs of war. Despite the jobs provided by the military-industrial complex, the PMOs insisted there are many reasons for working-class and poor people to stand against war. A strong peace movement theme was providing an economic analysis of how militarism misshapes national spending priorities. Because the working class and the poor are more in need of government assistance, the costs of war impact their daily lives. Moreover, a society at war, the PMOs argued, has little room for dissent and this limits all social movements, including trade unions. The cry of "all for one and one for all" during wartime suggests that all employees will accept the workhorse role with no complaint. Peace groups warned that since wars create national debt and can run for many years, workers' rights that might otherwise be gained are often lost, sometimes permanently. The PMOs also highlighted the "economic draft," explaining that wars continue because those who plan them are not losing their children on the battlefield. Finally they argued that combat soldiers, poorly paid and often disabled in battle, regularly experience downward mobility in times of war.

Religion

As suggested in chapter 5, appealing to people through their identity as a member of a faith group is difficult because of the overlaps between multiple faiths and faith-based perspectives. If the organization uses the more specific denominational appeal ("as Catholics we . . . ") rather than a more general appeal ("as Christians we . . . ") or a still more general appeal ("as people of faith we . . . "), there is an intensity of personalization that likely many followers will find familiar and attractive. However, the latter two approaches reach out to much broader bases and create a sense of cooperation and shared values among believers. These are not just strategic choices. They are also often deeply bound up with believers' sense of self, and even with their responsibility and "mission" to the world, to being true to and even advancing their religious values.

Several major themes emerged in the peace movement's use of religion as a way to appeal to potential and committed constituents. These included the following:

1. Principled opposition (e.g., nonviolence, alternative solutions)
2. Religion as a guide (e.g., for action, for foreign policy)
3. Religion as a resource (e.g., for reaching people, and for well-being through prayer)
4. Religion as a bridge between people
5. Religion as a means to social change and reconciliation (e.g., prayer, diplomacy)
6. Religion as a possible means of division, which must be challenged because various faiths share so much

Religious identity was thus used to make firmer a commitment to policy and actions that promoted values of fairness, compassion, reconciliation, and the basic dignity and connectedness of all people who practice a religious faith (see chapter 5 for more discussion of religion, discourse, and identity). The PMOs shaped collective responses to crises through religious symbols or language. Both subgroup identities and superordinate identities were developed by calling for people to respond through religious commitments.

DIASPORIC THINKING

A theme that runs through both the 9/11 data and the Iraq War data are the connections among people around the world who experience similar oppression. Such diasporic thinking is utilized particularly with the concepts of race/ethnicity and gender. For example, the BRC refers to "people of African descent world-wide" (Black Radical Congress 2001). Thus in our data we see the expansion of the identity deployment typology offered by Bernstein to include not only "identity for critique" and "identity for education" (1997, 538), but also what we are calling "identity for connection." For gender we also see this theme in the Gulf War conflict period. For class, the only discussion of links among all workers is found in documents from United States Labor Against the War. However, a more specific cross-national connection of U.S. workers with Iraqi workers is a prevalent theme during the Iraq War conflict period.

"Identity for connection" is the raising of awareness about how and why identity-based diasporas reach across time and place and give both immediate and historical sense of connection to members of a group that is larger and more diffuse than one's immediate territorial state. Diasporas cross state boundaries and are intended to secure bonds among people that supersede

Photo 6.2.   Unifying class analysis across state boundaries links war with victimization. (Photo by Patrick G. Coy)

nationalism. They are built on a sense of commonness. In this case the organizations were utilizing commonalities among people who by virtue of their membership in a particular category are denied full power in society. The concept that "we are connected to all other women by our gender" or "we are connected to all people of color" or "all workers are linked" carries that sense of common history and experience despite distance. Another source of connection is a sense of shared fate (Gamson 1992a), especially around the experience of exclusion from power and leadership. Malcolm X and later Martin Luther King Jr. viewed the Black freedom struggle as part of a worldwide struggle against capitalism and imperialism (Rod Bush 2003). The goal is an expanded consciousness of connection, intended to lead to agency for social change. Such an approach creates *transformative* oppositional knowledge by defining that sense of connectedness to the world, as exemplified below:

> Representatives of major US labor unions that have passed resolutions opposing a US invasion of Iraq will host a telephone press conference in which their counterparts from other countries, whose labor organizations have passed similar resolutions, will participate. (United States Labor Against War, February 19, 2003)

Counter-informative oppositional knowledge can utilize diasporic thinking to raise awareness of a shared oppression, as shown in the following example:

And as we come together in historic numbers to oppose these alarming developments, we march not only for ourselves, but for the women of the world because
we know that it isn't only the freedoms of U.S. women that are under attack, but
the women of Iraq and the world, as well. (CODEPINK, April 19, 2004)

And from that solidarity, the impression is given that there is understanding among the oppressed that crosses over boundaries of distance and culture.
Critical-interpretive oppositional knowledge includes making people aware of
shared experiences and calling into question the dominant power's definitions of group separations and adversarial politics. This happens in wartime
when cross-cultural understanding among the people on both sides is reached
despite government efforts to create an enemy consciousness. Women's International League for Peace and Freedom wrote a letter from the women of the
United States to the women of Iraq, which included this paragraph:

As women, as mothers and daughters, grandmothers and aunts, as sisters we are
reaching out to you, offering our friendship, support, and strength. You are not
alone in the struggle for peace and justice. (Women's International League for
Peace and Freedom, January 22, 2004, "To the Women of Iraq")

These passages show how the peace groups tried to raise identity consciousness and through that identity forge a connection to others around the world.
Perhaps through shared actions, as the first quote demonstrates; or perhaps
through shared oppressions, as the second quote outlines (see also chapter 3
on transnational allegiance).

"Pacifist" was another identity-based connection among people dispersed
throughout various regions that was appealed to by the PMOs. In discussions
of religious identity there were many references to nonviolence as the preferred response rather than violence. Not only did the pacifist groups inspect
and question the use of violence, but they practiced self-inspection as well.
As this passage, which takes a *radical-envisioning* approach to oppositional
knowledge and asks what are the implications of having a pacifist identity
shows, employment of these identities was itself fodder for analysis: "What is
the place for Quakers in this new situation? What does it mean to be a pacifist
in this particular time of war?" (American Friends Service Committee, March
27, 2003). Organizations with a pacifist identity also tried to educate the public about the global traditions of nonviolent action. The following quote is a
good example of the discussion of nonviolent action as having the dimensions
of a global diaspora:

In Iran in 1979, after 25 years of U.S.-supported dictatorship, nearly one million
Muslim fundamentalists took to the streets in the largest nonviolent demonstration in history and removed the Shah. In Manila in 1986, after 13 years of
U.S.-supported martial law, some one million Filipinos took to the streets and
removed Marcos. In Poland, people in the Solidarity labor movement had a new,
nonviolent vision of escape from their Russian masters. For years they reached

out to more and more different groups until the "critical mass" of nonviolent revolution was achieved. That same nonviolent revolution spread throughout the countries dominated by Communist rule. Even now, we are inspired by the February 15, 2003, nonviolent demonstrations for peace throughout the world (War Resisters League, October 3, 2003).

Diasporas tend to enhance and strengthen a single identity by showing its wide relevance across societies. Identity discourse can also focus on the relevance that the various identities have to each other. We turn now to look at that process of intersecting identities and how they emerge in the context of opposition to war.

INTERSECTIONALITY

Thus far we have discussed the data by looking at discrete categories, but the reality is that the organizations offered analysis that is much more complex and layered than a single-dimensional analysis can reveal. For example, concerns for the unfair burden of military service looked at both the politics of race and the politics of class. Critiques of spending priorities regularly noted the linkage of racism, sexism, and economic injustice. A potent theme across the conflict periods and one that was common among many organizations was the idea that experiences of violence are not limited to a single oppressed group but are familiar to all victims of racism, elitism, sexism, and religious intolerance. According to Patricia Hill Collins (1990), intersectionality represents how race/ethnicity, class, and gender operate together, *not* as an additive model of oppressions, but rather as a unique experience depending on which categories are relevant. That experience weaves together the various sources of oppression. Thus an African American poor woman does not have commonalities with all African Americans, all women, and all poor people. Rather her life is shaped by the interaction of her oppressions, that place where they intersect (Collins 1990). At the same time that essentialist definitions of oppression are challenged by intersectionality, these challenges have a second function, that is, enabling people to see how the various layers of oppression mutually reinforce each other. Rod Bush (2003) argues that this insight brought Martin Luther King Jr. and many of his followers to the realization that social transformation required not just civil rights but economic rights as well, especially on a global scale.

Discussions of oppressions afford many opportunities for peace organizations to introduce oppositional knowledge. Raising awareness of shared oppression is an important device for developing a sense of group, one that has the potential to act together to effect change. Groups typically express stronger or more adamant agendas regarding what is valuable than do individuals. The following example of *counter-informative* oppositional knowledge pulled to the surface of people's consciousness the interconnections of layers of violence:

We know from our own experience that people of color, poor people, women and children suffer most from the violence of militarism at home and abroad. It is simply not possible for us to do our work effectively without confronting this violence and the violence of racism, just as we confront the violence of homophobia and heterosexism. These struggles are intertwined. They are not separate. (American Friends Service Committee, November 8, 2002)

In combining *counter-informative* oppositional knowledge with *transformative* thinking, the definition of the problem is developed. In turn, the idea that the concern is better addressed collaboratively among oppressed groups opens an important "gate" for those who are focused on seeing the world through a single issue. That said, it is also difficult to achieve an action that has too broad of a mandate. Getting people to think about the world through the lens of intersectionality is not always easy. The countering of dominant assumptions that reject intersectionality is a long-term strategy to remove obstacles to thinking differently, shifting and remaking culture, and thus creating social change.

In many documents the expressions of intersections were not particularly sophisticated. Rather than analyzing the presence of these intersections, the typical list of "isms" was tagged by the PMO to a statement of opposition. However in the following excerpt, which mixes the *radical-envisioning* approach with the *critical-interpretive* approach, the BRC makes the more complex argument that social structures and cultural practices mix to shape the violent practices of discrimination:

These battles call on all black people to organize to struggle for peace in our homes, communities, churches, schools, work places, malls, temples, mosques, and other places. The road to peace is a long one. It is a road that requires a fundamental break with old practices. We must carve out spaces of peace and spaces of love. The present war challenges the present Peace Movement to grasp the reality that the U.S. military industrial information complex combines all the traditions of racism, genocide, masculinity, rape, homophobia, celebration of violence and wanton murder. (Black Radical Congress, March 20, 2003)

The statement also alludes to a concern that bias towards certain subgroups in society has not been a central issue in the peace movement. Not just the powerholders are critiqued for relying on hierarchical structures; the peace movement is often described as being itself built upon problematic stereotypes and assumptions that need to be challenged and further clarified.

SOCIAL IDENTITY: LONGITUDINAL ANALYSIS

The documents from the five organizations with data across all five of our conflict periods (AFSC, FOR, Pax Christi, Peace Action, and WILPF) show the ebb and flow of identity-based discourse practices (See also chapter 3, figure 3.1).[3] We found it interesting that there was an increased use of appeal to religious identity during conflicts involving major use of U.S. ground forces. Moreover, concerns over the justness and morality of war often accompanied heavy ground troop commitments. The post-9/11 spike in religious discourse by the PMOs probably related to the disproportionate emphasis by the Bush administration upon religious beliefs compared to previous administrations (see chapter 5). As Howard Fineman put it, "this Presidency is the most resolutely faith-based in modern times, an enterprise founded, supported and guided by trust in the temporal and spiritual power of God" (Fineman 2003, 22). In addition, the prevalent if not dominant construction by many of September 11th and the "war on terror" as having important religious dimensions was also likely a factor.

The five conflict-period analysis of five groups shows a mostly increasing appeal to gender identity over time. By the Iraq War, four of five groups contributed gender appeals, whereas in the Gulf War only two of the five did and the vast majority of the gender framing fell solely to WILPF. It is likely that sensitivity to gender analysis is a product of diffusion, especially from the very outspoken CODEPINK (not included in the longitudinal data but arguably influential on the tone of movement discourse), which pushed hard on gender identity. There is also much more attention to gender during the Kosova/o conflict compared to the Iraq 1998 conflict period. In Serbia there were active interethnic peacebuilding efforts by women's NGOs during the conflict. There was also extensive publicity about the use of rape as a war tactic during the Balkan wars.

These five groups paid little attention to the concept of class. Attention to class began to shift in response to 9/11 with the formation of specifically antiwar labor organizations (NYCLAW, USLAW), but these class-identified organizations are not able to be included in the five-period analysis. Statistical analysis of the five organizations over the five conflict periods shows a slight increase in class-identity discourse in the 9/11 conflict period. This recedes again during the Iraq War to a level similar to that of the Gulf War.

Applying a qualitative analysis to the data for the five groups reveals that the content as well as the extent of race/ethnicity discourse shifted by conflict period. In the 9/11 data, the framing around race/ethnicity (two passages) is both about racism and about anti-Arab demonization and discrimination. In the Iraq War data, the only two passages focus on anti-Arab discrimination. In the Gulf War data, a focus on African Americans is somewhat present. Typically discussion around race and racism was focused on who serves in the military and risks their lives. However, those organizations most likely to construct discourses containing analyses of race and ethnicity (BRC, BVFP, CAIR) are not included in the five-period longitudinal data set.

We also looked at discourse around race, class, and gender, comparing the 9/11 conflict period with the Iraq War. Because more of the organizations with strong identity politics concerns are included in that data, there is more identity-related framing.[4] An organization-by-organization comparison between the two conflict periods does not show a strong pattern in any single group between the two conflict periods. However, if we look broadly at the organizations, the concern for identity politics is more widely dispersed in the Iraq War period. In the 9/11 conflict period, only two of ten groups used the identity politics-class code, whereas in the Iraq War this tripled to six of ten. During 9/11, only three of ten groups used the identity politics-gender code whereas in the Iraq War this more than doubled to seven of ten groups. For race/ethnicity the evidence of diffusion was not as strong. In 9/11, five of the ten groups used identity politics-race, while during the Iraq War seven of ten groups used it. And for the identity politics-religion code, the exact same groups used the religious identity discourse in both conflict periods, showing that diffusion was not a factor in the case of religion.

Who Is Using Identity-Based Discourse?

Looking across the data set as a whole we can consider which organizations primarily use identity discourse. As table 6.1 shows, there is a strong pattern where organizations that regard specific categories of people and specific issues as central to their mission were the ones who engaged in identity politics the most.

One way to understand this pattern is that organizations have a strategic concern for framing the issues in a way that resonates to those possibly resistant to the ideas (e.g., trade union members). Or it may be fueled by a strong sense of responsibility to speak to the issues because as CODEPINK argues, women do what they do about protesting war because men are busy making

Table 6.1.   Overall Use of Identity-Based Codes

Organizations Using Identity Politics in Their Top Five Codes	Organizations Not Using Identity Politics in Their Top Five Codes
Black Radical Congress: Idpol[a]-race, Hcost[b]-race	American Friends Service Committee[c]
Black Voices for Peace: Idpol-race	Moveon.org
Council on American-Islamic Relations: Idpol-religion	Peace Action
CODEPINK: Idpol-gender	TrueMajority
Fellowship of Reconciliation: Idpol-religion	Women's Action for New Directions[d]
NYC Labor Against the War: Idpol-class	
Pax Christi: Idpol-religion	
US Labor Against the War: Idpol-class, Hcost-class	
Women's International League for Peace and Freedom: Idpol-gender	

Notes: Analysis based on weighted data. For weights formula, see appendix 2.
[a] Idpol = Identity Politics.
[b] Hcost = Human Cost of War.
[c] Though not a religious group itself, it is strongly connected to the Religious Society of Friends (Quakers).
[d] WAND seems to be an outlier from the pattern of the rest of the groups.

war. While CODEPINK's analysis is arguably oversimplistic, there is a sense in the dominant symbolic repertoire that women have a cultural role that gives them responsibility for peacemaking. Perhaps gender-oriented groups carefully exploited that stereotype because they expected it to resonate, even though it carries risks of reinforcing the dominant discourse around gender. A good example is the choice of pink as a symbolic color for a women's group, even though feminists have long fought against the pink-and-blue divide. Why does CODEPINK take this risk and how does it turn the color pink into a well-harnessed idea? Their own words explain it:

> We love our country, but we will never wrap ourselves in red, white and blue.
> Instead, we announce a Code Pink alert:
> signifying extreme danger to all the values of nurturing,
> caring, and compassion that women and loving men have held. We
> choose pink, the color of roses, the beauty that like bread is
> food for life, the color of the dawn of a new era when
> cooperation and negotiation prevail over force. (CODEPINK, "About CODEPINK")

Some groups also used the identity connection to introduce new, oppositional knowledge into discussions of peace, for example, when they connected the idea of reparations for racial inequalities directly to concerns about wartime spending, or when WILPF claimed that there is a particular *women's* foreign policy, which offers a more diplomatic approach to dealing with international conflicts. Identities can be salient either because of recent historical events or because organizations work to make their salience obvious to the general public. It does appear that, with the exception of Women's Action for New Directions (WAND) and the American Friends Service Committee (AFSC), the organizations with a race, class, gender, or religion connection were the primary participants in shaping their messages with the help of identity politics. This finding is not surprising, as membership in the social identities of race, class, and gender is likely to shape how people view and explain the world around them. For example, research conducted on responses to the attacks of September 11 found that racial/ethnic categories and the understandings of race and power in the United States deeply influenced reactions to the event (Harlow and Dundes 2004). In some cases, though, social identities were not pressed into service. The AFSC and WAND are examples of groups we expected to exhibit more use of identity discourse than they actually did.

We can also look at organizational contributions to identity-based discourse through the five conflict periods, as we do in table 6.2. As discussed in the previous section, these data show the diffusion through the peace movement of ideas around race, class, and gender politics, and even the use of religious referencing by secular groups.

It also reveals that the vast majority of the time the most consistent and largest amount of identity-based framing was done by organizations for which those ideas were likely to be highly salient to their targeted audiences.

Table 6.2. Identity Politics Use by Conflict Period (read across only)

Period	Identity Politics-Class	Identity Politics-Gender	Identity Politics-Race	Identity Politics-Religion
Gulf War	AFSC* FOR	AFSC WILPF*	AFSC FOR Peace Action WILPF*	AFSC FOR Peace Action Pax Christi*
Iraq 1998	WILPF	WILPF*		Pax Christi* WRL
Kosova/o		AFSC WILPF*		AFSC Pax Christi*
9/11	Peace Action NYCLAW*	AFSC FOR WILPF*	AFSC BRC* FOR NYCLAW WILPF	AFSC BRC CAIR* FOR Pax Christi
Iraq War	AFSC BRC CODEPINK FOR MoveOn NYCLAW Peace Action USLAW* WRL	AFSC BRC CODEPINK* FOR MoveOn Peace Action USLAW WAND WILPF WRL	BRC* CAIR FOR NYCLAW Peace Action USLAW WILPF WRL	AFSC BRC CAIR* CODEPINK FOR MoveOn Pax Christi TrueMajority USLAW WILPF WRL

Notes: Analysis based on weighted data. For weights formula, see appendix 2. Table lists all PMOs during a conflict period with one or more passages coded. Some of the identity-centered organizations had not been formed yet in earlier conflict periods. This analysis does not include Black Voices for Peace, because their small data set made them a statistical outlier.
* Highest occurrence of the code based on weighted data.

These organizations have explicit commitments to identity, which makes them responsible for articulating the intersection of war with identity-based concerns.

CONCLUSIONS ABOUT PMOS AND IDENTITY DISCOURSE

There is without doubt a need for further study with an even more representative data set that can give us a richer longitudinal view of identity-based discourse. However, even our profile of antiwar organizing during five conflict periods shows an emerging pattern of diffusion where more groups used identity-based discourse. For example, by the Iraq War, appeals to gender identities spread across the movement rather than being bounded inside the women-centered groups.

Despite some evidence of diffusion, we note that the normative values of certain groups shaped their stronger attachment to identity-based discourse. Clearly these groups believe that opposing war can be packaged to appeal to subgroup identities. In fact they spend a great deal of energy building on the salience of identities, or making arguments likely intended to push the identity salience higher.

Identity talk is well developed in the U.S. peace movement (Hunt and Benford 1994). Moreover, social identities such as religion, gender, race/ethnicity, and class are core to some organizations' very existence. Our data show that use of social identities by U.S. peace movement organizations rises and falls across conflict periods but never disappears. This suggests that identity-based discourse is constructed not only because it can be regularly counted on to resonate with the ongoing values and norms of movement members, but also because its salience and resonance with the wider public is thought to vary in response to political and cultural changes. The peace movement was both faithful to identity issues and responsive to perceived opportunities when identity talk was thought to be more or less effective. We also find use of diasporic thinking to create a sense of connection that is wider than identities based on location or constrained by national boundaries. The PMOs used social identities to create transnational links that are useful in helping people think creatively about social transformation.

In addition, we have uncovered an increasing use of the analytical framework of intersectionality (connecting the various social identities) in PMO analyses of military actions and U.S. foreign policy. This perhaps reflects the complexity of identity experienced by potential constituencies and the desire of the PMOs to appeal to cross sections of the population rather than to a single characteristic of a population. By using and encouraging intersectionality approaches, organizations made it easier for activists to embrace multiple identities. This may assist movement identities to become looser and more flexible (della Porta 2005). Increasing openness to intersectionality thinking and diffusion of identity discourses across the movement may in time help shape a peace movement that can appeal to a broader base of society than has happened in the past. These cross-over identity appeals help to further emphasize that at the root of the problem is a stratified social structure that leads to inequalities—in this case magnified by participation in the military-industrial complex and the machinations of war.

NOTES

1. Concerns over free trade policies and inequalities in the globalization process brought together a wide variety of social movement organizations in a series of protests at international economic policy meetings. Protests during the 1999 WTO meetings were an early example of this

transnational movement. A visual portrayal of this that serves as a helpful teaching tool is the film "This is What Democracy Looks Like," Independent Media Centers and Big Noise Films, 2000.

2. We agree with scholars who argue that race divisions are based on inaccurate beliefs that there are characteristics (e.g., hair color/texture, skin tone, eye shape) that can be used to identify biological separations among groups of people. Studies of DNA across racial groups have proved these divisions false. However, since U.S. society bases much of its evaluation of people on these "racial" characteristics, we choose to study them as a means for ideological expression and social movement mobilization.

3. This sample of five organizations does not include many of the organizations in the larger data set that are formed around social identities. Only religion and gender are represented in this sample. However, how groups with less emphasis on particular identities still make use of identity framing to achieve resonance with members of society is also worthy of note.

4. The 9/11 period did not include USLAW, a strong identity politics-class group. Nor did it include CODEPINK, a strong identity politics-gender group. It also did not include Black Voices for Peace, a strong identity politics-race group.

III

THE CHANGING PRESENT AND AN UNCERTAIN FUTURE

7

Real Solutions for a Safer World

The hens they all cackle, the roosters all beg,
But I will not hatch, I will not hatch.
For I hear all the talk of pollution and war
As the people all shout and the airplanes roar,
So I'm staying in here where it's safe and it's warm,
And I WILL NOT HATCH!

—Shel Silverstein, "Where the Sidewalk Ends"

The role of the state in the social contract is to provide its citizens with a secure way of life. Through time this has predominantly been envisioned as the state utilizing military means to protect its people. As discussed in chapter 3, the nation is often viewed as synonymous with the state. A nation and a state are different, but often people speak of them as the same, or refer to a "nation-state" to signify overlap and integration. States rely upon the construct of the nation in order to constitute themselves (Benedict Anderson 1991). Thus security includes not just physical safety but also protecting culture as expressed in nationalism and through identity as a people. The "we" that is the nation expects to be protected by the institutions of the state. While this is a common process among states, each state defines for itself what makes it secure, what threatens that security, and who is worthy of protection.

The concept of security is wrapped up in understandings of insecurity and threat. Threats come sometimes from within the state, but the primary focus is typically on external threats. At times the two levels of threat (internal and external) blur or become interconnected. For example, 1950s McCarthyism asserted that there was an internal Communist threat being engineered by forces external to the United States. Even earlier, during World War II, internment camps were established for Japanese Americans and Japanese people living in the United States. These camps were rationalized based on an alleged external threat being present within the residents and citizens of the United States. Another example is that the pilots in the September 11th, 2001, attacks attended flight schools on United States visas. Despite this blurring, understanding that threats can be either internal or external (or some combination) helps define what it means to be secure.

Security is a dynamic concept such that when external threats are considered low in salience, the sense of security within the nation-state is greater. Thus a state cannot float on its own but must view its level of security as related to the level of insecurity in the international system. The sources of insecurity can come from threats to political security—from real or imagined threats to the physical safety of borders or to the people within them. They may also come from threats to cultural security such as limitations on ritual traditions, forms of governance, or lifestyle.

In the United States today it is not unusual to hear the argument that since the 9/11 attacks, the concern for security has become more central than ever (Smith, Rasinski, and Toce 2001). Whereas referencing the security discourse has long been a favorite practice of governments, in the United States this became much more common and salient after 9/11. That attack gave many in the United States their first taste of feelings of national insecurity. And it made transparent that not all people in the world embrace the policies and priorities of the United States government. Much like during the height of the nuclear arms race of the mid-twentieth century, concerns for national security have risen to the surface throughout the general U.S. population. For example, a poll conducted by the Pew Internet and American Life Project from June 14 to July 3, 2004, found that 64 percent of the 465 respondents had heard or read frequently that an argument for the Iraq War was that "Iraq posed an imminent threat to American security." Conversely, only 9 percent of those polled had never heard or read such an argument in support of the war (Program on International Policy Attitudes 2006).

Meantime the George W. Bush administration hammered again and again on discourses of fear and insecurity and on his administration's foreign policy as the best response. Here are two examples:

And that's why we are all fighting. We are fighting to protect ourselves and our children from violence and fear. We're fighting for the security of our people and the success of liberty. We're fighting against men without conscience, but full of ambition—to remake the world in their own brutal images. For all the reasons we're fighting to win—and win we will. (George W. Bush, December 7, 2001)

The safety and security of America also faces a new threat, and that is the threat of terror. It is the calling of our time, to rid the world of terror. And it is the calling of our time to protect the American people. (George W. Bush, November 29, 2001)

With such a near-constant discourse, it is no surprise that security has become such an important issue in the United States.

With a notable segment of the U.S. population living in comfort relative to the rest of the world, U.S. security concerns have long focused more on political and cultural security than on human welfare or economic security. During the Gulf War the primary discourse on issues of threat was around protecting "freedom," not specifically about the concept of security. For example, President George H. W. Bush remarked in 1991:

> History is moving decisively in favor of freedom, thanks in large part to American ideals and perseverance—the touchstones of the modern world which the emerging democracies are now striving for: free markets, free speech, free elections. America has lived by these tenets for over 200 years. And they've given us both our power and our purpose. (George H. W. Bush 1991, 141)

Moreover the threat was presented by the president as the aggression of Iraq against Kuwait, a violation of the international understanding of the rule of law that states must follow. As a result, hope for peaceful coexistence in a post–Cold War world was also threatened since the international community was damaged (George H. W. Bush 1991).

Frequently, security concerns have focused upon international instability (e.g., Gulf War, Kosova/o). At other times, security concerns are based on threats of physical endangerment (Iraq 1998, post-9/11, Iraq War). Sometimes, security threats are presented as deeply cultural, as threats to a country's basic values or to its "way of life" (e.g., post-9/11). But rarely is the focus upon the daily economic well-being of the at-risk populations. On the question of whether human well-being leads to democracy or whether democracy must come first, the U.S. government stands clearly on the side of the democracy first model. This sets the United States apart from many of its peers on the international stage. As some human rights scholars point out, despite leadership by the United States on economic globalization (commodities, markets, and wages), the United States remains "on the margins of a new global discourse and emerging set of practices relating to human rights including food security, people's right to water, environmental sustainability, and other transnational projects that promote human security" (Blau and Moncada 2005, 4). While state security mainly focuses on protecting the integrity and sovereignty of the state, human security entails reducing or removing those things that make human lives insecure (Commission on Human Security 2003). This may or may not follow state boundaries, as the nation-state is more geographically bound than the concept of human community. There is also a tension between commitment to human security without boundaries and the demands of state sovereignty. This means states need to consider the question of global interdependence and how or whether both goals can coexist.

Human security interrelates with two other human-centered concepts: human development and human rights (Commission on Human Security 2003). Human security suggests a starker and more immediate response to the long-term goals that development seeks to achieve than does state security. Interpreting security as one subset of human rights strengthens the commitment to identifying what makes people insecure, where conflict comes from, and what the basic freedoms are that need to be protected (Commission on Human Security 2003).

In their criticisms of the state in recent years, peace movement organizations have asked what creates a secure society. The multiple fears engendered by the 9/11 attacks created a cultural context and political space for discourse on security and insecurity. Because how to be more secure was at the forefront of discourse in society, PMOs worked to refashion the concept of security and attempt to spur people to go beyond current definitions and ideologies (Armstrong and Bernstein 2008; Snow 2004a).[1] Their reformulations of what defines security are good examples of the power of creating and expressing oppositional knowledge. They broke from the traditional "national security" definition of being secure and refocused the conversation on the question of what will make the human community secure. PMOs have seen the security-insecurity dynamic as critical to defining a sense of safety. They offered oppositional knowledge that questions whether the traditional military approach can do anything more than make people *less* secure. What the PMOs said about where and why threats emerge diverged from what powerholders in society said. Even more important was the movement's attempt to transform the dialogue about security toward one that focuses on the interdependence of societies and on the concept that security requires that we respect and support other members of the global community.

One way to conceptualize these varieties of security is to consider the differences between what *military security* and *national security* mean compared to the concepts of *human security* and *global security*. The first two terms are directly embedded in the contemporary state system. They relate either to a single state or a coalition of states, whereas the third and fourth terms have the capacity to reach beyond the concept of a state system. These pairs of concepts are in tension with each other and provide the context for the dialogue between the peace movement and the government leadership over what "security" should mean. The PMOs worked on redefining security away from the nation and the military, replacing that concept with a sensibility for a global community based on the meeting of basic human needs. Our framework of oppositional knowledge as developed in chapter 1 helps lay plain the structure of this dialogue.

In this chapter we explore how the concepts of security and insecurity are formulated by the peace movement in opposition to hegemonic state-centered definitions of security. Our key questions are the following: How is security defined? On what basis (assumptions) does a definition of security develop? To what extent is security operationalized as "security with" or "security against"?

What does this tell us about the evaluation of foreign policies? What is seen as a source for security in the future? Has the peace movement discourse around security changed or expanded in recent decades?

THE PEACE MOVEMENT'S INCLUSIVE SECURITY: "SECURITY WITH"

While the U.S. government has been moving to further fortify its military might and the physical security of its borders, much of the rest of the world has been moving toward a very different conception of what it means to be secure (Commission on Human Security 2003). Our data show that the global impetus to redefine security toward the concept of "human security" resonates with the U.S. peace movement's broader agenda of peace with justice. The concept of human security distinguishes between state security and individual security, "and re-visions the latter as not merely the physical safety of individuals but their ability to secure and hold basic goods" (Gasper 2005, 222). Human security packages human development with peace, such that basic needs are met as well as safety addressed. Freedom from fear and freedom from want are focused on simultaneously. The goal is a society where humans have the full capacity to develop in dignity (Gasper 2005). For example, on September 11, 2001, the WRL argued: "We are one world. We shall live in a state of fear and terror or we shall move toward a future in which we seek peaceful alternatives to violence, and a more just distribution of the world's resources" (War Resisters' League, September 11, 2001).

The contributions made by the peace movement to security discourse strongly embrace the vision of human security. Yet this is not just simple individual well-being; it is human security in the context of a global community. Discourse around human security was done from two angles: (1) as an issue of spending priorities, and (2) as a concern that both individuals and nation-states each must recognize that their security is interdependent with the security of the rest of the world. Essentially the PMOs argued that when there is well-being, both at home and abroad, there will be peace. In making this argument, the peace groups articulated a variety of forms of oppositional knowledge.

The U.S. government's spending priorities were specifically criticized by the PMOs. They repeatedly explained the problems with investing in military equipment over social services. They also pointed out what the United States lacks socially because of the costs of investing in war and military equipment. We found this argument in four of the five conflict periods we studied (it is missing in the Iraq 1998 data). For example, utilizing the *radical-envisioning* approach to providing oppositional knowledge, the AFSC said:

> True national security is economic security. Government must play an essential role in helping meet the need for affordable housing, quality childcare, well-funded

public education, and strong safety-net programs such as TANF (welfare). . . .
Americans need health coverage, jobs with decent wages, and good educational op-
portunities, if our nation is to keep its people safe and out of harm's way. (American
Friends Service Committee, January 21, 2004)

This echoes a theme strongly evident in the Peace Action data from the Gulf
War period when the group argued: "President Bush's proposed 1992 federal
budget reflects a retreat from our domestic needs. We cannot afford to waste
tax dollars on unnecessary military programs. *These distorted priorities do not
add up to a secure future for our country*" (emphasis in the original; Peace Action,
1991). This example of *critical-interpretive* oppositional knowledge was played
out even more specifically in an argument for investing in a "peace economy"
at home rather than trying to secure foreign oil sources (Peace Action, January
7, 1991). Peace Action offered the *transformative* path of developing alternative
forms of energy in order to break from the need for foreign oil, a need that
involves the United States in conflicts like the Persian Gulf War. Both WILPF
and Peace Action talked about addressing our "real" security needs. These were
defined by WILPF as "housing, health care, education, environmental protection, and a humanitarian foreign policy" (Women's International League for
Peace and Freedom, October 1990).

The theme of global interdependence appeared in all five conflict periods.
However, we found it growing in complexity in the years following the September 11th attacks. During the Persian Gulf War, the PMOs spoke to the
role the United Nations can play in addressing conflicts (such as the invasion
of Kuwait by Iraq or the Israeli/Palestinian conflict). This theme repeated in
the Kosova/o 1999 conflict period, as Pax Christi argued for the UN as the
coordinator of the peacekeeping initiative (Pax Christi, May 4, 1999). In the
Iraq 1998 conflict period, the War Resisters' League used *transformative* oppositional knowledge when it pointed to disarmament on a global scale as the
way to establish peace and security. Iraq, they argued, is not the only threat;
all those with weapons of mass destruction threaten world security. Their *critical-interpretive* language clearly implicated the United States too as a source of
insecurity for the world (War Resisters' League, "No Military Action Against
Iraq," 1998, and December 17, 1998).

After September 11, 2001, the vision of security became one of global proportions as the PMOs recognized an opportunity for building community
worldwide. While the United Nations had a central role in their thinking,
the greater emphasis was on the people of the world. A growing dialogic
strategy emerged that linked global injustice to national *in*security for the
United States. This resonated with the trend in the United Nations, and in
general internationally during the 1990s, to expand the definition of security
toward a more humanitarian focus (Commission on Human Security 2003;
Basch 2004). In a statement just two weeks after the 9/11 attacks, Pax Christi
explored a response to terror that arguably would break the cycle of violence
at its beginning point. Their *radical-envisioning* approach rested on four prin-

ciples: (1) establish justice/respect for the law, (2) promote democracy, (3) provide for the common good, and (4) respect other cultures. They elaborated further: "These four principles articulate how we honor the victims. And practically speaking, they not only build our security in the U.S., but also global security" (Pax Christi, September 25, 2001).

During the Iraq War this global consciousness was called on again as the peace movement highlighted the UN along with international law and raised the importance of acknowledging the global interdependence of contemporary societies. More important, the language of security became not one of withdrawal as it was during the Persian Gulf War, but one of security "with," meaning a charge to work with the world proactively toward the achievement of justice. By hosting an international gathering to consult with people from around the world, Pax Christi introduced a *transformative* approach—the concept of "inclusive security." Dave Robinson, their executive director, was quoted as saying: "Building a truly inclusive and long-lasting security from terrorism is a multinational effort and requires the sharing of ideas from those who have lived and are living in areas of extreme conflict" (Pax Christi, May 5, 2004). This sentiment was echoed by Susan Shaer, executive director of WAND, who said you can either follow the unilateralist, "big guy on the block" path, "or you can become a leader, and work with others to build a community. This is real security" (Women's Actions for New Directions, March 18, 2004). Shaer gave the practical example of making change by referring to the congressional resolution by Lynn Woolsey (Sensible Multilateral Response to Terrorism—SMART) as a positive step.

THE GOVERNMENT'S PREEMPTIVE SECURITY: "SECURITY AGAINST"

U.S. policy across all administrations since 1945 has been to promote American values elsewhere while also safeguarding them from foreign interference at home (Ignatieff 2005). While state leaders have generally agreed that self-defense of sovereignty is a legitimate reason for a military response (as evidenced by the doctrine of collective security in the UN Charter), during both the Cold War era and following the 9/11 attacks the United States government used preemption as a basis for military strategy. In particular, the "preemptive strike" security policy of President George W. Bush seemed out of step with the world stance on what constitutes a legitimate threat and response. For example, international public opinion polls conducted in December 2005 in more than a dozen countries showed strong negative sentiment toward the U.S. attack on Iraq (Program on International Policy Attitudes 2006).

The irony of the preemptive strike policy is stark when compared to the complaints raised against Saddam Hussein in 1990 by the first President Bush. Justifying action against Iraq then, he said, "One big country can't bully its

neighbor and take it over. That's the principle that we're fighting for" (George
H. W. Bush 1990, 1622). Bush used many of his speeches in 1990 and 1991
to press home the issues of aggression and how Iraq was an aggressor and out
of step with the moral and diplomatic norms of the rest of the world (George
H. W. Bush 1990; 1991). Unlike the resounding concern over terrorism that
surfaced after 9/11, in the run-up to the Gulf War the frame most consistently
offered by the presidential office was a concern for aggression against sovereign states. The aggression of Iraq against Kuwait was also linked by President
Bush to the safety of U.S. citizens:

> First freedom: Protecting freedom means standing up to aggression. . . . Second:
> Protecting our future means protecting our national security and the stability and
> the security of the Gulf area that is so vital to all nations. . . . Iraq's aggression is
> not just a challenge to the security of our friends in the Gulf but to the new part-
> nership of nations we're hoping to build. Energy security is national security for
> us and for every country. (George H. W. Bush, November 22, 1990)

Emblematic of the international system in the 1990s was a move away from
unilateralism toward the creation of a community of nations that would exclude
"the bad guys." President Clinton also presented the discourse on national security in terms of global concerns. In several instances he argued that his policy on
Kosova/o was founded on the understanding that a risk to the Dayton Accords
threatened the United States. The following two quotes show his thinking:

> The current situation in Kosovo is fragile and, as yet, unresolved. It is of particular
> importance that developments in Kosovo would not disrupt progress in imple-
> menting the Dayton peace agreement. This threat to the peace of the region con-
> stitutes an unusual and extraordinary threat to the national security of the United
> States. (Clinton 1999, 10)

> Seeking to end this tragedy in Kosovo and finding a peaceful solution is the right
> thing to do. It is also the smart thing to do, very much in our national interests, if
> we are to leave a stable, peaceful, and democratic Europe to our children. We have
> learned a lot of lessons in the last 50 years. One of them surely is that we have a
> stake in European freedom and security and stability. I hope that can be achieved
> by peaceful means. If not, we have to be prepared to act. (Clinton 1999, 490)

Both George H. W. Bush and Bill Clinton stressed the union of the global
community in their discussions of getting involved in conflicts abroad. George
H. W. Bush emphasized the affront against the world community and the rule
of law among nations, while Bill Clinton argued for intervention in Kosova/o
in the interest of a stable European Community that in turn protected the security of the United States. We see a pronounced shift toward unilateral solutions in the interest of national security a decade later under the second Bush
administration. In all three cases, though, the primary means to security was
through militarism and violence.

The peace movement countered the preemptive stance taken by George W. Bush by first pointing to the cycle of violence and the likelihood that military responses make people less secure. Second, they raised concerns that security was being used as a pretext to eliminate freedoms and human rights. Third, they aimed to shift the conversation to take into account the security of others, particularly those civilians harmed by military responses.

The idea that government priorities for investment in security were misguided was a strong peace movement theme in the two conflict periods that encompass and follow 9/11. The PMOs made clear that they believe that military spending and the use of military solutions to conflict actually make the U.S. public less secure and cost them dearly. These costs include personal freedom such as lost civil liberties under the USA PATRIOT Act, the targeting of people of color and poor people as suspects, and the disinvestment in social welfare entitlements. One *critical-interpretive* argument offered by the PMOs is that "security" has become a pretext for acts of aggression abroad and repression at home. For example, the Black Radical Congress wrote:

> The dangers presented by the September 11th terrorist attacks do not restrict themselves to the external threat. We hear on television and radio calls for changing the laws and regulations in order to make it easier to conduct surveillance and to carry-out covert operations against potential opponents of the U.S. Rather than accomplishing anything in terms of reducing the threat of terrorism, such steps will eliminate basic civil liberties and strengthen the existing tendency toward a racist and classist police state. The police are already out of control and on the rampage in communities across the country. We cannot afford to further unleash their undemocratic and frequently murderous behavior in the name of national security. (Black Radical Congress, September 13, 2001)

United States Labor Against the War invoked a similar theme, accusing George W. Bush of using the Iraq War to "distract the American people from the anti-labor, anti-worker agenda" of his administration. Bush has, they argued, "launched a full-scale assault on our Constitutional protections in the name of national security. His war against Iraq serves as a cover for a war against working people here at home" (United States Labor Against the War, "Why Labor Opposes the War").

In all five conflict periods, the PMOs offered a *counter-informative* approach that in one way or another characterized the government's stance on security as *over*investing in military security to the detriment of human security. The government was consistently characterized as failing to offer the nation security because it viewed security as being against something or someone, hurting others instead of helping them. Moreover, while reflecting on the loss of civil and political liberties, the PMOs made it clear that it was not the terrorists holding society hostage but the policies abroad and at home that fueled frustration and led to violence. As Michael Ignatieff, professor of human rights, characterizes it, this is a developed sense of "American exceptionalism"

(2005). He argues that the United States views itself as supportive of certain principles of human rights but not subject to the limitations that respecting those rights places on government policies. Accordingly, there is perhaps a "broad popular sentiment that the land of Jefferson and Lincoln has nothing to learn about rights from any other country" (Ignatieff 2005, 8). In contrast, incidents like torture at Abu Ghraib prison, the secrets around Guantanamo Bay detentions, and the ambivalent attitude the United States has toward the United Nations reinforce the world's view that the United States is a maverick nation, out of step with the global consciousness.

ADDRESSING THE SECURITY RISK

Peace movement organizations countered government rhetoric in various ways. Mary Ellen McNish, executive director of the American Friends Service Committee, offered both criticism and a vision connected to a global identity (rather than the nation-state) in her address to Nobel Peace laureates:

> It is no longer only religious leaders and secular visionaries who say that neither militarism nor terrorism will give us security, that economic structures that create a new form of colonialism will not give the world prosperity. . . . I believe that we are witnessing the birth of a global, grassroots movement uniting those who long for peace, those who know our collective futures are intertwined and those who know in the deepest part of their soul *there can be no peace without justice.* (italics in original; American Friends Service Committee, December 2003)

PMO attempts to insert oppositional knowledge into the security dialogue did more than merely critique the failure of the state and the futility of military might as a solution. They also looked to redefine security as human security and pointed to practical changes that would move the world in that direction. In the Gulf War conflict period this meant investing in a "peace economy" and developing alternative energy sources that would reduce reliance on the resources of other states. In the Iraq 1998 conflict period this meant moving toward global disarmament. In the Kosova/o 1999 conflict period the PMOs stressed the importance of spending on development and diplomacy when addressing conflict, and on utilizing the UN for regional security issues. In the 9/11 conflict period this meant utilizing international institutions and international law to curb the threats to security and investing in humanitarian efforts to improve world opinion of the United States. Similarly, in the Iraq War conflict period alternate means of achieving security were emphasized such as utilizing international institutions (especially the UN) and norms, diplomatic or nonviolent solutions, and economic development both at home and abroad. For example, Pax Christi wrote:

> Moreover, Pax Christi USA fundamentally challenges the Bush administration's foreign policy doctrine. While the Bush doctrine says a strike on Iraq would

extend the benefits of freedom, democracy, prosperity and the rule of law, waging a war on Iraq will instead tear apart the very seams of international security, opening the door to the establishment of policies based solely on regime change in sovereign states. (Pax Christi, December 10, 2002).

Among PMOs, discussions of security centered on connecting the individual to the world community rather than to the nation-state. As CODEPINK suggested, the peace movement wants constructive investments at home and abroad, not destruction in the name of so-called "security":

If we cannot afford health care, quality education and quality of life, how can we afford to squander our resources in attacking a country that is no proven immediate threat to us? We face real threats every day: the illness or ordinary accident that could plunge us into poverty, the violence on our own streets, the corporate corruption that can result in the loss of our jobs, our pensions, and our security. In Iraq today, a child with cancer cannot get pain relief or medication because of sanctions. Childhood diarrhea has again become a major killer. 500,000 children have already died from inadequate health care, water and food supplies due to sanctions. (CODEPINK, "About CODEPINK")

This sense of global security and global unity emerges strongly in the movement to oppose the Iraq war. As MoveOn.org states, "We will continue waging

Photo 7.1.   Antiwar protestors in Chicago link security and spending priorities. (Photo by Lynne M. Woehrle)

peace, even if war comes. We have joined together to articulate a vision of how the world should be—of how nations should treat each other, of how we can collectively deal with threats to our security" (MoveOn, March 17, 2003).

The varying ideas put forward by the PMOs in each period about how to better achieve security developed from the social and political contexts of the time. In the Gulf War conflict period there was a sense that the end of the Cold War meant a downturn in the need for military spending, and thus a peace economy would offer a more constructive use of resources. The "no-fly zone" bombings of Iraq in 1998 were part of a long-term containment policy of sanctions against Iraq. The PMOs criticized this approach for being out of step with a global sensibility (again post–Cold War) that military answers to conflict were outdated and unacceptable. Close after that, the Kosova/o conflict period was perhaps shaped by the failure of the world community to give the UN adequate power to intervene in Rwanda a half decade before and by frustrations around the manipulations of the Dayton Accords. The statements of PMOs after 9/11 reflected the obsession in the United States with achieving security, the perfect door-opener for PMOs to introduce their oppositional ideas about alternative definitions for security and alternative mechanisms for achieving security. And in both the 9/11 and the Iraq War conflict periods, the dialogical processes that influenced the peace movement statements echoed an increasing global sensibility—the recognition of interdependence (see chapter 8).

LONGITUDINAL PERSPECTIVES ON SECURITY DISCOURSE

Our data allow for a longitudinal consideration of how security has been defined by the peace movement over fifteen years. Establishing the definition of security is a long-term dialogical process, and our data suggest that the peace movement has become increasingly invested in this definitional conversation over the years. As noted at the beginning of this chapter, security has long been considered the responsibility of the state to provide, and thus the state has assumed also the responsibility to define the meaning of security. This hegemonic definition of security as standing "against" perceived threats can be seen as the dialogical heritage that has provided for many decades the context for our understanding of the concept.

There are five organizations for which we collected data in each of the five conflict periods that we studied. Since they are fairly representative of the public voice of the peace movement in those moments, it is possible to analyze how the concept of security (both having it and not having it) played a role in the discourse of the groups. We expected the 9/11 attacks to result in pronounced increases in discussions about security by the U.S. peace movement, and in fact the data strongly support this hypothesis (see table 7.1).

Table 7.1. Use of Security Discourse by Five PMOs

Conflict Period	% of Documents Referencing Security	# of Passages (Median Weights)	# of Passages (Mean Weights)
Gulf War	15%	7.43	10.49
Iraq 1998	7%	6.83	9.63
Kosova/o 1999	16%	13.23	18.68
Post-9/11	44%	47.41	66.90
Iraq War	44%	30.85	43.11

Notes: Analysis based on weighted data. For weights formulas, see appendix 2. Only data from the five PMOs issuing statements in all five conflict periods are included (American Friends Service Committee, Fellowship of Reconciliation, Pax Christi, Peace Action, Women's International League for Peace and Freedom).

The table makes clear that there was a sharp rise in the use of the concept of security following the 9/11 attacks. Whether we consider the percentage of documents in which language about security appears, or the relative average number of occurrences of the code, there is a consistent trend that supports our hypothesis on the changes after 9/11. What is interesting is that even in the context of an offensive war in Iraq, security continued as a strong theme for the peace movement. We surmise that this is because after 9/11 the national leadership in the United States leaned heavily on fear factors to justify the so-called War on Terrorism (see chapter 4 for more on this). Security issues were very salient for most in the United States, so it made sense for the peace movement to participate in the dialogical process of defining what it meant to be secure and what posed threats to security.

We analyzed seventy-five speeches by President George W. Bush from September 11 to December 31, 2001. We found that President Bush often presented his policies in terms of responding to threats to national security: for example, 192 paragraphs contained instances of security framing (23.6 percent of threat-related code occurrences; 5.6 percent of all code occurrences). After references to terrorists, the security code appeared more frequently in presidential speeches than any other code related to intensifying threat salience. His security discourse posed an external attack as one instance of a larger threat to public safety and asserted that the state must use force and suspend civil liberties to "heighten security" in the face of that threat. For example, in a televised address on November 8, 2001, President Bush used security framing to generate support for repressive legislation and for invading Afghanistan: "Our nation faces a threat to our freedoms and the stakes could not be higher. We are the target of enemies who boast they want to kill—kill all Americans, kill all Jews, and kill all Christians. We've seen that type of hate before—and the only possible response is to confront it, and to defeat it." Such framing not only has high threat salience, but also resonates with the familiar, authoritative assumption that the state protects the nation and its way of life from danger.[2]

The occurrence of security discussions by the PMOs dramatically increased in the last two conflict periods. This reflected growing national and global concerns about how to address and control terrorism and the vast investment of resources to provide security. We found that what the PMOs said about the core definition of security—security is with rather than against—was fairly consistent throughout the five conflict periods. What clearly and starkly changed was the emphasis given to security concerns by the PMOs in the fourth and fifth conflict period of our study compared to the first three. This shift serves as evidence that the peace movement is not simply singing the same refrain in response to every war. Rather, widespread concerns among publics influence the themes that PMOs choose to invoke. So misguided was the understanding of security offered by nation-state leaders that the PMOs invested considerable dialogic energy into opening space for a new and different definition of security. They accomplished this by providing the oppositional knowledge that struck down old meanings and buttressed the new definition. Specifically we note that during the Iraq War, four of the organizations in our study mounted campaigns focused on creating a discursive shift: Peace Action had material titled "Three Steps to a Safer World;" Pax Christi coined the term "inclusive security" and held a conference on it; USLAW developed information under the rubric of "A Just Foreign Policy;" and WAND released material on "Women's Perspective on Security in a Changing World."

We found that as the prominence of the discussion grew, its complexity of presentation by the PMOs did as well. We can analyze this by considering which other codes co-occur with the code for security within the same passage or document. This co-occurrence tells us what concepts the PMOs were linking to the idea of security (see table 7.2). For example, connecting security to militarism happens in four of the five conflict periods, but what counts as important in discussing national security widens measurably, as the peace movement added concerns that U.S. policies besides military spending had become problematic aspects of the U.S. approach to insuring national security.

Connecting security with the human rights and freedoms articulated both in the U.S. Constitution and in international law is a trend we see in our data almost exclusively after 9/11. This security/human rights linkage was also happening internationally from the 1990s onward (Commission on Human Security 2003). But for the U.S. peace movement, it seemed to emerge as the movement was increasingly internationalized and as security issues became more salient and thus more resonant with the average citizen (see chapter 8 for further discussion). This broke from the strong tradition in the United States of seeing individual rights only in the context of the nation-state (Blau and Moncada 2005). Buttressed by political opportunities and a supportive cultural context, the PMOs pushed for the definition of security to include a more global vision of rights. The data suggest that the PMOs harnessed the concept of security, reworked it, and aimed to make it their own. In doing

Table 7.2.   Code Concurrence with Security by Time Period for Five PMOs

Code Bundle	Conflict Period				
	Gulf War	Iraq 1998	Kosova/o	9/11	Iraq War
National/Military Security:					
Militarization	2 (9%)*	0	1 (25%)	14 (33%)	20 (15%)
U.S. Imperialism	0	0	0	4 (9%)	14 (10%)
Boomerang	0	0	0	3 (7%)	17 (13%)
War on Terrorism	0	0	0	2 (5%)	14 (10%)
Pretext	4 (18%)	0	0	3 (7%)	10 (7%)
Unilateralism by U.S.	0	0	0	0	14 (10%)
National/Military Insecurity:					
Threat from U.S.	0	1 (100%)	0	1 (2%)	20 (15%)
Threat from non-U.S.	0	1 (100%)	0	2 (5%)	14 (10%)
Cause of Terrorism	0	0	0	11 (26%)	19 (14%)
Cycle of Violence	2 (9%)	0	0	5 (12%)	15 (11%)
WMD	0	1 (100%)	0	0	8 (6%)
Human Security:					
Civil Rights	0	0	0	5 (12%)	19 (14%)
Human Rights	1 (4%)	1	0	1 (2%)	6 (5%)
Relief	0	0	0	1 (2%)	20 (15%)
Global Response	2 (9%)	0	0	4 (9%)	19 (14%)
International Law	0	0	0	5 (12%)	19 (14%)
Global Justice	1 (4%)	0	0	4 (9%)	18 (13%)
UN-positive	1 (4%)	0	1 (25%)	2 (5%)	18 (13%)
Nonviolence	1 (4%)	0	0	3 (7%)	12 (9%)
Human Insecurity:					
Human Cost-domestic	8 (36%)	0	0	0	23 (17%)
Human Cost-nation	0	1 (100%)	1 (25%)	4 (9%)	22 (16%)
Fear	0	0	0	3 (7%)	14 (10%)
Scapegoat	0	0	0	2 (5%)	5 (4%)
Civilian Casualty	0	0	0	3 (7%)	13 (10%)

Notes: Analysis based on weighted data. For weights formula, see appendix 2. Only data from the five PMOs issuing statements in all five conflict periods are included (American Friends Service Committee, Fellowship of Reconciliation, Pax Christi, Peace Action, Women's International League for Peace and Freedom).
* # of passages (% of total passages coded as Security)

so they incorporated a vision more common outside the United States: that security comes from global cooperation while insecurity comes from unilateralism. Ideas such as civil rights, human rights, globalism, adhering to international law, multilateralism, and using diplomacy emerge in the 9/11 data but really become salient in the data from the Iraq War conflict period. When we look across the five conflict periods the dramatic rise of security as an important discourse is evident. In addition, it is not expressed merely in traditional military terms, as it parallels the global trend toward human security rather than state-centered military security.

CONCLUSION

It is our premise that in a nation-state system based on sovereignty, institutional power has shaped a security discourse that has the function of legitimating the state and its policies. For example, faced with a growing threat of terrorism, the United States has utilized military intervention, mass incarceration, and heightened surveillance as its methods for trying to protect the physical and material well-being of its residents. As discussed in chapter 2, the U.S. government has promoted the dominant security discourse through its privileged access to the mainstream media along with the high levels of time, money, and organized effort devoted to influencing public opinion. Regular exposure to this discourse predisposes the general public to viewing war and repression as reasonable, fair, and just. The investment of the state in defining security presents both obstacles and opportunities for the peace movement, especially in those conflict periods when events and salient emotions make the topic relevant to the general public.

Our analysis suggests that the U.S. peace movement responded to these obstacles by harnessing security concerns as it tried to more persuasively convey its own ideas on foreign policy. Much of the reworking of the meaning and implications of security by PMOs can be better understood within the context of conversations within the international community (individuals and institutions) about security as a humanitarian issue, not just a military issue. These internationally discussed concerns appear to be an important source in the development of oppositional knowledge by the peace movement in the United States.

In addition, this study of the dialogical processes of defining security provides a dramatic example of a social movement harnessing an important element of the dominant symbolic repertoire in response to the 9/11 attacks. The data in tables 7.1 and 7.2 show the increasing importance that security discourse played in the rhetoric of the PMOs. The tables also show the increasing complexity in how the PMOs understood concepts of military and human security and insecurity. But we should be clear that this redefinition of security is not simply a matter of strategically using the discursive opportunity afforded by the 9/11 attacks. Certainly the peace movement's leap into the dialogic process of defining security is a response to 9/11, the War on Terrorism, and the rising focus of policymakers on fear-mongering to excuse war. But it is also the work of a movement elaborating and extending its discourse to connect with an international community which had already been engaged in refashioning the meanings of security. The increased investment in discussing security shows a dialogical shift in how the PMOs were presenting their case against war. And the way security was discussed in the last two conflict periods mirrored cultural shifts toward a more global view of the self in the world. The traditional concept of security was harnessed by the PMOs to develop a salient but dramatically different explanation of the meaning of U.S. foreign policy.

Oppositional knowledge provided by the PMOs pointed out the limi
traditional definitions of security and provided what was presented as a more
inclusive vision. Our research shows the peace movement moved toward a
more complex definition of peace not merely as the absence of war, but as a
process of deeper change that bends society toward justice and a moral basis
for existing in peace.

NOTES

1. Snow's argument is that the ideational work of social movements is often "innovative articu-
lations and elaborations of existing ideologies or sets of beliefs and ideas, and thus [functions] as
extensions of or antidotes to them" (Snow 2004a, 401). Our data analysis suggests that PMOs do
much more than merely amplify or extend frames (Maney, Coy, and Woehrle forthcoming).

2. A similar analysis of this quote appears in some of our other work (Maney, Coy, and Woehrle 2005, 2008; Maney, Woehrle, and Coy, forthcoming).

8

Going Global?

Discourses Beyond the State

> The idea that you surrender your identity when you relinquish national powers is unhelpful. No, indeed, precisely the opposite is the case: if done in an intelligent way, you attain the sovereignty to better solve national problems in cooperation with others.
>
> —Ulrich Beck

A MOVEMENT AT THE CROSSROADS

As prior chapters have illustrated, U.S. peace movement discourses are shaped by domestic cultural and political processes. The movement has gone on the offensive by challenging hegemony when the confidence of the U.S. public in the government is waning and while deep differences of opinion exist among policymakers. On the other hand, the movement has taken a more subtle course by harnessing hegemony during periods when the U.S. public is highly supportive of military intervention abroad and political repression at home.

At the same time, there exist cultural and political processes beyond the United States that also affect movement discourse. Starting with the Universal Declaration of Human Rights approved by the General Assembly of the United Nations in 1948 and continuing through the Millennium Development Goals adopted by the General Assembly in 2000, successive international declarations and conventions have expanded and elaborated upon a set of guaranteed opportunities and protections for all human beings, regardless of their countries of origin or residence. Along with the acceptance of universal human rights has come an increasing recognition of global responsibilities. Global interdependence means that domestic-level or even local problems require cooperation across territorial boundaries for their resolution. For instance, the negative environmental effects of global warming in one society cannot be addressed without major reductions of greenhouse gas emissions in most societies. Recognition of global interdependence has contributed to an increasing number of international governmental organizations as well as multilateral treaties that address issues of global significance.

Transnational social movements have played vital roles in strengthening international political institutions, lobbying for the passage of international laws, and assisting in the monitoring and enforcement of human rights norms (Jackie Smith 1995; Coy 1997; Risse, Ropp, and Sikkink 1999). The peace movement organizations in the United States that have contributed to these developments and that are included in our study are the AFSC, FOR, Pax Christi, WRL, and WILPF, with the latter playing the most significant role (Alonso 1993).

Domestic- and transnational-level cultural and political contexts do not always coincide. Because nationalist discourses emphasize national sovereignty and national interest, they often run contrary to transnational discourses that assume that international law should supersede national laws and that the needs of all persons and societies are of equal importance. Similarly, domestic and transnational political contexts can vary in terms of the opportunities and constraints that they impose. Domestic policymakers may oppose a peace movement demand that policymakers in international political institutions are receptive to and vice versa.

Because of these contradictions, peace activists can find themselves at the crossroads between two powerful, countervailing social forces. On the one hand, embracing nationalist discourses and taking advantage of domestic political opportunities can create tensions with activists residing in other societies. For example, the emphasis placed by U.S. PMOs upon superpower competition and the need for a bilateral nuclear weapons freeze in the 1980s created rifts with European nuclear disarmament activists stressing multilateral disarmament (Cortright and Pagnucco 1997). On the other hand, stressing global interdependence and multilateral solutions during periods of heightened nationalism and insularity would likely relegate peace groups to the margins of a national debate over foreign policy.

This chapter analyzes how the U.S. peace movement responds to the sometimes contradictory logics of domestic and transnational contexts. Longitudinal and comparative organizational analyses offer four important findings. First, while outward looking in its overall orientation, U.S. peace movement organizations adjust the focus of their statements based on the anticipated or actual domestic costs of military intervention. Second, domestic and transnational contexts generally encourage the same type of responses to hegemony. Third, when these contexts diverge, the domestic context is more influential. Fourth, the U.S. peace movement appropriates prominent discourses used by transnational social movements when they are widely circulating, strategically useful, and ideologically compatible with core components of oppositional knowledge. We now look at each of these findings in turn.

 ## LOOKING WITHIN, LOOKING BEYOND

Military interventions abroad have important domestic consequences in terms of government spending priorities; ethnic, class, and gender relations; and civil and political rights. Military interventions also have grave consequences for societies where armed conflict physically takes place in the form of casualties, destruction of infrastructure, economic dislocation, and social instability. Relations between combatant and bystander states are also frequently altered.

Even though the internal and external consequences of war are each important, peace movement discourses tend to vary in their spatial orientations across conflict periods. What explains the relative internal versus external orientation of statements by peace activists? We theorize that the geographic orientation depends upon the anticipated domestic costs associated with the conflict. Even when the national-level polity is closed, financially expensive wars with high levels of U.S. casualties and heightened political repression at home encourage activists to orient their focus inwards. Inward discourses endeavor to spark mass resistance by presenting domestic costs as exceptional threats to the public's well-being (Staggenborg 1986). In contrast, when the domestic costs of military intervention are fairly low, frames that stress these costs are likely to be perceived as lacking in empirical credibility and experiential commensurability (Snow and Benford 1992). With their lives not noticeably affected by the war, few in the general public will be persuaded that the domestic costs of the war are high enough to warrant opposition. Consequently, peace activists must attempt to gain mass appeal by emphasizing the costs of war to those living in invaded societies as well as to the foreign interests and international reputation of the United States.[1]

To assess the effects of domestic costs on the geographic orientation of U.S. peace movement discourses, we classified the five conflict periods by the magnitude of domestic costs associated with the conflict. In three of the five conflicts, domestic costs associated with the conflict were considerable. The Gulf War, the war in Afghanistan, and the Iraq War all involved the deployment of sizeable numbers of ground troops, raising the possibility of large casualties among U.S. soldiers. Congress also debated and eventually appropriated several billion dollars to fund military intervention in each of these conflicts. In comparison, the domestic financial and human costs of the "no-fly zone" bombings of northern Iraq and the NATO bombing of Kosova/o were smaller. Neither operation involved significant levels of ground troops. The financial costs related to the operations were also considerably less. As such, we expected U.S. peace movement discourses to be more internally oriented during

Table 8.1.   Geographic Orientation by Conflict Period and Domestic Costs

Conflict Period	Domestic Costs	Ratio of External to Internal Code Frequencies
Gulf War	High	2.5
Iraq 1998	Low	7.4
Kosova/o	Low	11.2
9/11	High	2.1
Iraq War	High	2.9
Mean	—	5.2

Notes: Analysis based on weighted data. For weights formula, see appendix 2. Only data from the five PMOs issuing statements in all five conflict periods are included (American Friends Service Committee, Fellowship of Reconciliation, Pax Christi, Peace Action, Women's International League for Peace and Freedom). Table has rounding errors.

the Gulf War, 9/11, and Iraq War conflict periods than during the Iraq 1998 and Kosova/o conflict periods.

To assess the accuracy of these expectations, we divided eighteen weighted codes into two orientation categories—internal and external.[2] We then looked for differences in the ratio of the external code frequencies to internal code frequencies across the five conflict periods. Table 8.1 presents the findings. The results indicate that statements were consistently more externally than internally focused. In each of the conflicts, PMOs collectively devoted substantially more text to discussing matters involving people and practices outside the United States than inside. Considerably more attention was devoted to civilian casualties and other humanitarian costs of war to invaded societies, violations of human rights and international law, and the damage inflicted upon the international reputation of the United States than to the negative repercussions at home.

At the same time, the table also shows that the ratio of externally to internally focused text varied considerably across conflict periods. These variations are attributable to differences in the magnitude of domestic costs associated with each conflict. As expected, a higher percentage of the code frequencies were internally oriented during the Gulf War, 9/11, and Iraq War periods than during the Iraq 1998 and Kosova/o bombings. The PMOs shifted their spatial orientation in response to the most significant costs associated with a given conflict period. Greater domestic costs associated with military intervention promoted internally focused statements. Lesser domestic costs promoted externally oriented statements. We maintain that these shifts illustrate the strategic nature of peace movement discourses in the United States.

Chi-square tests (not shown here) indicate that both the Kosova/o bombing period and the 9/11 period were significantly different ($p < .01$) from the mean code frequency distributions for all five conflict periods. We attribute the exceptional external orientation of the Kosova/o period to the fact that it was a multilateral military intervention by the North Atlantic Treaty Organization (NATO) with the stated purpose of stopping genocide. With the responsibility for the operation more diffuse and domestic costs paling in comparison to the specter of genocide, peace groups were compelled to focus mainly upon the negative effects of military intervention for the people of Kosova/o and the prodemocracy movement in Serbia. For instance, the War Resisters League proclaimed that "THE BOMBING DESTROYED THE PRO-DEMOCRACY MOVEMENT" (emphasis in the original). The statement goes on to explain the proclamation:

> Within Yugoslavia's civil society, the bombing undid nearly a decade of effort by pro-democracy and nonviolent civilian groups from all ethnic backgrounds working to ease tension and to change Yugoslavia from within. The ethnic cleansing of Albanians from Kosovo/a could have been stopped by concerted efforts at negotiation. Lacking reconciliation, Serb residents of Kosovo/a now flee their homes in fear. (War Resisters League, "The People of the Region and the Global Community Will Feel the Effects of this U.S./NATO Action for a Long Time," n.d.)

In contrast, the internal orientation of statements from the 9/11 period are exceptional and reflect concerns that the unusual attack against civilians on U.S. soil would result in the stripping away of civil liberties, greater government secrecy under the guise of protecting national security, and attacks upon Muslim Americans (see chapter 7).

TRANSNATIONAL DIMENSIONS OF
RESPONSES TO HEGEMONY

Different domestic conditions affect the likelihood of the U.S. peace movement challenging or harnessing hegemony. For instance, in the hyperpatriotic and repressive 9/11 period, PMOs harnessed nationalist ideas from the dominant symbolic repertoire to a greater extent than during other conflict periods (see chapter 3). International conditions have also impacted how other social movements have responded to hegemony. For example, throughout the 1950s, the civil rights movement in the United States used opportunities at the United Nations, at conferences of newly independent former colonies, and in numerous other venues to challenge the U.S. government's commitment to the principles of freedom and democracy. The activists thus took advantage of Cold War competition to pressure the U.S. government to dismantle Jim Crow laws (Layton 2000). Accordingly, we hypothesize that the response by the peace movement to hegemony is influenced by the intersection of public opinion and political access at both the domestic and transnational levels.

Legitimacy and Political Access

Cultural and political changes are overlapping, mutually constitutive processes.[3] Sidney Tarrow (1998) identifies dynamic dimensions of the political opportunity structure that alter the likelihood of protest by affecting expectations for failure or success. Political access is the degree to which political elites are vulnerable or receptive to demands from challenger movements. Political openings entail a higher degree of political access. Examples of political openings include increasing civil and political rights, the destabilization of political alignments, splits among policymakers, the emergence of influential allies, sporadic or medium levels of repression, and facilitation. Conversely, political closure entails a lower degree of political access. Examples of political closure include decreasing civil and political rights, the stabilization of political alignments, unity among policymakers, the absence of influential allies, high-intensity repression, and the absence of facilitation. According to Tarrow, political closure discourages collective action by negatively affecting expectations regarding the costs and benefits of resistance.

While the origins, trajectories, and outcomes of many social movements can be explained partly in terms of structures of political opportunities, there have been instances when social movements have arisen and flourished in the context of political closure (Kurzman 1996). Structural conditions of political closure may be widely perceived as opportunities to bring about social change. Even when political closure is understood as an obstacle to change, popular disillusionment with a regime and its policies can fuel a sense of promise and efficacy among the excluded and repressed. If the powerful deny access, then the people will sweep the powerful and their policies away. Social movement discourses tend to both shape and react to changes in political access and mass public sentiment.

For these reasons, scholars must take into account both structural political conditions and macro-level trends in meaning construction when explaining social movement discourses. The conjunction of these two factors at a given historical moment impacts a movement's response to hegemony. On one end of the spectrum is *legitimated political closure* (figure 8.1). Organizers face an uphill climb when political elites unite around a policy agenda and appear immune to pressure (Meyer 2004). The climb becomes particularly steep when policymakers, the mainstream media, and much of the public view political closure as reasonable, fair, and just. Activists must convince targeted elites, bystanders, and reference publics to break with consensus and assume greater risks, even when such risks are widely regarded as unnecessary, futile, and counterproductive. Challenging hegemony in the context of legitimated political closure invites incomprehension, ridicule, and intensified repression. A more promising strategy is to somehow convince potential supporters that rather than protecting deeply held values, beliefs, and identities, consensus on war and heightened repression actually present grave threats to cherished ideals. By constructing the political context as antithetical to authoritative ideas frequently used by powerholders to generate popular legitimacy, harnessing hegemony uses the salience of the dominant symbolic repertoire to create space for dissent (see chapter 2).

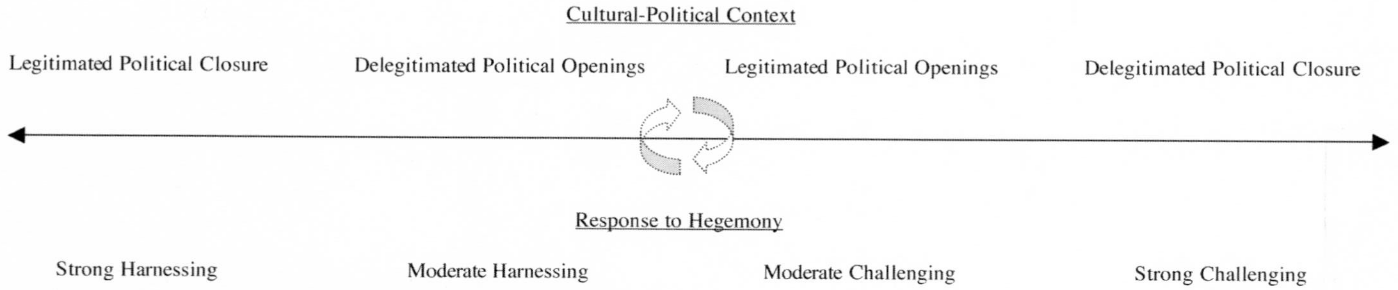

Cultural-Political Context

Legitimated Political Closure   Delegitimated Political Openings   Legitimated Political Openings   Delegitimated Political Closure

Response to Hegemony

Strong Harnessing   Moderate Harnessing   Moderate Challenging   Strong Challenging

Figure 8.1. Cultural-Political Context and Movement Discourse

On the other end of the spectrum is *delegitimated political closure.* Delegitimated political closure occurs when influential public figures, the mainstream media, and much of the public come to regard high levels of exclusion and repression of civil and political rights to be unreasonable, unfair, and unjust (Maney, Woehrle, and Coy 2005). With growing opposition to the existing regime, harnessing hegemony is likely to be viewed as pointless if not evidence of co-optation. Disillusionment with the status quo brings an opportunity to realize oppositional cultures on a society level, both symbolically and in practice. Challenging hegemony forms part of a deeper transformative project.[4]

It is also possible that there are historical moments where political access increases for social movements. In cases of *legitimated political openings,* the general public favors greater institutional access and political rights accorded to challenger movements. On the one hand, high levels of public support encourage activists to challenge and repudiate ideas that for so long were used frequently and effectively to justify their exclusion. On the other hand, by referencing peace movement concerns, a regime can strengthen hegemony, reinforcing the empirical credibility and experiential commensurability of claims that the regime embodies the values and beliefs that it has drawn upon for legitimacy. As a result, we expect social movements in these conditions to cautiously challenge hegemony.

The opposite will often prevail in cases of *delegitimated political openings.* Delegitimated political openings occur when powerholders include challengers despite high levels of opposition from the general public. In these circumstances, groups will likely appropriate and reinforce familiar, authoritative ideas from the dominant symbolic repertoire to shore up powerholder support for their policy positions while seeking to reverse the current of public sentiment. On the other hand, fears of unwittingly strengthening hegemony by harnessing it, along with concerns of co-optation, will encourage a cautious approach.

While our conceptual framework adds a greater degree of nuance to explaining social movement discourses than previous frameworks, the analysis remains deficient in two respects. First, it assumes that the general public is aware of changes in policies and cares about them. There are situations, however, where censorship prevents the general public from being aware of government policies. There are also situations in which the general public is aware of a policy, but low levels of personally experienced costs along with framing by policymakers and the media encourage vacillation, apathy, or disinterest (Gitlin 1996). In these circumstances, social movements are likely to strongly challenge hegemony. When they are firmly ensconced in the doldrums with little chance of attracting mass support from new constituencies, traditional movement adherents belonging to oppositional cultures make bold statements that bear witness to alternative values and ideas (Rupp and Taylor 1987). Second, political access and cultural trends can vary across levels of analysis. The framework, therefore, needs to be situated within a multilevel analysis.

Nested Opportunity Structures

As separate systems of governance, national states and international governmental organizations (IGOs) have their own distinctive policy discourses and culturally infused structures of political opportunity. At the same time, national and transnational processes and structures are nested in that they often shape one another (Rothman and Oliver 1999). For instance, a movement can strategically maneuver to take advantage of a state's vulnerability to international pressure to increase receptivity to policy changes at the national level (Maney 2001). Accordingly, we must look at the transnational public opinion and access to international political institutions to understand peace movement framing at a given historical moment. Even in domestic conditions of legitimated political closure, receptivity towards peace movement demands by IGOs and the transnational public may encourage peace movement organizations to challenge familiar, authoritative ideas on the domestic level. Conversely, even in domestic circumstances of legitimated political openings, hostility toward peace movement demands by IGOs and the international public may encourage PMOs to harness familiar, authoritative ideas in international political discourse such as international law and human rights.

Analysis of Nested Contexts and Responses to Hegemony

We gathered a wide range of data to operationalize domestic and transnational contexts. On the domestic level, we used the average absolute difference between votes in the U.S. House of Representatives for and against legislation related to military intervention as our primary measure of political access. A larger average absolute difference suggests unity among elected officials and domestic political closure for the U.S. peace movement. Conversely, a smaller average absolute difference suggests deep splits among policymakers and, therefore, higher levels of domestic political access. On the transnational level, we compared the percentage of United Nations General Assembly member states voting against resolutions supportive of military intervention for each conflict period.

As a measure of trends in how the mass public reacted to dominant policy discourses, we took the mean of monthly averages of public opinion polls in which respondents answered favorably to questions regarding the advisability of military intervention in each of the five conflict periods included in the study. Domestic opinion polls were generally available for each month in which PMOs issued statements for a particular conflict. For transnational public opinion, we used the mean of the average approval rating in six countries (Canada, France, Germany, Great Britain, Italy, and Russia) for each military intervention. These polls were available less frequently than domestic polls. As a result, differences in transnational opinion across conflict periods could be an artifact of the timing of the polls included in the data set.

Table 8.2 classifies the five conflict periods by the intersection of political access and popular legitimacy at both the domestic and transnational levels. In addition, the table applies our conceptual framework to generate hypotheses regarding how each context will impact peace movement responses to hegemony. Using one standard deviation from the mean to assist us in defining contexts, we ranked both domestic and transnational contexts on a scale of 0 to 10, with 0 being a context that our theoretical framework suggests strongly encourages harnessing hegemony and 10 being a context that our framework suggests strongly encourages challenging hegemony. More cautious or moderate harnessing and challenging are placed closer to the middle of the scale (2.5 and 7.5 respectively). For example, during the Gulf War period, the domestic contextual measures suggest a context of moderately delegitimated minor political openings. A slightly higher than average percentage of U.S. public opinion favored military intervention in Iraq, though over one quarter of the public opposed it. At the same time, slightly greater than average numbers of congressional representatives voted against legislation authorizing and funding military intervention. Our conceptual typology suggests that delegitimated political openings encourage the cautious harnessing of hegemony (see figure 8.1). The fact that neither domestic public opinion nor political access was significantly beyond the mean further reinforced this expectation.

The data reveal a convergence between policy positions of the general public and powerholders on both the domestic and international levels. High levels of public support for military intervention were strongly correlated with high degrees of unity among policymakers. For instance, the 9/11 period had both the highest public approval ratings for military intervention and virtually no dissent among policymakers in both the U.S. House of Representatives and the United Nations General Assembly. Conversely, a lower level of public support for military intervention is strongly correlated with greater divisions among policymakers. For example, both the general public and policymakers were deeply divided over the NATO bombing of Kosova/o.

In addition, applying our conceptual framework to each of the five conflict periods, both domestic and transnational contexts encouraged U.S. PMOs to respond to hegemony in a similar manner. In some instances, this convergence reflected parallel contexts. For example, the general public and policymakers on both levels became increasingly critical of U.S. military intervention during the Iraq War period compared to the 9/11 period. Average domestic public support for military intervention dropped 32.4 percent while average international public support dropped by 11.2 percent. These declines in public support are particularly dramatic given the temporal proximity of the two conflict periods. In terms of policymakers, members of the U.S. House of Representatives were more divided in their voting on military and security

Table 8.2. Nested Cultural-Political Contexts by Conflict Period

Conflict Period	Domestic Public Opinion % respondents in favor of war	Domestic Political Access Mean absolute difference in house voting	Domestic Context[a] Score on scale of 0–10; 0 =strong harness 10 =strong challenge	Transnational Public Opinion % respondents in favor of war	International Political Access UN GA in favor of US position	Transnational Context[a] Score on scale of 0–10; 0 =strong harness 10 =strong challenge
Gulf War	71.8	248.0	moderately delegitimated minor political openings (2.5)	57.1*	77.7*	strongly legitimated major political closure (0.0)
Iraq 1998	71.3	284.8	moderately legitimated minor political closure with neglect (7.5)	40.4	55.7	moderately legitimated minor political openings (7.5)
Kosova/o	53.8*	100.2*	strongly legitimated major political openings with neglect (10.0)	39.4	57.4	moderately legitimated minor political openings (7.5)
9/11	88.6*	362.0*	strongly legitimated major political closure (0.0)	54.4*	b	strongly legitimated major political closure (0.0)
Iraq War	56.2	302.2	moderately delegitimated minor political closure (7.5)	43.2	50.8c	moderately legitimated major political openings (7.5)
Mean (SD)	68.3 (14.1)	259.4 (98.1)		47.2 (8.6)	60.4 (11.9)	

Notes: Analysis based on weighted data. For weights formula, see appendix 2. Only data from the five PMOs issuing statements in all five conflict periods are included (American Friends Service Committee, Fellowship of Reconciliation, Pax Christi, Peace Action, Women's International League for Peace and Freedom). Table has rounding errors.

[a] Public opinion is categorized as strongly legitimated/delegitimated if the measure is > ±1 standard deviation from the mean (otherwise moderately legitimated/delegitimated). Political access is categorized as having major openings or closure if the measure is > ±1 standard deviation from the mean or for other reasons noted in notes below (otherwise minor openings or closure).

[b] The General Assembly (GA) adopted a resolution criticizing the human rights record of the Taliban without voting. The Security Council voted unanimously in favor of a resolution calling for regime change in Afghanistan.

[c] US government efforts to get the Security Council to authorize military intervention in Iraq failed.

* > ±1 standard deviation from the mean.

related legislation during the Iraq War period than the 9/11 period. Similarly, the UN General Assembly passed Resolution 232 condemning the human rights practices of Saddam Hussein's Ba'athist regime only by the narrowest of margins, while the Security Council refused to authorize military intervention as sought by the Bush Administration. Yet less than two years earlier, the General Assembly adopted a similar resolution against the Taliban regime without a vote while the Security Council voted unanimously for Resolution 1378 supporting regime change in Afghanistan. The finding supports our assertion that domestic and transnational contexts are nested. Greater support for military intervention on the domestic level contributes to stronger support transnationally and vice versa. Similarly, strong transnational opposition to U.S. military intervention encourages dissent on the domestic level.

At other times, however, the domestic and transnational contexts did not align as closely. In these instances, mutual encouragement of certain responses to hegemony appears to be coincidental. For instance, during the 1998 Iraq "no-fly zone" conflict period, the domestic context was less hospitable to dissent than was the transnational context. However, a lack of awareness or interest in the conflict among the general public encouraged U.S. PMOs to challenge hegemony. Greater degrees of opposition to the bombings among the transnational public and within the United Nations further supported this approach (see table 8.2).

To assess the impact of nested cultural and political contexts, we examined the statements of five PMOs issuing statements in each of the conflict periods (AFSC, FOR, Pax Christi, Peace Action, and WILPF). We divided codes according to whether they presented instances of harnessing hegemony or instances of challenging hegemony. We excluded codes that contained instances of both responses. To further ensure comparability across conflict periods, we also excluded codes that were not coded in any paragraphs for one or more conflict periods. Table 8.3 presents the results. Actual responses to hegemony closely conformed to our expectations for three of the five conflict periods. The U.S. peace movement challenged hegemony most during the Iraq air strikes and Kosova/o periods. A Republican-controlled Congress and talks of impeachment over the Lewinsky affair generated considerable opposition to military intervention. Observers, both on and off Capitol Hill, believed that President Clinton was using military intervention in both Iraq and Kosova/o as distractions from his domestic woes. U.S. PMOs echoed this theme. A press release issued by the War Resisters League, for instance, stated:

> Many of the administration's opponents also believe that in a scenario eerily congruent with the plot of the movie Wag the Dog (nominated this week for an Academy Award), Clinton is attempting to distract the nation from the Monica Lewinsky scandal that refuses to go away. "If it happens, it will be the War of the President's Zipper," says [Rep. Robert] Ney. "But bombing Baghdad for no good reason would be the worst scandal of Clinton's presidency." (War Resisters League, February 12, 1998)

Table 8.3. Expected and Actual Responses to Hegemony by Conflict Period

Conflict Period	Expected Response to Hegemony[a]	Actual Response to Hegemony[b]
Gulf War	1.25	4.7
	strong harness	mild harness
Iraq 1998	7.5	6.0
	mild challenge	mild challenge
Kosova/o	8.75	6.7
	strong challenge	strong challenge
9/11	0.0	3.7
	strong harness	strong harness
Iraq War	7.5	3.8
	mild challenge	strong harness

Notes: [a] Average of scale of scores from Table 8.2.
[b] Transformed ratio of challenging to harnessing.
Analysis based on weighted data. For weights formula, see appendix 2. Only data from the five PMOs issuing statements in all five conflict periods are included (American Friends Service Committee, Fellowship of Reconciliation, Pax Christi, Peace Action, Women's International League for Peace and Freedom). Data transformed by equating the mean of the conflict period ratios to the midpoint of the scale (5).

Transnational opinion was also unenthusiastic, particularly in Russia where the public strongly supported their government's opposition to air strikes against Iraq as well as NATO bombings of Kosova/o.

On the opposite end of the discursive spectrum, U.S. PMOs harnessed hegemony most during the 9/11 period. At this historical moment, international norms against targeting civilians along with the doctrine of collective security produced a widespread outpouring of sympathy for the people of the United States and support for a military response to terrorism. Responding with disregard for the loss of life or the right of a state to protect the security of its people would not have resonated with international public opinion or policymakers. Consequently, U.S. PMOs harnessed concerns for the rights of civilians as well as resolve for multilateral cooperation to combat terrorism. They argued that a military invasion of Afghanistan would likely endanger civilians in much the same way that the attacks of 9/11 did. Moreover, the PMOs suggested that collective security could best be accomplished through multilateral cooperation to enforce international law. In calling for an international tribunal to put on trial those involved in the attacks, Peace Action stated: "Legal prosecution holds criminals accountable, and punishes the responsible parties, without killing more innocent civilians" (Peace Action, "Real Solutions for a Safer World," n.d.).

During the Iraq War period, we anticipated that as the war and occupation unfolded, an increasingly receptive context to opposing war and occupation would have translated into peace groups challenging hegemony more strongly than what we found. The five groups included in our longitudinal analysis harnessed hegemony only slightly less than they did during the 9/11 period when the context was considerably more hostile. We suspect that the anomaly reflects the discursive restraints imposed by the temporal proximity of the conflicts. While the 1998 Iraq "no-fly zone" and the 1999 Kosova/o bombings occurred within a span of one year, contextual factors simply encouraged an intensification of the predominant approach of challenging hegemony. In contrast, the Iraq War context required a dramatic discursive shift from the strong harnessing of hegemony during the 9/11 period to a strong challenge of it. Such a shift could undermine understandings and resonances generated by oppositional discourses constructed during the 9/11 period. Moreover, a strong challenging would likely invoke stiff opposition due to the continued appeal of prowar discourse from the 9/11 period. Many in the U.S. public continued to believe that Saddam Hussein was involved in the attacks of 9/11 and that the war in Iraq was simply an extension or expansion of "the war on terror."

In two conflict periods (Gulf War and Kosova/o), domestic and transnational contexts diverged slightly in terms of their expected impact upon responses to hegemony (see table 8.2). In both cases, the actual response to hegemony was more in line with the mandates of the domestic context than the pressures of the international context. The result provides further support that it would be premature to dismiss the influence of domestic-level factors even in an era of rapidly widening and deepening exchange of ideas across territorial boundaries. Nonetheless, the increasing use of human rights and global justice discourses suggests movement toward a systematic challenge to the national logic that has pervaded since 9/11.

THE DIFFUSION OF TRANSNATIONAL SOCIAL MOVEMENT DISCOURSES

Regional and international political and economic integration, coupled with technological advances in mass communications and transportation since World War II, have brought growth in the numbers and size of transnational social movements (TSMs; Jackie Smith 2004). TSMs involve collective action coordinated by organizations based in more than one society. Often demanding social changes in more than one society, transnational movements frequently pressure multinational corporations and international governmental organizations. Because of the considerable cultural and socioeconomic differences among participants, TSMs must develop discourses that are flexible yet sufficiently coherent to attain resonance and potency in multiple contexts with different audiences (Jackie Smith 2002; della Porta 2005).

Given this flexible coherence and the expanded scope of mobilization, the discourses of transnational movements may diffuse to other movements. Donatella della Porta and Sidney Tarrow (2005, 3) define diffusion as a process whereby "challengers in one country or region adopt and adapt the organizational forms, collective frames, or targets of those in other countries or regions." We theorize that five factors increase the likelihood that the U.S. peace movement will appropriate discursive elements generated by transnational movements organized around other issues: exposure, overlapping social networks, demonstrated efficacy, discursive opportunities, and ideological compatibility. First, regarding exposure, activists will not appropriate discourses that they do not know exist or know little about. Rapid and extensive online dissemination, coupled with widespread television, newspaper, and radio coverage of mass protests across the globe, encourages diffusion. The advent of alternative media sources on the Internet has cast transnational social movements in a positive light, offsetting the tendency of mainstream media to characterize these movements as deviant or extremist (Bennett 2005).

Second, in terms of overlapping social networks, protest ideas are transmitted not only indirectly through modes of mass communication, but also directly through relationships (McAdam and Rucht 1993). Social movements with high degrees of overlapping memberships, organizational interaction, and cooperation often converge in their framing practices (Meyer and Whittier 1994; Carroll and Ratner 1996; Bennett 2005). The peace movement of the Iraq War period was marked by this sort of overlap and coordination. The coordinated, worldwide demonstrations against the impending war on the weekend of February 15–16, 2003, brought out the largest crowds ever in a number of major cities worldwide, and the largest crowds since the Vietnam era in many others.[5] This global coordination was made possible in large part by the Internet. We expect that partly due to the mobilizing capacities of the Internet, peace movement organizations and activists in the United States will increasingly diversify their organizational and personal networks across territorial boundaries. As U.S. PMOs become more fully part of a transnational peace movement, they will become increasingly exposed to the language and ideas of other progressive TSMs. In addition, sometimes individuals who do not participate in the same movement may still belong to the same social network and oppositional culture. In both cases, the language and ideas of one movement are likely to be constructed and transmitted in online and face-to-face conversations with members of another. Strong ties, along with shared beliefs and collective identities, facilitate diffusion.

Third, regarding efficacy, even dismissive media coverage of large numbers of people protesting and demanding changes is likely to highlight the mobilization potential of movement discourses. Thus, the greater the extent to which a discourse is perceived as being effective in generating pressure for the goals of its originator, the more likely that it will be appropriated by other movements.

Yet one discourse does not necessarily fit the needs of all movements. Different movements have separate targets and opponents who often construct their issue positions quite differently. An oppositional discourse that responds persuasively to the dominant discourse on one issue may lack resonance and potency in response to the dominant discourse on another issue. Similarly, unusual public events and heightened media attention to an issue may bring emotional and discursive opportunities for achieving resonance and potency that were not available to another movement (Maney, Woehrle, and Coy 2005). In order for a discourse to diffuse, it must be perceived as assisting the appropriating activists in taking full advantage of these discursive opportunities available to them.

Fifth and lastly, many social movement activists reject Machiavelli's maxim that the ends justify the means. Even if activists believe that the adoption of a discourse will help them achieve their political objectives, if it violates their deeply held beliefs and principles, it is unlikely to be adopted. Some of these same activists would argue that little will change if discourses pander to the prejudices of misinformed publics and fail to expose the underlying causes of social problems (Coy, Maney, and Woehrle 2003). Not surprisingly, activists possessing different ideologies will react differently to the same discourse (Benford 1993). These concerns lead us to conclude that discourses will not be appropriated if they are incompatible with the predominant ideologies of a movement.

To assess the impact of transnational social movements addressing separate issues upon the discourses of the U.S. peace movement, we examined statements included in our data set for evidence of diffusion from two TSMs—the human rights movement and the global justice movement.[6] We selected these two movements because they satisfy the first three criteria that would lead us to expect that elements of their discourses would be appropriated by the U.S. peace movement (exposure, overlapping social networks, and demonstrated efficacy). We now look at each of these movements and their possible influence upon the discourses of the U.S. peace movement.

As measured by the number of international human rights organizations, the human rights movement experienced rapid growth in the 1970s and the 1980s (Keck and Sikkink 1998). With the end of the Cold War in the early 1990s, many activists saw the opportunity to at last fulfill the promise of the United Nations' 1948 Universal Declaration of Human Rights. Rather than merely being used selectively to vilify political opponents, a codified set of individual and collective rights would be equitably and universally enforced through coordinated international efforts. In the face of intensified pressure by the human rights movement, several targeted regimes began to use human rights discourse. Ironically, the use of the rhetoric placed a high degree of moral pressure upon these regimes to change their practices (Risse, Ropp, and Sikkink 1999; Davis and Rosan 2004; Morgan 2004). High-profile international human rights campaigns and the subsequent successful institutionalization of human rights norms exposed most peace movement activists to human rights discourse by the mid-1990s. Human rights discourse dovetailed not only with the peace movement's traditional emphasis upon protecting the rights of noncombatants, but also with the emerging conception of human security as discussed in chapter 7. By 1999, the Hague Appeal for Peace held a conference titled "Peace is a Human Right" (Jackie Smith 2006).[7] Seven of the fifteen PMOs included in our study have websites that offer the ability to search site pages (AFSC, CAIR, Pax Christi, Peace Action, USLAW, WAND, and WILPF). All seven websites included multiple references to Amnesty International (AI)—a leading international human rights organization. Several of these references revealed direct organizational contact with AI. Both Peace Action and WILPF mentioned coordinating efforts with AI on developing a global code of conduct for arms transfers. Pax Christi noted its efforts to support the group's access to the Gaza Strip to monitor human rights practices by the Israeli military. WAND noted its work with AI to pressure then U.S. attorney general Alberto Gonzales to sign a Declaration Against Torture. We expect this familiarity and interaction with human rights groups to facilitate the incorporation of human rights framing into U.S. peace movement discourse.

Nonprofit organizations, however, were not the only ones to see the advantages of creating multilateral agreements. As multinational corporations sought to develop legal regimes that would facilitate trade and investment across borders, activists began to question whether multilateral agreements served the interests of profit more than people. In mobilizing against meetings of the Organization for Economic Cooperation and Development (OECD), the World Trade Organization (WTO), the International Monetary Fund (IMF), and the World Bank, activists developed a common set of attributions that have come to be known as global justice discourse. Global justice discourse emphasizes structural inequalities in international governmental organizations and the global economy as a source of a wide range of social problems, including poverty, repression, global warming, genocide, and depletion of biodiversity. In this discourse, the answer to these ills is a fair, equitable, and democratic global order. The year 1998 brought a major protest against the WTO during its meeting in Geneva and the defeat of a proposed Multilateral Agreement on Investment. The following year featured even larger protests in what has became known as the "Battle of Seattle" where massive protests contributed to the failure of the WTO to make further progress on trade liberalization (Jackie Smith 2001).

The WTO meeting in Seattle, meetings of the IMF and World Bank in Washington, DC, in April of 2000, the World Economic Forum in New York City in 2002, and the Free Trade Area of the Americas (FTAA) negotiations in Miami in 2003 presented exceptional opportunities for U.S. members of the global justice movement to use negative publicity to pressure states not to sign the proposed trade agreements. On- and offline mobilization for these protests and their coverage by the media exposed many peace movement activists to global justice discourse by the early 2000s. Direct organizational ties and coordinated action had also started to develop between the two movements. According to W. L. Bennett (2005), peace organizations attended the European Social Forum (ESF) in Florence, Italy, in November of 2002 where they called for a day of international protest against the war in Afghanistan, which eventually came to fruition on February 15, 2003. Representatives of United for Peace and Justice also met with ESF organizers in Copenhagen. The peace coalition includes six of the PMOs in our data set (AFSC, FOR, Peace Action, Pax Christi, WRL, and WILPF).

Because of their high levels of exposure, overlapping networks, and demonstrated efficacy, we expected increasing use of both human rights and global justice discourses by peace activists over time. To test this hypothesis, we coded statements for the number of paragraphs making specific references to human rights as well as to global justice–related themes.[8] Table 8.4 presents the frequencies. Neither human rights nor global justice was a prominent theme during the Gulf War period. The frequency of passages referring to human rights nearly tripled during the Iraq 1998 conflict, and then more than tripled again during the Kosova/o conflict. And while references to human rights declined during the 9/11 period, there was a resurgence during the Iraq War. Reference to global justice themes increased significantly after 9/11, accounting for well over one-third of the code frequencies in both the 9/11 and Iraq War periods.

The findings support our expectations. Consistent with the exposure, overlapping networks, and demonstrated efficacy hypotheses, major increases in the usage of human rights language followed shortly after the widespread institutionalization of human rights norms in the early 1990s. Moreover, human rights language appeared most during the two conflict periods that presented opportunities to heighten the resonance of peace movement statements by referencing human rights. The pro-war framing of the NATO bombing of Kosova/o as a humanitarian intervention also encouraged PMOs to emphasize humanitarian concerns in response. Groups like Peace Action argued that instead of protecting human rights and its supporters, NATO bombings undermined both: "The tragedy in Kosovo clearly demonstrates that reaching for a gun or dropping bombs are not solutions to conflict; that U.S./NATO military attacks do not protect human rights, foster dialogue, nor lay the foundation for sustainable peace" (Peace Action, "Beyond the Bombs," n.d.).

Extensive media coverage of torture and abuses of Iraqi prisoners at Abu Ghraib also presented major discursive opportunities to highlight human rights in the debate over U.S. foreign policy. With human rights being part of the prevailing political discourse both in the United States and internationally, framing prisoner abuses and military intervention in general as human rights violations would likely increase pressure upon the U.S. government to change its policies. A countrywide survey of 892 adults in the United States taken by Steven Kull (2004) in July of 2004 found that large majorities of respondents supported "having international laws governing the treatment of detainees in principle and support specific requirements for detainee registration, the right to a hearing, access by the Red Cross, and the right to communicate

Table 8.4. Relative Frequency of Discourses across Conflict Periods

Conflict Period	Human Rights Discourse			Global Justice Discourse			Militarism Discourse			Total
	N	Col.%	Row%	N	Col.%	Row%	N	Col.%	Row%	N (Row%)
Gulf War	3.3	4.9	8.3	5.9	10.0	15.1	30.1	20.1	76.6	39.3 (100)
Iraq 1998	9.1	13.6	63.0	1.0	1.7	7.1	4.3	2.9	29.9	14.4 (100)
Kosova/o	29.1	43.5	35.1	1.5	2.5	1.8	52.4	34.9	63.2	83.0 (100)
9/11	5.7	8.6	7.3	27.7	46.8	35.3	45.0	29.9	57.4	78.4 (100)
Iraq War	19.7	29.4	32.2	23.1	39.0	37.7	18.4	12.3	30.1	61.2 (100)
Total	66.9	100.0	24.2	59.2	100.0	21.4	150.2	100.0	54.4	276.3 (100)

Note: Analysis based on weighted data. For weights formula, see appendix 2. Only data from the five PMOs issuing statements in all five conflict periods are included (American Friends Service Committee, Fellowship of Reconciliation, Pax Christi, Peace Action, Women's International League for Peace and Freedom). Table has rounding errors.

with relatives." PMOs attempted to foster public dissent by constructing the mistreatment of prisoners as a moral outrage that required immediate rectification and restitution (Jasper and Poulsen 1995). AFSC and CAIR referred to the treatment as "horrific" while FOR called it "shocking." In assigning blame, FOR and WAND suggested that the Bush administration's demonizing of Al Qaeda and questioning of the applicability of the Geneva Conventions to terrorist suspects created an environment conducive to the violation of human rights. This type of framing was likely to resonate with if not inform the opinions of a large segment of the U.S. public. The study by Kull also found that 51 percent of respondents believed that memos written by the Department of Justice arguing that international laws against torture and abuse were not fully applicable to terrorists contributed to what occurred at Abu Ghraib prison. CAIR demanded an immediate congressional investigation while MoveOn called for the firing of Secretary of Defense Donald Rumsfeld.

Consistent with the exposure and demonstrated efficacy hypotheses, the rise in global justice themes followed many high-profile, successful mass protests by the global justice movement beginning in the late 1990s. Moreover, sustained high levels of global justice themes after 9/11 coincided with increasing organizational interaction between the global justice and peace movement. Prowar discourse during the 9/11 period also encouraged peace activists to appropriate elements of global justice discourse. The geographic scope of the "war on terrorism" lent itself to a systematic critique of the global economic and political order, as illustrated by the following Pax Christi statement:

> For terrorism to end we must help create the economic mechanisms that will insure that the wealth and resources of this world are distributed in a way that all people can live in dignity. As long as the wealthy elite of the U.S. consume and control a sinfully disproportionate amount of the world's resources, there will be terrorism. (Pax Christi, September 25, 2001)

Would the U.S. peace movement have appropriated global justice and human rights discourses if they were incompatible with core oppositional knowledge? To answer this question, we included militarism in the analysis because of its long-standing presence in peace movement discourse. A steady decline in references to militarism would suggest that peace movement discourses are primarily strategically driven and not constrained ideologically. To the contrary, we found that passages containing references to militarism occurred more frequently than passages containing human rights or global justice themes, not only during the Gulf War, but also during the Kosova/o and 9/11 periods. The belief that a military-industrial complex in the United States engages in conflicts worldwide for the purposes of power and profit clearly remains a core component of the peace movement's production of oppositional knowledge. Human rights and global justice discourses have diffused to the U.S. peace movement precisely because of their compatibility with long-standing beliefs firmly rooted within the movement. Our findings demonstrate that discourse is not only a strategic exercise in persuasion, but also an expression of deeply felt values and beliefs.

Instead of replacing existing oppositional knowledge within the movement, both human rights and global justice language and ideas now supplement it. Increasingly, U.S. PMOs have argued that the use of military force serves the interests of the world's rich and powerful at the expense of human rights and the needs of the poor. The 9/11 attacks are implicitly interpreted as a product of an unjust and militarized global order:

> No one should suffer what we experienced on September 11. Yet war will inevitably harm countless innocent civilians, strengthen American alliances with brutal dictatorships and deepen global poverty—just as the United States and its allies have already inflicted widespread suffering on innocent people in such places as Iraq, Sudan, Israel and the Occupied Territories, the former Yugoslavia and Latin America. (New York City Labor Against War, September 27, 2001)

The proposed solution, in turn, is to create a more equitable, fair, humane, and democratic global system. Consistently, PMOs defined problems in global terms and proposed solutions based upon transnational cooperation. In a playful "fantasy statement," TrueMajority offered a mock White House press release with excerpts from a State of the Union speech by President Bush:

> Tonight I pledge the support of my administration to a new plan of action that recognizes the interdependency of this and all nations. We will attack world hunger and poverty as if our lives depend on it. Through compassion and generosity, we will reduce poverty and win over potential terrorists to the side of democracy and the rule of law. We are scrapping our plans to invade Iraq. We will fight Iraq and other enemies with integrity, generosity, and idealism—working in full cooperation with the United Nations and international community. We will end our obstructionism to the world's treaties on landmines and chemical and biological weapons and on the environment. We will reduce our dependence on oil and lead the world into an age of renewable energy and energy independence. (True Majority, January 24, 2003)

Paralleling developments in the global justice movement (della Porta 2005), PMOs are increasingly emphasizing the important role that ordinary people have to play in creating a new global order. Just as all people are endowed with the same rights, they argue that all have the same responsibilities toward one another, regardless of nationality. For example, an AFSC spokesperson stated:

> The events of the last two years have made it clear that it is no longer enough for states to support international institutions. These institutions that will guide our future must be bolstered by the strength of tens of millions of voices. . . . As civil society within nations has been the mother of liberty and equality, a new global

citizenship must now call the current world order to account for itself. (American Friends Service Committee, December 2003)

This globalized construction of citizenship emerging after 9/11 constitutes an important instance of oppositional knowledge production. It harnessed the concept of citizenship while challenging the traditional delineation and confinement of its commitments to those belonging to one nation. In the process, the identity of the U.S. peace movement changed, not only in terms of its geographic scope, but also in terms of viewing the movement as part of a larger movement for global human progress.

Photo 8.1.   Global dimensions of peace expressed at Peace Action–sponsored march in Wisconsin. (Photo by Lynne M. Woehrle)

CONCLUSION

The bulk of this chapter makes it clear that dismissing the impact of domestic cultures and polities upon social movements would be premature. The U.S. peace movement responds first and foremost to domestic considerations. Higher domestic costs associated with a conflict encourage more internally oriented discourses. When the domestic cultural-political context diverges from the transnational context, the peace movement responds more to domestic concerns and exigencies. Nonetheless, post-9/11 trends suggest that the U.S. peace movement will increasingly highlight global systems and their implications for conflict transformation. Exposed to efficacious discourses used by the transnational human rights movement and the global justice movement, peace activists have increasingly appropriated their elements, not only because of their ability to heighten the resonance and potency of peace movement messages in certain contexts, but also because of their compatibility with long-standing beliefs in the peace movement. If post-9/11 trends continue, we expect to see peace activists in the United States defining themselves more and more as part of a global polity that will obviate military intervention by creating a humane and just set of relations across borders.

NOTES

1. To assess whether strong transnational ties would encourage PMOs to be more externally oriented, we compared the Iraq War period statements of five PMOs with international chapters (AFSC, FOR, Pax Christi, WILPF, and WRL) with those of nine PMOs without international chapters (BRC, BVP, CAIR, CODEPINK, MoveOn, NYCLAW, Peace Action, USLAW, TrueMajority, and WAND). While PMOs with strong transnational ties had higher ratios of external code frequencies to internal code frequencies compared to groups with weak or nonexistent transnational ties, a chi-square test (not shown here) indicates that the difference was not statistically significant.

2. We included all codes that could unambiguously be categorized as either being internally or externally oriented. The following codes were placed in the internal orientation category: domestic human costs of war; civil liberties; scapegoating; democracy in the United States; and expressions of concern for U.S. soldiers. The following codes were placed in the external orientation category: civilian casualties; global justice; human rights; international law; international opinion; multinational corporations; the Palestinian-Israeli conflict; humanitarian relief; U.S. imperialism; global democracy; spreading democracy; the United Nations (both positive and negative references); and negative references to the practices of deployed U.S. soldiers. Given that most of our codes were arrived at inductively, the greater number of externally oriented codes suggests that U.S. PMOs used a wider variety of themes in externally oriented text than in internally oriented text. A greater number of codes, however, does not necessarily mean that there will be a larger number of paragraphs containing externally oriented text. To assess the independence of our two code categories, we conducted a chi-square test comparing code frequencies for both categories for the five conflict periods. The test found the categories to be significantly different at the $p < .001$ level ($\chi^2 = 68.84$; $df = 4$).

3. In the explanation that follows of our framework for understanding the intersection of political and cultural processes, we draw directly from, and then build upon Maney, Woehrle, and Coy (2005).

4. The Iranian Revolution provides an example of delegitimated political clos opposition to the Shah's repressive policies encouraged a more critical examination ɔ, une beliefs that the regime used to legitimate its rule. As activists became more emboldened to speak openly and critically of the regime, they generated even higher levels of public disapproval. See Kurzman (1996).

5. As Derrick Jackson wrote in the *Boston Globe*, "The London demonstration—England is America's biggest ally for a military strike against Iraq—was the largest political demonstration in the nation's history. The turnout at the Brandenberg Gate was the largest German political rally since World War II. The 70,000 in Amsterdam was the largest demonstration in that city since antinuclear rallies in the 1980s. The 200,000 protesters in Sydney, Australia, was that city's biggest rally since Vietnam" (Jackson 2007).

6. In fact, some scholars have argued that protests against corporate globalization encompass a family of several progressive social movements. See della Porta (2005). Most participants in these protests now refer to themselves as being part of either a global justice movement or a global social justice movement.

7. We thank Jackie Smith for this and other insights that have heavily informed the analysis in this section of the chapter.

8. We coded paragraphs as containing instances of global justice discourse when they (1) critiqued the current global economic order, including multinational corporations and corporate profiteering; or (2) referred to the need for, a vision for, or making a world based on global democracy, justice, or eradicating poverty.

9

Peace Movement Discourses

Unraveling Hegemony, Spinning New Threads

We must be the change we wish to see in the world.

—Mohandas Gandhi

To resort to power one need not be violent, and to speak to conscience one need not be meek. The most effective action both resorts to power and engages conscience.

—Barbara Deming

When taken together, the chapters of this book show the steep hill the peace movement faces when confronting hegemony in the United States. Hegemony entails cultural processes that contribute to the legitimacy of powerholders and their policies (Gramsci 1971; Perry Anderson 1976; Raymond Williams 1982). The dominant discourse pigeonholes patriotism by defining it as remaining in lockstep with military intervention abroad and political repression at home, even in times of failed policy. Heightened emotions, intergroup conflict, and strong norms associated with wartime present powerholders with opportunities to further limit and mold public discourse. Aided by mainstream media pundits, government spokespeople weave a picture of binary opposites such as "good vs. evil" and "you are either with us or against us." These choices, as presented, encourage both uncritical thinking and uncritical emotions that arise from the need to belong, to avoid chaos, and to affirm moral order.

While freedom of speech protects the right to openly voice opinions, it does not promise that all voices hold equal power. At times, hegemony can function like a heavy blanket covering the body politic. It tends to muffle and flatten most attempts to separate and pierce through what is considered customary. Especially during wars and other crises that potentially threaten the state and the status quo, hegemony marginalizes oppositional voices and dampens resistance.

Our study acknowledges the strength of dominant discourses while also revealing the innovations of the peace movement in finding ways to subvert them and communicate alternative views to the public. We have suggested two important typologies for understanding peace movement discourses in this regard. The first identifies four types of oppositional knowledge produced by the fifteen organizations in our analysis: *counter-informative, critical-interpretive, radical-envisioning,* and *transformative.* Our results suggest that PMOs weave these four strands of oppositional knowledge together in presenting their criticisms of U.S. foreign policy in times of war. These four types of oppositional knowledge are intended to help the public to expand their understanding of the big picture and to consider possible alternatives. The content of the dominant discourse is turned inside out, criticized, and replaced.

For example, in chapter 1, we apply the oppositional knowledge framework to capture the rich and various ways that the U.S. peace movement has contributed to the discourse on democracy. PMOs not only utilize the rhetoric of democracy to attain their goals, but they care deeply about the nature and implementation of democracy. They are highly critical of democracy that is imposed or that feels false and culturally inappropriate. They integrate concerns about civil liberties and electioneering with their outspoken opposition to war. Many of the PMOs in our study argue that further democratization of the political system in the United States is necessary for addressing what they see as not just an ideology of domination and unilateralism, but an ideology of a total war system as well. Actions of dominance abroad are linked to actions of dominance at home. Few issues cut to the heart of democratic citizenship as deeply as do the decisions to go to war and the decisions about how to wage a war. Peace movement discourse on democracy is best understood as a deliberative partner in the struggle over meaning creation through the development of oppositional knowledge and the weakening of hegemony. To the extent that this resistance is successful (i.e., oppositional knowledge informs policies to some degree), policy formation is more inclusive and more representative. In short, it is more democratic.

Our second typology is based on a continuum of choices, ranging from challenging hegemony on one end to harnessing hegemony on the other. This framework allows a nuanced analysis of the methods that PMOs use when they confront hegemony. We find direct challenges to the dominant discourse, as well as ideas from the dominant discourse being harnessed and refashioned, and hybrid responses, too. Our results lead us to conclude that the oppositional messages are variegated, reflecting strategic dilemmas, context-specific opportunities, collective identities, and organizational ideologies.

For instance, in chapter 7, we examine the responses of the U.S. peace movement to the dominant discourse of national security. The data suggest that *out of oppositional knowledge*

PMOs have harnessed the concept of security, reworked it, deepened and expanded its meanings, and aimed to make it their own. In so doing, they have fashioned a discourse that is more familiar outside the United States—that security comes from global cooperation while insecurity comes from unilateralism.

Looking across the five conflict periods reveals a dramatic rise in the movement's security-related discourses. While the attacks of 9/11 had the political effect domestically of closing off debate on certain topics, they also had the corresponding effect of invigorating discussions on other topics, including security. The data in chapter 7 also definitively demonstrate that the peace movement challenged hegemony, undermining and subverting the logic of a state-centered militarily based security. This challenge to hegemony was followed by putting forward alternative visions of security with potential to appeal, not only to subgroup identities, but also to a broader national collective identity. Taken together, our analysis of harnessing and challenging the dominant discourse about the security concept shows how the movement acted both to unravel hegemony and to offer alternative visions.

The challenge/harness typology, along with the oppositional knowledge typology, allows us to chart and to interpret the multiple ways that peace movement organizations engage the dominant discourse on war and peace. The use of any of the four forms of oppositional knowledge may occur while challenging and/or harnessing hegemony. It is the integrated nature of these two frameworks that give them their explanatory power as social movement theory, and their political power as applied social movement practice.

For example, as discussed in chapter 3, rather than reject patriotism itself (i.e., challenge hegemony), many peace movement organizations have harnessed the power of patriotism and offered constructive, alternative ways to define it during wartime. They highlighted the importance of protecting the freedom of dissent by speaking out and resisting. Dissent is transformed as evidence of love for one's country and the willingness to stop wrongs about to happen. This creation of oppositional knowledge about patriotism during wars suggests the potential moderating effects of social movements on nationalist assumptions over time.

Some of the approaches that we took to our research were motivated, at least in part, by our desire to help the peace movement think critically about its discourses. We outline some of those potential contributions below.

THE MOVEMENT LENS: LESSONS AND OBSERVATIONS FOR ACTION AND ACTIVISTS

By highlighting specific facets of dominant discourses that encourage support for military intervention abroad and political repression at home, we show how strengthened hegemony poses problems for peace activists seeking to build a mass movement. We also identify and explain strategic dilemmas associated with different responses to hegemony (e.g., harnessing responses may inadvertently reinforce the salience of dominant discourses, while challenging responses may weaken the overall appeal of the movement). Peace activists often assume that appropriating the language and ideas of powerholders not only plays into the hands of the powerful, but also has a moderating effect upon movement goals and forms of collective action. Our analysis, however, suggests that such responses to hegemony can result in the envisioning of fundamental alterations in power relations along with the championing of disruptive means of social transformation. Returning to the root of what defines democracy, patriotism, religion, and security can expose fertile ground for activists to engage otherwise hostile audiences in fundamental critiques of the status quo.

Moreover, our longitudinal research design isolates and emphasizes the ways that specific historical contexts encourage certain types of responses to hegemony. Dominant discourses present opportunities for movements to gain more support. For instance, the heavy use of religious discourse by the Bush administration after 9/11 provided opportunities for PMOs to emphasize religious bases for opposing the administration's policies (see chapter 5). Ironically, the power of dominant discourses to generate public consensus also presents movements with opportunities to generate dissent by using the weight of familiar and authoritative ideas on behalf of their oppositional claims.

The peace movement can also heighten its appeal by linking strong emotions in the general public with oppositional claims in ways consistent with dominant norms governing the expression of emotions (see chapter 4). For example, after 9/11, most PMOs in our analysis linked strong emotions about the attacks with a determination to ensure that there would be no more civilian victims—American or otherwise.

Beyond discursive and emotional opportunities, we highlight the potential of harnessing hegemony as a discursive strategy for effecting social change during times of legitimated political closure (such as during the 9/11 period) as well as the promise of challenging hegemony during times of delegitimated political closure (such as during the unfolding of the Iraq War). More conscious development and application of context-appropriate responses to hegemony can help the peace movement to carve out additional political spaces during inhospitable moments, while also launching direct, frontal challenges to dominant discourses during moments of growing public disillusionment. In these ways, our book better equips activists as they negotiate their way through the thorny complex of choices associated with discursive politics.

In addition to being contextually adaptive, several trends in responding to hegemony that we identify suggest that movement discourse is also a dynamic, innovative product of shared learning by activists. Our longitudinal study illuminates specific forms of oppositional knowledge developed by peace activists over the last fifteen years. We view these emergent forms as part of the peace movement's long-term project of cultural transformation. Peace movement discourses can be viewed as attempts to define a peace culture and eliminate a war culture. We highlight a few of these attempts below.

Peace Is Patriotic: Harnessing Nationalism

As discussed in chapter 3, in three out of five conflict periods, PMOs challenged nationalism more than they harnessed it. The peace movement's harnessing of nationalism increased dramatically after 9/11, and remained high even during the much less popular Iraq War. In addition, there was only a very modest increase in the use of American identity-negative discourse from 9/11 to the Iraq War. These findings suggest that the experience of effectively harnessing nationalism during 9/11 helped the peace movement to overcome a conceptual hurdle of sorts in affirming and harnessing basic American principles to support oppositional claims.

Facing Fears: Developing Critical Feeling

In chapter 4, we point to the expanding volume and increasingly sophisticated emotional work by peace activists in the United States. In particular, peace movement organizations have developed multilevel approaches for using emotions in ways that encourage the development of what we call the faculty of "critical feeling." We also show the manifold ways that PMOs have provided opportunities for the constructive expression of emotion.

In the aftermath of 9/11, we found that PMOs responded with innovative alternative framing to the culture of exaggerated fear and to the public's concern for security. While acknowledging and apparently sharing feelings of fear, they also pointed to the importance of a sense of global community and interdependence (not an "us vs. them" stance) for addressing violence and building security. The structures, institutions, and powerholders that many see as the solution were labeled as deeply connected to the problem. The movement presented the limits imposed by the U.S. government on civil liberties and human rights as greater threats to the public.

Connecting Struggles: Intersectional Thinking

Since identity in its many forms is key to why people participate in social groups, it is useful for movement organizations to think about their use of identity appeals. Our analysis of antiwar organizing during five conflict periods holds up a mirror so that the peace movement can engage in critical self-reflection. We show an emerging pattern of diffusion, where more groups participate in turning collective identities into widely relevant messages (see chapter 6). Perhaps this increased identity construction work reflects internal processes pressuring the movement to diversify its membership, a deeper consciousness of the linkages between social inequalities and war, and a growing awareness of intersectionality. That their use of social identity is still somewhat limited suggests that there remains ample opportunity for the peace movement to more effectively engage the ideas of race, class, and gender. The increasing diffusion of identity appeals across the peace movement suggests that the movement's ability to foster cultural change may also be improving. More openness to and sophisticated use of intersectional thinking and the diffusion of identity discourses across the peace movement may in time help shape a peace movement that can appeal to a broader base of society than has happened in the past. The movement's highlighting of the many places where collective identities intersect creates useable oppositional knowledge.

In addition, over time, intersectional thinking gradually dismantles the artificial boundaries between collective identities that are promoted by dominant discourses that keep people separate and divide and conquer oppositional movements. Through discourse, alternative cultural spaces are created within these intersections while old, dominant ones are dismantled or simply abandoned. The more these fertile intersections of identity are cultivated by movement discourses, the more bountiful the harvest of resistance to social inequalities and the war system will be.

Expanding Movement Reach

Chapter 8 highlights both the ways in which and the reasons why the peace movement has more and more adopted the language of human rights and global justice. By showing empirically that traditional peace movement themes remained prominent even as new ones increased in usage, we definitively establish that in this social movement, discourse is both opportunistic and faithful to its own traditions. From this understanding, peace movement activists may improve their means for reaching nonmembers and be better able to articulate their goals to them. Moreover, the weaving of these newer strands with older, more traditional movement themes helps to connect the peace movement in the United States to progressive social movements throughout the world. This development constitutes the discursive underpinnings of a transnational oppositional culture, with activists in multiple movements and societies drawing from a variegated yet coherent body of oppositional knowledge. As such, this trend in U.S. peace movement discourse represents an important contribution to cultural transformation at the global level.

Beyond our attempt to help the movement think critically about its discourses, we have also structured our research so as to contribute to building theory on social movements. We turn to a brief discussion of those contributions below.

THE THEORY LENS: CONTRIBUTIONS TO UNDERSTANDING SOCIAL MOVEMENTS

Following the lead of movements themselves, some theorists recently have focused more on the symbolic dimensions of politics, challenges to non-state institutions, and efforts to transform cultures (Goodwin and Jasper 2003; Myers and Cress 2004; Armstrong and Bernstein 2008). In what follows we highlight ways that our research contributes to this new focus by offering insights into the dynamic processes of social movements and social change.

Cultural Sources of Control and Dissent

In this book, we contribute to social movement theorizing that recognizes how power is generated through contested cultural processes that can either encourage or discourage widespread dissent.[1] Social movement theorists have emphasized how powerholders use inclusion and exclusion as tools for limiting dissent. We argue that a symbolically oriented tool of social control, persuasion, has received less attention than it should. When many are persuaded that they either have no "real" grievances or that powerholders across society are successfully addressing their concerns, efforts to mobilize dissent are less likely to succeed. The concept of hegemony highlights persuasion as a form of social control. When powerholders and their preferred policies are regarded as legitimate, challenges are perceived as superfluous or counterproductive. Conceptualizing social movement discourses as responses to hegemony that attempt to encourage dissent by producing and disseminating oppositional knowledge leads to several additional insights with important implications for social movement theory.

The Discursive Dimension of Contention

Social movements research has focused primarily on physical forms of contention that challenge powerful opponents (e.g., strikes, boycotts, rallies, sit-ins). Yet resistance does not occur only in the street through discrete and overt acts. It also occurs in continuous contests over public discourses and their multiple meanings. Producing and disseminating oppositional knowledge constitute the discursive dimensions of challenges to cultural processes that legitimate powerful opponents, whether they be the government, multinational corporations, the mainstream media, organized religion, or other authorities (Myers and Cress 2004; Armstrong and Bernstein 2008). Given the importance of hegemony as an obstacle to social movement organizing, scholars should pay more attention to movement discourses. Doing so provides concrete evidence of the dialogical processes of persuasion that take place in a variety of institutional settings.

Intersecting Political and Cultural Processes

In addition to acknowledging discourse as a dimension of contention, it is important to recognize the ways that movement discourses are related to intersecting political and cultural processes. Chapter 8, for instance, highlights ways that public attitudes about levels of political access interact with peace movement discourses. As with other political processes, the effects of political access on mobilization simply cannot be understood without reference to symbolic processes of interpretation and contention.

At the same time, peace movement discourses often engage with cultural processes influenced by but extending beyond politics. Chapter 5, for example, underscores how peace movement discourses not only responded to presidential discourses on religion, but also addressed religious institutions, identities, and symbols in ways that created new language and meanings. And in chapters 6 and 7 we show that PMOs recognize the larger definitional shifts necessary to achieve policy changes.

The Interplay of Agency, Structure, and Culture

The analytical path that we have followed in this book has taken advantage of the best of what have often been considered to be competing approaches in social movement research. Many structural and cultural approaches have relied on interpretations that don't give proper attention to the agency of movement actors. We accord considerable agency to actors (both powerful and less powerful) in influencing power relations through their choices in writing and talking. Activists have options in response to dilemmas. Jasper (2004, 2006) emphasizes dilemmas as being at the heart of strategy and agency in collective action. We show that movements frequently face a dilemma of whether to harness or to challenge hegemony. We also argue that these dilemmas often result in statements that mix the two responses. The use of hybrid arguments or of pure harnessing suggests that the strength of dominant discourses is an obstacle to movement organizing. Direct challenging is seldom resonant across the entire cultural landscape. There may be too much of a gap between what PMOs ideally would like to say and what would appeal to the wider public. We have shown that harnessing responses provide a bridge across that gap.

Myra Ferree (2003) and others have warned about the dangers for challenging movements when they appropriate discursive opportunities. While acknowledging the possibility of inadvertently strengthening hegemony, we also have identified instances where harnessing responses may create considerable power for movements. Rather than moderating oppositional messages, these responses often entail making radical claims in ways that are familiar and authoritative to others. As such, this response has enormous subversive potential, not only in terms of generating widespread resistance, but also in terms of fundamentally altering symbolic culture (Maney, Woehrle, and Coy 2005).

In addition to neglecting the role of activist agency, structuralist approaches to analyzing movements often obscure the deeply symbolic components of social context within which movements must operate. Activists are rewarded by appropriating familiar and authoritative language and ideas generated in previous rounds of discursive contention. Conversely, they may be penalized for challenging or circumventing this language and ideas. For example, we show that the peace movement regularly harnessed familiar language and ideas (e.g., freedom, civil rights, support for the troops, democracy, justice, religion, motherhood, American identity) to talk back to presidents and other powerholders and to undercut policies and positions from perspectives that would be widely understood. We go beyond framing analysis in acknowledging and explaining how macro-level symbolic contextual factors encourage certain responses to these dilemmas. We show how PMO discourses drew upon shared culture to appeal to individual sensibilities through their fidelity with core movement narratives, their consonance with widely circulating and deeply felt emotions, and their appeals to salient collective identities.

On the other hand, overly cultural approaches to movement analyses fall prey to discounting the many powerful structural constraints that influence movement actors. Powerholders' disproportionate access to and influence over mass communications provides them with the ability not only to legitimate their policy agendas but also to discredit resistance. Accordingly, we have paid attention not only to both structural and cultural factors, but also to the dynamic intersections of these forces as they were engaged by the same U.S. peace movement organizations in different conflict periods. We argue that it is in these intersections that social movement decision making about tactics and discourses is at its most robust. The combination of longitudinal and comparative organizational analysis of peace movement statements allows us to utilize the best in each interpretive approach while avoiding their respective blind spots. It reveals a peace movement that constructs its public statements with care in order to broaden the appeal of its arguments by taking advantage of emotional opportunities, discursive opportunities, and the declining popular legitimacy of political closure. At the same time, movement participants actively honor core movement values, beliefs, and oppositional identities.

Discourse as Dynamic and Contested

Dominant discourses are reproduced, challenged, and transformed through interactive, contested, and cumulative discursive processes by multiple actors. The production of oppositional knowledge is a response to constricting cultural processes that legitimate powerholders' rule and their policies. As noted by Antonio Gramsci (1971), however, the appropriation of oppositional knowledge by powerholders can also bolster hegemony. Our study adds an additional wrinkle by suggesting that such instances provide discursive opportunities by adding credibility to challenging responses to hegemony. Moreover, just as powerholders can appropriate oppositional knowledge to strengthen hegemony, challengers can appropriate elements of the dominant symbolic repertoire to weaken hegemony. These nuances confirm Michel Foucault's (1980) assertions regarding the multisided nature of discourse as an instrument of power as well as points of resistance. Through their discourses, both powerholders and challengers provide opportunities for the other to gain broad appeal. Our analytical accounts of the dialogical dimensions of discourse show it to be dynamic and continuously contested.

Despite the fact that movements are nested within multiple social sites, analysis of the framing and discourse work of social movements has too often been sterile in a sense that it has removed the movements' work from their social context. This is particularly true with regard to discourse analysis, which has, with a few notable exceptions (Coles 1998; Steinberg 1999), seldom been done in a deeply dialogical way. The inclusion of presidential statements in our data set breaks this mold and allows us to both demonstrate and to analyze how peace movement discourses respond to dominant discourses. We show, to cite but one example, that President Bush ramped up his religious discourse following the attacks of 9/11. Our weighted, quantitative analysis also demonstrates that the peace movement strategically responded in kind, taking advantage of discursive opportunities created by the president's religious discourse. PMOs, including some secular groups, harnessed religious symbols to talk back to President Bush and to undercut his policies and positions from a religious perspective. They also created oppositional knowledge by educating the U.S. public about the many positive dimensions of Islam. Religious discourses were not the only site of struggle that we identified. The U.S. government and the peace movement also tussled with each other to control the meanings of citizenship, emotions, support for the troops, democracy, global interdependence, freedom, nationalist identity, and security.

From a research methods standpoint, our project shows the importance of gathering data from different perspectives and subjecting them to rich qualitative study and rigorous quantitative measures in a dialectical analysis that brings together both dominant discourses and the production of oppositional knowledge. In this way, our book fills a largely empty space that has endured for too long in social movement research: an empirical approach to the epistemological processes of movements.

Discourse as Consistent and Adaptive

What may make the oppositional knowledge of PMOs powerful is their ability to produce ideas that are both consistent and adaptive. The PMOs frequently relied on their traditional appeals while they also shaped their messages to match historical events and cultural contexts. We found, for example, deep fidelity to core PMO beliefs and values. At the same time, our longitudinal analysis suggests that the historical context in which the movement statements were released influenced the production of oppositional knowledge. In times when dissent is less welcome by the general public, PMOs may shift their emphasis more toward building on dominant cultural themes. This strategy helps these organizations to portray themselves as cultural insiders. At times when dissent is more welcome they aim to cut deeper, articulating a clear challenge as they work to "speak truth to power" by formulating a "truth" that more directly counters the familiar, authoritative scripts for that situation.

A picture emerges of consistent patterns in U.S. peace movement discourse regarding patriotism. During times of heightened national pride and unity and closure to dissent, the movement as a whole rides the patriotic wave, trying to turn its power toward the movement's own goals. Through the use of hybrid statements, however, the movement also sends messages below the surface that seek to stem the tide of uncritical, destructive patriotism. When nationalism wanes and divisions materialize, these hybridized messages are strengthened with challenging messages that stand tall against destructive forms of patriotism, further weakening its dissipating currents.

Multilevel Responses to Emotional Components of Hegemony

Emotions form an important component of hegemony. Powerholders try to heighten certain emotions through their discourses and, in turn, link these emotions to their rule and policies. For example, in the United States, powerholders long have attempted to instill a sense of fear along with the belief that only they can quell fear through war abroad and repression at home. Fear often dominates the emotional climate during times of war; it is also nurtured by policymakers in support of war, as it was during 9/11 and in the run-up to the invasion of Iraq.

As a hegemonic device, well-defined enemy images with religious or moralized overlays divert awareness from potentially problematic domestic policies (e.g., civil liberties repression) outwards toward a shared enemy (see Coy, Maney, and Woehrle 2008). Thus war supports binary discourses and the limiting of space for dissent. Fear discourse also opens the door to a stronger relationship between the nation and the people. Many regard allegiance to the state as being rewarded with protection from threats to their lifestyle. This dominant construction of security legitimates military intervention abroad and domestic political repression.

Our study suggests that the successful mobilization of resistance in times of war hinges upon the ability of activists to challenge, at the macro level, the climate of fear fostered by powerholders; to create, at the meso level, alternative emotional dispositions; and to develop, at the micro level, the capacity for critical feeling. We believe we are the first to develop a multilevel theory of the emotional work by social movements.

CONTESTING PATRIOTISM AND
PROMOTING A PEACE CULTURE

Surprisingly, American nationalism has not received as much scholarly attention as its influence suggests it deserves; the impact of nationalism upon social movements in the United States is even less studied. We advance the literature by highlighting specific ways that taken-for-granted assumptions underpinning the dominant nationalist discourse in the United States encourage not only broad support for war and repression but also opposition to the peace movement. Typically, nationalist assumptions envelope discussions about whether to wage war or to wage peace. These assumptions are deeply rooted, formed over decades and even centuries, and somewhat resistant to change. Since they can be counted on to figure prominently in the discourses of any major conflict—as they did in the five conflict periods covered in this study—they provide an ideal framework for longitudinal analysis.

Our identification of these assumptions and investigation of how the peace movement interacted with them would be the first of its kind even if we had data for only one conflict period. But our longitudinal data make it possible to reveal the creative and increasingly sophisticated ways that the U.S. peace movement has contested dominant constructions of patriotism over time. War, by its very nature, is destructive. Dominant discourses in the service of war-making also articulate destructive conceptions of patriotism. Peace movement organizations oppose war because it is destructive. Consequently, through discourse they reconstruct patriotism by creating new understandings about it. This is a deeply cultural process. More specifically, PMOs remold patriotism to represent a global vision, compassion for those who are different, judicious use of power, preference for peaceful alternatives, privileging of diplomacy in times of conflict, protection of civil liberties and human rights, willingness to dissent in times of destructive leadership, and cooperation instead of imperialism. They also show the errors and failures of powerholders to truly support the nation, its soldiers, and its people. PMOs then put these reconstructed understandings to work on behalf of what the movement sees to be more positive and constructive purposes. The peace movement's discursive practices use the facilities of democracy to put forward both cultural- and structural-level critiques that move the society from exclusion toward participation, from injustice toward justice, and from war toward peace.

Both PMO members and analysts might question the success of movements, but our research can help them step back and see the bigger picture of how PMOs contribute to changing cultural practices, to the development of public dialogue, and to the demand for accountability in foreign policy. We argue that ongoing and flexible discursive pressure by oppositional figures is needed to shift dominant discourses. PMOs provide that pressure during conflict periods by highlighting the human costs of war and repression, and by demonstrating how those costs negatively impact U.S. interests in both the short and the long term. Our results show that peace movement discourses include criticism and vision. As we have also shown, sometimes the peace movement also aims its oppositional discourse inwards. An example is our analysis of the movement's use of identity politics to oppose not just war but also a deeper societal shift. Identity claims help turn a critical eye on U.S. policies as well as on the historical homogeneity of the peace movement. In effecting the collective change of self and others, peace movement discourses may facilitate the transformation of a war-oriented culture to a peace-oriented culture.

NOTE

1. Much of this paragraph is taken from Maney, Woehrle, and Coy (2005).

Appendix 1

Profiles of Peace Movement Organizations Included in the Study

AMERICAN FRIENDS SERVICE COMMITTEE (AFSC)

Founded in 1917 by Quakers, the American Friends Service Committee provided young Quakers and other conscientious objectors an opportunity to serve those in need instead of fighting during World War I. The AFSC is a practical expression of the faith of the Religious Society of Friends (Quakers). Pacifist and committed to the principles of nonviolence and justice, the organization seeks to draw upon the power of love, human and divine. AFSC works to transform conditions and relationships both in the world and between individuals that threaten to overwhelm what is precious in human beings. They believe that conflicts can be resolved nonviolently, and that enmity can be transformed into friendship, strife into cooperation, poverty into well-being, and injustice into dignity and participation.

Prior to the Iraq War, AFSC conducted relief work inside Iraq and advocated an end to economic sanctions. In anticipation of a United States–led war with Iraq, AFSC stockpiled a cache of emergency supplies in Jordan that were distributed in Iraq after hostilities began. The search for regional peace has been a major focus of AFSC's highly regarded international affairs work. The group has a long history of working for peace and reconciliation in an atmosphere of war, winning the Nobel Peace Prize in 1948.

Contact information:

AFSC National Office
1501 Cherry Street
Philadelphia, PA 19102
215-241-7000

Fax: 215-241-7275
afscinfo@afsc.org
www.afsc.org

BLACK RADICAL CONGRESS (BRC)

The Black Radical Congress was founded in Chicago in June 1998 with the objective of bringing together varied sections of the Black radical tradition. The BRC aims to promote dialogue among Black activists and scholars on the left; to discuss critical issues on the national and international scene that pertain to the Black community; to explore new strategies and directions for progressive political, social, and cultural movements; and to renew the Black radical movement through increased, unified action. The main emphasis is on finding concrete mechanisms to build dialogue and alliances, bringing diverse radical traditions to bear on contemporary realities. The BRC tries to deal seriously with political, social, cultural, and theoretical issues in an accessible way. It recognizes the centrality of antiracist politics and movements of people of color to social change in the United States and elsewhere.

The BRC called on its members to join antiwar activities in their communities, registering their opposition to the Iraq War. Activities included supporting a selective boycott of U.S. products, joining the peace movement, and clarifying the linkages between reparations, peace, and justice. BRC worked with labor and peace movements to link the Iraq War to global racism.

Contact information:

The Black Radical Congress–National Office
P.O. Box 24795
St. Louis, MO 63115
314-307-3441
brcnatl@blackradicalcongress.org
www.blackradicalcongress.org

BLACK VOICES FOR PEACE (BVFP)

BVFP was founded in 2001 at Howard University by Muslims and Christians, academics and grassroots organizers, and lawyers and students. BVFP is a national network of people of African heritage and others working for peace with justice at home and abroad. BVFP worked to end the war in Afghanistan and the secret military tribunals and trials, as well as the "preventive" measures resulting in the detention of persons based on nationality, race, or religious beliefs. They see race- and religious-based profiling as an assault on civil liberties, constitutional rights, and democracy. BVFP is opposed to U.S.

financial and military support for Israeli occupation and new settlements in Palestine.

BVFP organizes and supports educational forums, training workshops, action campaigns, political protests, and economic development programs to achieve its goals. When going to press the authors noticed that the BVFP website had temporarily been suspended. BVFP is part of the United for Peace and Justice coalition, which may be able to provide further updates on BVFP. www.unitedforpeace.org

Contact information:

BVFP
1750 Columbia Rd. NW
Washington, DC 20009
202-232-5690
www.blacksforpeace.org/

CODEPINK

Founded in October 2002, CODEPINK is a women-initiated grassroots peace and social justice movement working to end the war in Iraq, stop new wars, and redirect resources into healthcare, education, and other life-affirming activities. CODEPINK rejects the Bush administration's fear-based politics justifying violence, calling instead for policies based on compassion, kindness, and a commitment to international law. With an emphasis on joy and defiant humor, CODEPINK women and men seek to inspire a community of peacemakers through creative campaigns and a commitment to nonviolent action and civil disobedience.

In 2003, as the world prepared for war, CODEPINK initiated a four-month rolling vigil at the White House to oppose the war in Iraq. CODEPINK also created a signature "pink slip" action that gained nationwide momentum: presenting those who were not doing their jobs to represent the people's interests with pink slips (women's lingerie), demanding they do their jobs or the people will "fire" them. There are over 250 local CODEPINK chapters, from Fayetteville, Arkansas, to Boise, Idaho, and internationally from Brazil to Ireland to Iran.

Contact information:

CODEPINK
2010 Linden Ave
Venice, CA 90291
310-827-4320
info@codepinkalert.org
www.codepink4peace.org

COUNCIL ON AMERICAN-ISLAMIC RELATIONS (CAIR)

Founded in 1994, the Council on American-Islamic Relations is the largest Islamic civil liberties group in the United States. CAIR's mission is to enhance understanding of Islam, encourage dialogue, protect civil liberties, empower American Muslims, and build coalitions that promote justice and mutual understanding. CAIR has worked to promote a positive image of Islam and Muslims in the US. Through media and government relations, education, and advocacy, CAIR puts forth an Islamic perspective to ensure the Muslim voice is represented. In turn, CAIR seeks to empower the Muslim community in the US and encourage their participation in political and social activism.

CAIR counsels, mediates, and advocates on behalf of Muslims and others who have experienced religious discrimination, defamation, or hate crimes. The organization monitors legislation and government activities and lobbies on behalf of the Muslim community in the United States. CAIR has thirty-two chapters in twenty states and one in Canada. CAIR's national office and chapters employ more than sixty staff, more than 300 active volunteer board or executive committee members, and numerous interns.

Contact information:

Council on American-Islamic Relations
453 New Jersey Avenue SE
Washington, DC 20003
202-488-8787
202-488-0833
cair@cair-net.org
www.cair-net.org/

FELLOWSHIP OF RECONCILIATION (FOR)

FOR-USA was founded in 1915 by religious pacifists in response to the outbreak of World War I. FOR claims to be the largest and oldest interfaith peace and justice organization in the United States. FOR is composed of women and men who recognize the essential unity of all creation and have joined together to explore the power of love and truth for resolving human conflict. Vigorous in its opposition to war, the FOR also insists that this effort must be based on a commitment to the achieving of a just and peaceful world community, with full dignity and freedom for every human being. The fellowship is an interfaith organization committed to active nonviolence as a transforming way of life and as a means of radical change. FOR publishes a magazine, *Fellowship*. Well-known leaders of the organization at various times include A. J. Muste, Reinhold Neibuhr, James Farmer, and James Lawson.

Other influential organizations have grown directly out of the FOR, including the American Civil Liberties Union in 1916–1917 and the Congress on Racial Equality in the 1940s. In the 1940s, the fellowship opposed internment of Japanese Americans and helped Jews and political refugees escape the Nazis. They provided important resources and nonviolent action training to the U.S. civil rights movement, and advocated for a "third way" during the Vietnam War. In the 1990s, the FOR advocated for Iraqi children affected by sanctions and brought Bosnian students to the United States during the war in the Balkans. FOR currently engages in work in Latin America and the Middle East, including the Arab-Israeli conflict, Iraq, and Iran.

Contact information:

Fellowship of Reconciliation
521 N. Broadway
Nyack, NY 10960
845-358-4601
www.forusa.org/

MOVEON.ORG

MoveOn.org was initially formed in 1998 in response to the impeachment hearings for President Bill Clinton. MoveOn.org has two functional arms. One focuses on education and advocacy while the other mobilizes people across the country to fight important battles in Congress and help elect candidates who reflect progressive values. MoveOn.org seeks to provide individuals an opportunity to aggregate their contributions with others to gain a greater voice in the political process.

As its name implies, MoveOn.org makes extensive use of the Internet through its cyberactivism campaigns. In addition, MoveOn.org has aired many television commercials and published newspaper ads on issues associated with war, militarism, energy independence, social security, political corruption, torture, and so on.

Contact information:

MoveOn.org
www.moveon.org

NEW YORK CITY LABOR AGAINST THE WAR

New York City Labor Against the War emerged at "Ground Zero" as the first antiwar labor body established in the United States after 9/11. NYCLAW is committed to unambiguous opposition to the war; multiracial leadership; participation of both union officers and rank-and-file members; broad alliances; and democratic processes. NYCLAW advocated an independent international tribunal to impartially investigate, apprehend and try those responsible for the 9/11 attacks. The group called for stopping terror, racial profiling, and legal restrictions against people of color and immigrants, and for defending democratic rights. NYCLAW promoted government aid for the victims' families and displaced workers, not the wealthy, stating that New York City should be rebuilt with union labor with special concern for new threats to worker health and safety. NYCLAW suggested that the cost of 9/11 should not be borne by working and poor New Yorkers. NYCLAW has been a leading labor voice in the peace movement.

Contact information:

nyclaw@comcast.net

PAX CHRISTI

Pax Christi U.S.A. was founded in 1972. As its Latin name suggests, it strives to create a world that reflects the Peace of Christ by exploring, articulating, and witnessing to the call of Christian nonviolence. Pax Christi believes this work begins in personal life and extends to communities of reflection and action to transform structures of society. The organization rejects war, preparations for war, and every form of violence and domination. Pax Christi has four primary foci: primacy of conscience, economic justice, social justice, and respect for creation. The organization employs a prayer/study/action model for personal and social transformation through these four priority areas. Pax Christi U.S.A. promotes the gospel imperative of peacemaking as a priority in the Catholic Church in the United States.

Contact information:

Pax Christi U.S.A.
532 West Eighth Street
Erie, PA 16502
814-453-4955
info@paxchristiusa.org
www.paxchristiusa.org

PEACE ACTION

Originating in disarmament and antiwar organizations founded during the Cold War (including SANE in the 1950s and the FREEZE campaign in the

1980s), the organization that would be Peace Action was formed in 1987, and then renamed again in 1993. The earliest leaders included Norman Cousins and Benjamin Spock. For more than fifty years, Peace Action and its predecessor organizations have campaigned to end the nuclear threat, create a more peaceful economy, and apply nonviolent resolutions to international conflicts. Peace Action is committed to the idea that every person has the right to live without the threat of nuclear weapons, that war is not a suitable response to conflict, and that the United States has the resources to both protect and provide for its citizens.

Peace Action has led issue advocacy efforts in congressional districts throughout the nation as part of its Peace Voter Campaign. Peace Action's 85,000-person membership has addressed issues such as landmine legislation, the Comprehensive Test Ban Treaty, the Nuclear Nonproliferation Treaty, a weapons trade code of conduct, and military budget cuts.

Contact information:

Peace Action
1100 Wayne Avenue Suite 1020
Silver Spring, MD 20910
301-565-4050
Fax: 301-565-0850
www.peace-action.org/

TRUEMAJORITY

TrueMajority was founded by Ben Cohen, cofounder of Ben and Jerry's Ice Cream. TrueMajority was started to compound the power of all those who believe in social justice, giving children a decent start in life, protecting the environment, and having the United States work in cooperation with the world community. Based on the principles of peace, justice, and sustainability, True Majority monitors politics in Washington. When additional voice is needed, TrueMajority sends e-mail alerts to members, who then add their voice to political debates, primarily through cyberactivism. TrueMajority claims a membership of over 500,000.

Contact information:

TrueMajority.org
191 Bank Street
Third Floor
Burlington, VT 05401
802-860-6858
info@truemajority.com
www.truemajority.org

UNITED STATES LABOR AGAINST THE WAR (USLAW)

Founded in 2003, United States Labor Against the War is a national network of sixty-nine national, regional, and local unions and other labor organizations opposed to the Iraq War. USLAW wants a just foreign policy that will bring genuine security and prosperity to working people, an end to U.S. government occupation of foreign countries, and redirect the nation's resources from inflated military spending to meeting the needs of working families for health care, education, a clean environment, housing, and a decent standard of living based on principles of equality and democracy. USLAW is committed to supporting U.S. troops and their families by bringing the troops home now. It advocates protecting workers' rights, civil rights, civil liberties, and the rights of immigrants by promoting democracy, not subverting it. USLAW maintains solidarity with workers and their organizations around the world who are struggling for their own labor and human rights, and with those in the United States who want U.S. foreign and domestic policies to reflect the nation's highest ideals.

USLAW provides information to and mobilizes its members to engage in a variety of protest activities aimed at ending the Iraq War.

Contact information:

USLAW
1718 M Street NW #153
Washington, DC 20036
202-521-5265
info@uslaboragainstwar.org
www.uslaboragainstwar.org

WOMEN'S ACTION FOR NEW DIRECTIONS (WAND)

WAND was founded in 1982 as Women's Action for Nuclear Disarmament. Following the end of the Cold War, the group was renamed Women's Action for New Directions. WAND claims 10,000 members and supporters dedicated to redirecting federal budget priorities away from the military and toward human needs. WAND promotes alternatives to militarism and violence as solutions to conflict and shifting from a military- to a civilian-based economy that will meet human, economic, and environmental needs. WAND highlights the deleterious environmental effects of nuclear weapons production while promoting elimination of testing, production, sale, and use of weapons of mass destruction. WAND also promotes the prevention of violence against women as well as increasing women's political leadership. WAND works with progressive women state legislators working to influence federal policy and budget

priorities. It creates educational materials for training and briefing individuals, elected leaders, and the media.
Contact information:

WAND National Office
691 Massachusetts Avenue
Arlington, MA 02476
781-643-6740
info@wand.org
www.wand.org

WAR RESISTERS LEAGUE (WRL)

The War Resisters League was organized in 1923 by secular pacifists who opposed World War I, many of whom had been jailed for refusing military service. Believing that war is a crime against humanity, the league works for a society that is democratic and free of economic, racial, and sexual oppression. The methods WRL uses range from education to demonstrations to lobbying to nonviolent direct action. WRL is committed to eliminating not only war, but the causes of war. The organization argues that the suffering of homelessness, hunger, lack of medical care, and poverty are forms of violence comparable to war.

WRL centers its work on education and action. Education involves publishing pacifist literature on the Internet and in the organization's magazine, *WIN*. WRL's emphasis is on action, war resistance, and individual conscience. WRL organizes demonstrations, cooperates in coalition with other peace and justice groups, opposes conscription and all forms of militarism, and supports men and women who resist the military at all levels. WRL helps train people in civil disobedience, war tax resistance, and other forms of putting conscience into action. WRL cosponsors the Fund for Education and Training (FEAT), which assists young men who for reasons of conscience do not comply with laws requiring registration for the draft.
Contact information:

War Resisters League
339 Lafayette Street
New York, NY 10012
212-228-0450
Fax: 212-228-6193
wrl@warresisters.org
www.warresisters.org

WOMEN'S INTERNATIONAL LEAGUE FOR
PEACE AND FREEDOM (WILPF)

The Women's International League for Peace and Freedom was founded in 1915 by women from warring countries to address the root causes of World War I and to redefine the notion of security. Jane Addams was the organization's first president. WILPF rejects war-making and military domination as the path to security. WILPF advocates the equality of all people in a world free of sexism, racism, classism, and homophobia as well as the guarantee of fundamental human rights, including the right to sustainable development. WILPF promotes an end to all forms of violence, including rape, battering, exploitation, military intervention, and war. WILPF also promotes the transfer of world resources from the military to meeting human needs, leading to economic justice within and among nations, and world disarmament and peaceful resolution of international conflicts via the United Nations.

WILPF's Middle East campaign examines the role of U.S. government policy in the dynamics of current conflicts. They explore economic interests that underlie the power struggles in the region and identifies U.S. government policy changes that will end violence and promote justice.

Contact information:

Women's International League for Peace and Freedom
U.S. Section Office
1213 Race Street
Philadelphia PA 19107
215-563-7110
wilpf@wilpf.org
wilpf.org/

Appendix 2

Explanation of Weights Applied to Code Frequencies

WEIGHTS FOR COMPARATIVE ORGANIZATIONAL ANALYSES

To control for differences in the number of words and average paragraph size across peace movement organizations (PMOs), we used weights based upon the following formulas:

Median-based Formula for Weights = (Median # Words for all PMOs/Total Words for Individual PMO) * (Mean # Words per Paragraph for Individual PMO/Median of PMO Means)

Mean-based Formula for Weights = (Mean # Words for all PMOs/Total Words for Individual PMO) * (Mean # Words per Paragraph for Individual PMO/Mean of PMO Means)

WEIGHTS FOR LONGITUDINAL ANALYSES

To control for differences in the number of words and average paragraph size across conflict periods, we developed a two-step weighting process. After applying the weights listed above to the code frequencies for each PMO within a specific conflict period, we applied weights based upon the following formulas:

Median-based Formula for Weights = (Median # Words for all Conflict Periods/Total Words for Individual Conflict Period) * (Mean # Words per Paragraph for Individual Conflict Period/Median of Conflict Period Means)

Mean-based Formula for Weights = (Mean # Words for all Conflict Periods/ Total Words for Individual Conflict Period) * (Mean # Words per Paragraph for Individual Conflict Period/Conflict Period Means)

Unless specifically stated otherwise, data provided in tables and figures for both comparative organizational analyses and for longitudinal analyses are weighted using the median-based formulas.

Appendix 3

Codes Included in Bundles Analyzed in Chapter 3

CHALLENGING NATIONALISM BUNDLE

Abu Ghraib: References to Abu Ghraib.

Alternative response_multilateral: Multilateral and/or global systemic responses to conflict.

American identity_negative: Negative references to specific U.S. political and moral traditions, the "American spirit," or assumptions about what is normatively American. Negative self-reference to organization as Americans (e.g., as Americans, we . . .). Includes critiques of gluttonous lifestyle, ethnocentrism, superpower complex, world cop, and so on.

Democracy_failure: Statements about democracy or attempts at democracy outside the United States failing or having problems.

Human costs of war_race: Costs of war to racial minority groups.

Occupation: References to U.S. presence in Iraq as an occupation.

Oil: References to oil, the West's need for it, as a variable in war, War for Oil, and so on.

Pretext: Observation that publicly stated reasons for policies have little or nothing to do with the actual reasons for policies.

Scapegoating: Critiques of anti-Arab, anti-Middle Eastern, and anti-Muslim attitudes and actions.

Sorry: Making and requesting expressions of sorrow, regret, guilt; asking for forgiveness or for an apology.

Terror condemned_state: State terror condemned. Direct state violence or state-sponsored paramilitary violence explicitly labeled as terror.

Threat_unreal: Observation that threats to the U.S. public stated by authorities are not real.

Threat_U.S.: United States government, policies or lifestyle as a threat or a danger (as opposed to a cost) to either persons, property, political or economic stability, moral or political principles.

Torture: References to use of torture.

Troops_negative: Comments that criticize U.S. troops or that evaluate troop behavior negatively.

U.S. foreign policy condemned_failure: Comments that classify U.S. foreign policy as a failure or ineffective. Also includes criticism of specific strategies or policies (e.g., preemptive strike, shock and awe, sanctions) and comments criticizing the timing of a policy or an initiative.

U.S. foreign policy condemned_wrong: Comments that classify U.S. foreign policy as a crime, illegal, unjust, or immoral.

U.S. imperialism: Critiques of U.S. policies (historic, current, proposed) as imperialistic. Includes words like empire and hegemony. References to abuse of superpower status for self-interest or negative U.S. interventions in several societies. On its own the use of the word "occupation" is not sufficient. Do not use code if coding passage as instance of U.S. foreign policy condemned.

Violence condemned_unilateral: Violence conducted unilaterally without international support.

HARNESSING NATIONALISM BUNDLE

Alternative response_self-determination: Calls for withdrawal/self-determination

American identity_positive: positive references to specific U.S. political and moral traditions, the "American spirit," and assumptions about what is normatively American. Positive self-reference to organization as Americans (e.g., as Americans, we . . .).

Civil liberties: Access to information, freedoms to act, human rights, references to war potentially limiting them; constitutional rights or limits.

Democracy_action: Calls for people in the United States to voice their opinions and exercise their democratic rights. Must include specific request for action (otherwise code as Democracy_U.S.).

Democracy_global: References to the need for global democracy.

Democracy_self-rule: References to a people's right to self-determination (non-U.S.).

Democracy_spread: References to the desire or responsibility to spread democracy abroad.

Democracy_U.S.: References for need for democratic debate in the United States, comments about democracy as a right for U.S. people, concern over status of democracy in the United States.

Freedom: Specific references to freedom or being free.

Hero: Portrayals of people as heroes or of acts as heroic.

Leadership_state: What qualities (e.g., values or actions) make a government a strong global leader among nation-states.

Patriotism: Specific references to patriotism or national loyalty.

Pride: Specific references to pride or being proud.

Sacrifice: References to sacrifices made by or for someone or something.

Security: Definitions of what leads to safety, security or insecurity, perception of an event as loss of security, expression of need to feel more secure.

Terror condemned_paramilitary: Terror by non-state actors condemned.

Threat_not U.S.: Something other than the United States government, policies, or lifestyle as a threat or a danger (as opposed to a cost) to either persons, property, political or economic stability, or moral or political principles.

Troops_betrayal: References to those actions of the U.S. government and defense contractors that are claimed to result in increased dangers and costs incurred by the U.S. troops serving in the war, including such things as insufficient equipment, poor training, inadequate medical care, and poor planning leading to increased risks.

Troops_positive: Includes expressions of support or concern for U.S. soldiers (including simple references to numbers of dead or wounded). Simply mentioning how many troops are deployed is not sufficient. On its own, a simple statement of support for withdrawal of troops is also not sufficient, without an expression of concern. The phrase "Bring them home now" would, however, be coded given its historical resonance and meanings.

U.S. foreign policy condemned_leadership: Criticism of policy that names specific government officials.

References

Adorno, Theodor, Else Frenkel-Brunswik, Daniel Levinson, and Nevitt Sanford. 1950/1993. *The Authoritarian Personality.* New York: W. W. Norton & Company.

Ahlstrom, Sydney. 1975. *A Religious History of the American People.* Vol. 1. Garden City, N.Y.: Image Books.

Allen, Barbara, Paula O'Loughlin, Amy Jasperson, and John L. Sullivan. 1994. The Media and the Gulf War: Framing, Priming, and the Spiral of Silence. *Polity* 27 (2): 255–84.

Alonso, Harriet H. 1993. *Peace as a Women's Issue: A History of the U.S. Movement for World Peace and Women's Rights.* Syracuse, N.Y.: Syracuse University Press.

Aminzade, Ronald, and Doug McAdam. 2001. Emotions and Contentious Politics. In *Silence and Voice in the Study of Contentious Politics,* ed. R. Aminzade et al., 14–50. New York: Cambridge University Press.

———. 2002. Emotions and Contentious Politics: Introduction to the Special Issue. *Mobilization* 7 (2): 107–9.

Anderson, Benedict. 1991. *Imagined Communities: Reflections on the Origin and Spread of Nationalism.* Rev. ed. London: Verso.

Anderson, Perry. 1976. The Antinomies of Antonio Gramsci. *New Left Review* 100 (November–December): 5–78.

Andrews, Molly. 1997. Fighting for "The Finest Image We Have of Her": Patriotism and Oppositional Politics. In *Patriotism in the Lives of Individuals and Nations,* ed. D. Bar-Tal and E. Staub, 271–92. Chicago: Nelson Hall.

Arendt, Hannah. 1951. *The Origins of Totalitarianism.* New York: Harcourt, Brace.

Armstrong, Elizabeth A., and Mary Bernstein. 2008. Culture, Power, and Institutions: A Multi-Institutional Politics Approach to Social Movements. *Sociological Theory* 26 (1): 74–99.

Azmon, Yael. 1997. War, Mothers, and a Girl with Braids: Involvement of Mothers' Peace Movements in the National Discourse in Israel. *Israel Social Science Research* 12 (1): 109–28.

Barbalet, Jack M. 1998. *Emotion, Social Theory, and Social Structure.* Cambridge, UK: Cambridge University Press.

Bar-Tal, Daniel, and Ervin Staub. 1997. Introduction: Patriotism: Its Scope and Meaning. In *Patriotism in the Lives of Individuals and Nations,* ed. D. Bar-Tal and E. Staub, 1–19. Chicago: Nelson-Hall.

Basch, Linda. 2004. Human Security, Globalization, and Feminist Visions. *Peace Review* 16 (1): 5–12.

Baumgardner, Jennifer, and Amy Richards. 2000. *Manifesta: Young Women, Feminism, and the Future*. New York: Farrar, Straus and Giroux.

Bellah, Robert N. 1967/2005. Civil Religion in America. *Daedalus* 134 (4): 40–55.

Bellah, Robert N., Richard Madsen, William M. Sullivan, Ann Swidler, and Steven M. Tipton. 1985. *Habits of the Heart: Individualism and Commitment in American Life*. New York: Perennial Library.

Benford, Robert D. 1993. Frame Disputes within the Nuclear Disarmament Movement. *Social Forces* 71 (3): 677–701.

Benford, Robert D., and David A. Snow. 2000. Framing Processes and Social Movements: An Overview and Assessment. *Annual Review of Sociology* 26: 611–39.

Bennett, W. L. 2005. Social Movements Beyond Borders: Understanding Two Eras of Transnational Activism. In *Transnational Protest and Global Activism*, ed. D. della Porta and S. Tarrow, 203–26. New York: Rowman & Littlefield.

Berezin, Mabel. 2002. Secure States: Towards a Political Sociology of Emotion. In *Emotions and Sociology*, ed. J. M. Barbalet, 33–52. Oxford, UK: Blackwell.

Bernstein, Mary. 1997. Celebration and Suppression: The Strategic Uses of Identity by the Lesbian and Gay Movement. *American Journal of Sociology* 103(3): 531–65.

Billig, Michael. 1995. *Banal Nationalism*. Thousand Oaks, Calif.: Sage.

Billings, Dwight B. 1990. Religion as Opposition: A Gramscian Analysis. *American Journal of Sociology* 96 (1): 1–31.

Billings, Dwight B., and Shaunna L. Scott. 1994. Religion and Political Legitimation. *Annual Review of Sociology* 20 (August): 173–201.

Blain, Michael. 1989. Power and Practice in Peace Movement Discourse. In *Research in Social Movements, Conflicts and Change*, Vol. 11, ed. L. Kriesberg, 197–218. Stamford, Conn.: JAI Press.

Blau, Judith, and Alberto Moncada. 2005. *Human Rights: Beyond the Liberal Vision*. Lanham, Md.: Rowman & Littlefield.

Brecher, Jeremy, Jill Cutler, and Brendan Smith, eds. 2005. *In the Name of Democracy: American War Crimes in Iraq and Beyond*. New York: Metropolitan Books.

Burkitt, Ian. 1997. Social Relations and Emotions. *Sociology* 31 (1): 37–55.

———. 2002. Complex Emotions: Relations, Feelings and Images in Emotional Experience. In *Emotions and Sociology*, ed. J. M. Barbalet, 151–67. Oxford, England: Blackwell.

———. 2005. Powerful Emotions: Power, Government and Opposition in the "War on Terror." *Sociology* 39 (4): 679–95.

Bush, George H. W. 1990. *Weekly Compilation of Presidential Documents*. Washington, D.C.: Office of the Federal Register.

———. 1991. *Weekly Compilation of Presidential Documents*. Washington, D.C.: Office of the Federal Register.

Bush, George W. 1999. *A Charge to Keep*. 1st ed. New York: Morrow.

———. 2001. Address to a Joint Session of Congress and the American People. Washington, D.C. www.whitehouse.gov/news/releases/2001/09/print/20010920-8.html (accessed July 12, 2003).

Bush, Rod. 2003. African Americans, Social Justice and the Aftermath of September 11, 2001. *Socialism and Democracy* 17:1. www.sdonline.org (accessed January 26, 2005).

Carroll, William K., and Robert S. Ratner. 1994. Between Leninism and Radical Pluralism: Gramscian Reflections on Counter-Hegemony and the New Social Movements. *Critical Sociology* 20 (2): 3–26.

———. 1996. Master Framing and Cross-Movement Networking in Contemporary Social Movements. *Sociological Quarterly* 37 (4): 601–25.

———. 2001. Sustaining Oppositional Cultures in "Post-Socialist" Times: A Comparative Study of Three Social Movement Organizations. *Sociology* 35 (3): 605–29.

Chatfield, Charles. 1971. *For Peace and Justice: Pacifism in America, 1914–1941*. Knoxville: University of Tennessee Press.

Clark, Howard. 2000. *Civil Resistance in Kosovo*. London, UK: Pluto Press.

Clinton, William. 1999. *Weekly Compilation of Presidential Documents*. Washington, D.C.: Office of the Federal Register.

Coe, Kevin, and David Domke. 2006. Petitioners or Prophets? Presidential Discourse, God, and the Ascendancy of Religious Conservatives. *Journal of Commmunication* 56 (2): 309–30.

Coles, Roberta L. 1998. Peaceniks and Warmongers' Framing Fracas on the Home Front: Dominant and Opposition Discourse Interaction during the Persian Gulf Crisis. *Sociological Quarterly* 39 (3): 369–91.

———. 1999. Odd Folk and Ordinary People: Collective Identity Disparities between Peace Groups in the Persian Gulf Crisis. *Sociological Spectrum* 19 (3): 325–57.

Collins, Patricia H. 1990. *Black Feminist Thought*. Boston: Unwin Hyman.

Commission on Human Security. 2003. *Human Security Now*. New York: United Nations.

Cortright, David. 1991. Assessing Peace Movement Effectiveness in the 1980s. *Peace & Change* 16 (1): 46–63.

———. 1993. *Peace Works: The Citizen's Role in Ending the Cold War*. Boulder, Colo.: Westview Press.

Cortright, David, and Ron Pagnucco. 1997. Limits to Transnationalism: The 1980s Freeze Campaign. In *Transnational Social Movements and Global Politics*, ed. J. Smith, C. Chatfield and R. Pagnucco, 159–74. Syracuse, N.Y.: Syracuse University Press.

Coy, Patrick G. 1997. Cooperative Accompaniment by Peace Brigades International in Sri Lanka. In *Transnational Social Movements and Global Politics*, ed. Jackie Smith, Charles Chatfield, and Ron Pagnucco, 81–100. Syracuse, N.Y.: Syracuse University Press.

Coy, Patrick G., and Timothy Hedeen. 2005. A Stage Model of Social Movement Cooptation: Community Mediation in the United States. *Sociological Quarterly* 46 (3): 405–35.

Coy, Patrick G., Gregory M. Maney, and Lynne M. Woehrle. 2003. Contesting Patriotism by the Post 9/11 Peace Movement in the United States. *Peace Review: A Transnational Quarterly* 15 (4): 463–71.

———. 2008. Blessing War and Blessing Peace: Religious Discourses in the U.S. During Major Conflict Periods, 1990–2005. *Research in Social Movements, Conflicts and Change* 29.

Coy, Patrick G., and Lynne M. Woehrle. 1996. Constructing Identity and Oppositional Knowledge: The Framing Practices of Peace Movement Organizations During the Gulf War. *Sociological Spectrum* 16 (3): 287–327.

———, eds. 2000. *Social Conflicts and Collective Identities*. Lanham, Md.: Rowman & Littlefield.

Coy, Patrick G., Lynne M. Woehrle, and Gregory M. Maney. 2008a. Discursive Legacies from the Vietnam War and the Iraq War: The U.S. Peace Movement and "Support the Troops." *Social Problems* 55 (2): 161–89.

———. 2008b. A Typology of Oppositional Knowledge: Democracy and The U.S. Peace Movement. *Sociological Research Online* 13, no. 4. www.socresonline.org.uk/ 13/4/3.html.

Cress, Daniel M., and Daniel J. Myers. 2004. Authority in Contention. *Research in Social Movements, Conflicts and Change* 25:279–93.

Davies, James C. 1962. Toward a Theory of Revolution. *American Sociological Review* 27 (1): 5–19.

Davis, Darren W., and Brian D. Silver. 2004. Civil Liberties vs. Security: Public Opinion in the Context of the Terrorist Attacks on America. *American Journal of Political Science* 48 (1): 28–46.

Davis, Diane E., and Christina D. Rosan. 2004. Social Movements in the Mexico City Airport Controversy: Globalization, Democracy, and the Power of Distance. *Mobilization: An International Journal* 9 (3): 279–93.

Davis, Flora. 1991. *Moving the Mountain*. New York: Simon & Schuster.

DeBenedetti, Charles, and Charles Chatfield. 1990. *An American Ordeal: The Antiwar Movement of the Vietnam Era*. Syracuse, N.Y.: Syracuse University Press.

della Porta, Donatella. 2005. Multiple Belongings, Tolerant Identities, and the Construction of Another Politics: Between the European Social Forum and the Local Social Fora. In *Transnational Protest and Global Activism*, ed. D. della Porta and S. Tarrow, 175–202. New York: Rowman & Littlefield.

della Porta, Donatella, and Sidney Tarrow. 2005. Transnational Processes and Social Activism: An Introduction. In *Transnational Protest and Global Activism*, ed. D. della Porta and S. Tarrow, 1–17. New York: Rowman & Littlefield.

de Rivera, Joseph, Rachel Kurrien, and Nina Olsen. 2007. The Emotional Climate of Nations and Their Culture of Peace. *Journal of Social Issues* 63 (2): 255–71.

Domke, David S. 2004. *God Willing? Political Fundamentalism in the White House, The War on Iraq, and the Echoing Press*. London; Ann Arbor, Mich.: Pluto Press.

Edelman, Murray. 1988. *Constructing the Political Spectacle*. Chicago: University of Chicago Press.

Einwohner, Rachel L. 1999. Gender, Class, and Social Movement Outcomes: Identity and Effectiveness in Two Animal Rights Campaigns. *Gender & Society* 13 (1): 56–76.

Einwohner, Rachel L., Jocelyn A. Hollander, and Toska Olson. 2000. Engendering Social Movements: Cultural Images and Movement Dynamics. *Gender & Society* 14 (5): 679–99.

Eisinger, Peter K. 1973. The Conditions of Protest Behavior in American Cities. *American Political Science Review* 67: 11–28.

Eley, Geoff. 1994. Nations, Publics, and Political Cultures: Placing Habermas in the Nineteenth Century. In *Culture/Power/History: A Reader in Contemporary Social Theory*, ed. Nicholas B. Dirks, Geoffrey Eley, and Sherry B. Ortner, 297–335. Princeton, N.J.: Princeton University Press.

Epstein, Barbara. 1990. The Politics of Moral Witness: Religion and Nonviolent Direct Action. In *Peace Action in the Eighties: Social Science Perspectives*, ed. S. Marullo and J. Lofland, 106–24. New Brunswick, N.J.: Rutgers University Press.

Esacove, Anne W. 2004. Dialogic Framing: The Framing/Counterframing of "Partial Birth" Abortion. *Sociological Inquiry* 74 (1): 70–101.

Evans, Sara M. 2003. *Tidal Wave: How Women Changed America at Century's End*. New York: The Free Press.

Eyerman, Ron, and Andrew Jamison. 1991. *Social Movements: A Cognitive Approach*. University Park: Pennsylvania State University Press.

Fairbanks, J. D. 1981. The Priestly Functions of the Presidency: A Discussion of the Literature on Civil Religion and its Implications for the Study of Presidential Leadership. *Presidential Studies Quarterly* 11 (2): 214–32.

Fendrich, James M. 2003. The Forgotten Movement: The Vietnam Antiwar Movement. *Sociological Inquiry* 73 (3): 338–58.

Ferree, Myra M. 2003. Resonance and Radicalism: Feminist Framing in the Abortion Debates of the United States and Germany. *American Journal of Sociology* 109 (2): 304–44.

Ferree, Myra M., and David A. Merrill. 2000. Hot Movements, Cold Cognition: Thinking about Social Movements in Gendered Frames. *Contemporary Sociology* 29 (3): 454–62.

Ferree, Myra M., and Frederick D. Miller. 1985. Mobilization and Meaning: Toward an Integration of Social Psychological and Resource Perspectives on Social Movements. *Sociological Inquiry* 55:38–61.

Fine, Gary A. 1995. Public Narration and Group Culture: Discerning Discourse in Social Movements. In *Social Movements and Culture*, ed. H. Johnston and B. Klandermans, 127–43. Minneapolis: University of Minnesota Press.

Fineman, Howard. 2003. Bush and God: A Biography of Bush's Faith. *Newsweek*, March 10, 22.

Flynn, M. Kate. 2000. *Ideology, Mobilization and the Nation: The Rise of Irish, Basque and Carlist Nationalist Movements in the Nineteenth and Early Twentieth Centuries*. New York: Palgrave Macmillan.

Foucault, Michel. 1978. *The History of Sexuality: An Introduction*. New York: Vintage.

———. 1980. *Power/Knowledge: Selected Interviews and Other Writings, 1972–1977*. New York: Pantheon Books.

Fowler, Robert B., Allen D. Hertzke and Laura R. Olson. 1999. *Religion and Politics in America: Faith, Culture, and Strategic Choices.* 2nd ed. Boulder, Colo.: Westview Press.

Friedman, Debra, and Doug McAdam. 1992. Collective Identity and Activism: Networks, Choices, and the Life of a Social Movement. In *Frontiers in Social Movement Theory,* ed. A. D. Morris and C. McClurg Mueller, 156–73. New Haven, Conn.: Yale University Press.

Gamson, William A. 1988. Political Discourse and Collective Action. In *International Social Movement Research,* Vol. 1, ed. B. Klandermans, 219–44. Greenwich, Conn.: JAI Press.

———. 1992a. The Social Psychology of Collective Action. In *Frontiers in Social Movement Theory,* ed. A. D. Morris and C. McClurg Mueller, 53–76. New Haven, Conn.: Yale University Press.

———. 1992b. *Talking Politics.* New York: Cambridge University Press.

———. 1995. Constructing Social Protest. In *Social Movements and Culture,* ed. H. Johnston and B. Klandermans, 85–106. Minneapolis: University of Minnesota Press.

Gamson, William A., David Croteau, William Hoynes, and Theodore Sasson. 1992. Media Images and the Social Construction of Reality. *Annual Review of Sociology* 18 (August): 373–93.

Gamson, William A., and David S. Meyer. 1996. Framing Political Opportunities. In *Comparative Perspectives on Social Movements: Political Opportunities, Mobilizing Structures, and Cultural Framings,* ed. D. McAdam, J. D. McCarthy, and M. N. Zald, 275–90. New York: Cambridge University Press.

Gasper, Des. 2005. Securing Humanity: Situating "Human Security" as Concept and Discourse. *Journal of Human Development* 6 (2): 221–45.

Gaventa, John. 1980. *Power and Powerlessness: Quiescence and Rebellion in an Appalachian Valley.* Urbana: University of Illinois Press.

Geertz, Clifford. 1973. *The Interpretation of Cultures: Selected Essays.* New York: Basic.

Gitlin, Todd. 1996. Television's Anti-Politics: Surveying the Wasteland. *Dissent* 43 (1): 76–85.

Glassner, Barry. 2004. Narrative Techniques of Fear Mongering. *Social Research* 71 (4): 819–26.

Goffman, Erving. 1974. *Frame Analysis.* Cambridge, Mass.: Harvard University Press.

Goodwin, Jeff, and James M. Jasper, eds. 2003. *Rethinking Social Movements: Structure, Meaning, and Emotion.* New York: Rowman & Littlefield.

Goodwin, Jeff, James M. Jasper, and Francesca Polletta. 2000. Return of the Repressed: The Fall and Rise of Emotions in Social Movement Theory. *Mobilization* 5 (1): 65–84.

Goodwin, Jeff, and Steven Pfaff. 2001. Emotion Work in High-Risk Social Movements: Managing Fear in the U.S. and East German Civil Rights Movements. In *Passionate Politics: Emotions and Social Movements,* ed. J. Goodwin, S. Pfaff and F. Polletta, 282–302. Chicago: University of Chicago Press.

Gordon, David. 2003. America First: The Anti-War Movement, Charles Lindbergh and the Second World War, 1940–1941. Paper presented at a joint meeting of the Historical Society and The New York Military Affairs Symposium, September 26, New York, N.Y.

Gould, Deborah. 2004. Passionate Political Processes: Bringing Emotions Back into the Study of Social Movements. In *Rethinking Social Movements: Structure, Meaning and Emotion,* ed. J. Goodwin and J. M. Jasper, 155–75. New York: Rowman & Littlefield.

Gramsci, Antonio. 1971. *Selections from Prison Notebooks.* London: New Left Books.

Gregg, Richard. 1935/1966. *The Power of Nonviolence.* New York: Schocken Books.

———. 2001. The Ego-Function of the Rhetoric of Protest. In *The Ego-Function of the Rhetoric of Protest,* ed. C. E. Morris and S. H. Browne, 45–60. State College, Penn.: Strata.

Griffin, Leland M. 2001. The Rhetoric of Historical Movements. In *Readings on the Rhetoric of Social Protest,* ed. C. E. Morris and S. H. Browne, 5–10. State College, Penn.: Strata.

Groves, Julian M. 2001. Animal Rights and the Politics of Emotion: Folk Constructions of Emotion in the Animal Rights Movement. In *Passionate Politics: Emotions and Social Movements,* ed. J. Goodwin, J. M. Jasper and F. Polletta, 212–29. Chicago: University of Chicago Press.

Gurtov, Mel. 2006. *Superpower on Crusade: The Bush Doctrine in US Foreign Policy.* Boulder, Colo.: Lynne Rienner Publishers.

Hackett, Robert A., and Yuezhi Zhao. 1994. Challenging a Master Narrative: Peace Protest and Opinion/Editorial Discourse in the US Press During the Gulf War. *Discourse and Society* 5 (4): 509–41.

Hallin, Daniel C., and Todd Gitlin. 1994. The Gulf War as Popular Culture and Television Drama. In *Taken By Storm: The Media, Public Opinion, and U.S. Forign Policy in the Gulf War*, ed. W. L. Bennett and D. L. Paletz, 149–63. Chicago: University of Chicago Press.

Hansen, Olaf, and Randolph Bourne. 1977. *The Radical Will: Selected Writings 1911–1918.* New York: Urizen Books, Inc.

Harlow, Roxanna, and Lauren Dundes. 2004. United We Stand: Responses to the September 11 Attacks in Black and White. *Sociological Perspectives* 47 (4): 439–64.

Harris, Adrienne, and Ynestra King, eds. 1989. *Rocking the Ship of State: Toward a Feminist Peace Politics.* Boulder, Colo.: Westview Press.

Hedges, Chris. 2006. *American Fascists: The Christian Right and the War on America.* New York: Free Press.

Hewitt, Lyndi, and Holly J. McCammon. 2004. Explaining Suffrage Mobilization: Balance, Neutralization, and Range in Collective Action Frames, 1892–1919. *Mobilization* 9 (2): 149–66.

Heyer, Kristin. 2003. US Catholic Discipleship and Citizenship: Patriotism or Dissent? *Political Theology* 4 (2): 149–74.

Hochschild, Arlie R. 1983. *The Managed Heart: Commercialization of Human Feeling.* Berkeley: University of California Press.

Huebner, Andrew J. 2002. Support Unseen: Rhode Island and the Vietnam War, 1965–1973. *Rhode Island History* 60 (Winter): 2–24.

Hunt, Scott A., and Robert D. Benford. 1994. Identity Talk in the Peace and Justice Movement. *Journal of Contemporary Ethnography* 22 (4): 488–517.

Huntington, Samuel. 1969. *Political Order in Changing Societies.* New Haven, Conn.: Yale University Press.

Ignatieff, Michael, ed. 2005. *American Exceptionalism and Human Rights.* Princeton, N.J.: Princeton University Press.

Jackson, Derrick. 2007. "Protestors Worldwide Send a Message." *Common Dreams.* February 19. www.commondreams.org/views03/0219-01.htm (accessed May 24, 2007).

Jackson, Stevi. 1993. Even Sociologists Fall in Love: An Exploration in the Sociology of Emotions. *Sociology* 27 (2): 201–20.

Janowitz, Morris. 1985. *The Reconstruction of Patriotism: Education for Civic Consciousness.* Chicago: University of Chicago Press.

Jasper, James. 2004. A Strategic Approach to Collective Action: Looking for Agency in Social Movement Choices. *Mobilization* 9 (1): 1–16.

——. 2006. *Getting Your Way: Strategic Dilemmas in the Real World.* Chicago: University of Chicago Press.

Jasper, James M., and Jane D. Poulsen. 1995. Recruiting Strangers and Friends: Moral Shocks and Social Networks in Animal Rights and Anti-Nuclear Protests. *Social Problems* 42 (4): 493–512.

Johnson, Chalmers. 1964. *Revolution and the Social System.* Stanford, Calif.: The Hoover Institution.

Keck, Margaret E., and Kathryn Sikkink. 1998. *Activists Beyond Borders.* 1st ed. Ithaca, N.Y.: Cornell University Press.

Keen, Sam. 1986. *Faces of the Enemy: Reflections of the Hostile Imagination.* San Francisco, Calif.: Harper & Row.

Kelman, Herbert C. 1995. Decision Making and Public Discourse in the Gulf War: An Assessment of Underlying Psychological and Moral Assumptions. *Peace and Conflict: Journal of Peace Psychology* 1 (2): 117–30.

Kent, Stephen A., and James V. Spickard. 1994. The "Other" Civil Religion and the Tradition of Radical Quaker Politics. *Journal of Church & State* 36 (2): 373–88.

Kornhauser, William. 1959. *The Politics of Mass Society.* New York: Free Press.

Ku, Agnes S. 2001. Hegemonic Construction, Negotiation and Displacement: The Struggle Over Right of Abode in Hong Kong. *International Journal of Cultural Studies* 4 (3): 259–78.

Kull, Steven. 2004. *Americans on Detention, Torture, and the War on Terrorism.* College Park, Md.: Program on International Policy Attitudes.

Kunstler, James H. 1993. *Geography of Nowhere: The Rise and Decline of America's Man-Made Landscape.* New York: Simon & Schuster.

Kurzman, Charles. 1996. Structural Opportunities and Perceived Opportunities in Social-Movement Theory: Evidence from the Iranian Revolution of 1979. *American Sociological Review* 61 (1): 153–70.

Kutz-Flamenbaum, Rachel. 2007. Ideology, Identity and Issues: Feminist Ideologies Among Women's Peace Activists. Paper presented at the annual meeting of the American Sociological Association, New York City, August 11.

Layton, Azza S. 2000. *International Politics and Civil Rights Policies in the United States, 1941–1960.* 1st ed. New York: Cambridge University Press.

Leach, Colin W., and Larissa Z. Tiedens. 2004. Introduction: A World of Emotion. In *The Social Life of Emotions,* ed. L. Z. Tiedens and C. W. Leach, 1–16. Cambridge, UK: Cambridge University Press.

Leatherman, Janie. 2005. Global Arrogance and the Crises of Hegemony. In *Charting Transnational Democracy: Beyond Global Arrogance,* ed. J. Leatherman and J. A. Webber, 3–27. New York: Palgrave Macmillan.

Le Bon, Gustave. 1897/2002. *The Crowd.* Mineola, N.Y.: Dover.

Lipset, Seymour M. 1996. *American Exceptionalism: A Double-edged Sword.* 1st ed. New York: W. W. Norton.

Loseke, Donileen. 1993. Constructing Conditions, People, Morality, and Emotion: Expanding the Agenda. In *Constructionist Controversies,* ed. J. Holstein and G. Miller, 207–16. Hawthorne, N.Y.: Aldine de Gruyter.

MacDougall, John, Stephen D. Minicucci, and Doug Myers. 1995. The U.S. House of Representatives' Vote on the Gulf War, 1991: Measuring Peace Movement Impact. *Research in Social Movements, Conflicts and Change* 18:225–84.

Maney, Gregory M. 2001. Transnational Structures and Protest: Linking Theories and Assessing Structures and Evidence. *Mobilization* 6 (1): 83–100.

Maney, Gregory M., Patrick G. Coy, and Lynne M. Woehrle. 2008. Pursuing Political Persuasion: War and Peace Frames in the United States after Sept. 11th. Working paper, Hofstra University.

Maney, Gregory M., Lynne M. Woehrle, and Patrick G. Coy. 2005. Harnessing and Challenging Hegemony: The U.S. Peace Movement after 9/11. *Sociological Perspectives* 38 (3): 357–81.

———. forthcoming. Ideological Consistency and Contextual Adaptation: U.S. Peace Movement Emotional Work before and after 9/11. *American Behavioral Scientist* 52, no. 4.

Mansbridge, Jane J. 2001. The Making of Oppositional Consciousness. In *Oppositional Consciousness: The Subjective Roots of Social Protest,* ed. J. J. Mansbridge and A. D. Morris, 1–19. Chicago: University of Chicago Press.

McAdam, Doug. 1982. *Political Process and the Development of Black Insurgency, 1930–1970.* Chicago: University of Chicago Press.

McAdam, Doug, and Dieter Rucht. 1993. The Cross-National Diffusion of Movement Ideas. *Annals of the American Academy of Social and Political Science* 528 (July): 56–74.

McAdam, Doug, Sidney Tarrow, and Charles Tilly. 2001. *Dynamics of Contention.* New York: Cambridge University Press.

McVeigh, Rory, and Christian Smith. 1999. Who Protests in America: An Analysis of Three Political Alternatives: Inaction, Institutionalized Politics, or Protest. *Sociological Forum* 14 (4): 685–702.

Melucci, Alberto. 1989. *Nomads of the Present: Social Movements and Individual Needs in Contemporary Society.* Philadelphia: Temple University Press.

———. 1996. *Challenging Codes: Collective Action in the Information Age.* New York: Cambridge University Press.

Merskin, Debra. 2004. The Construction of Arabs As Enemies: Post-September 11 Discourse of George W. Bush. *Mass Communication and Society* 7 (2): 157–75.

Meyer, David S. 2004. Protest and Political Opportunities. *Annual Review of Sociology* 30:125–45.

Meyer, David S., and Sam Marullo. 1992. Grassroots Mobilization and International Politics: Peace Protest and the End of the Cold War. *Research in Social Movements, Conflicts and Change* 14:99–147.

Meyer, David S., and Suzanne Staggenborg. 1996. Movements, Countermovements, and the Structure of Political Opportunity. *American Journal of Sociology* 101 (6): 1628–60.

Meyer, David S., and Nancy Whittier. 1994. Social Movement Spillover. *Social Problems* 41 (2): 277–98.

Meyer, David S., Nancy Whittier, and Belinda Robnett, eds. 2002. *Social Movements: Identity, Culture, and The State.* Oxford, UK: Oxford University Press.

Meyers, John P. 2002. *Dominant-Minority Relations in America.* New York: Allyn and Bacon.

Milbank, Dana. 2001. Religious Right Finds its Center in the Oval Office. *Washington Post,* December 21, A.

Morgan, Rhiannon. 2004. Advancing Indigenous Rights at the United Nations: Strategic Framing and Its Impact on the Normative Development of International Law. *Social & Legal Studies* 13 (4): 481–500.

Morris, Charles E., and Stephen H. Browne, eds. 2001. *The Ego-Function of the Rhetoric of Protest.* State College, Penn.: Strata.

Muhlhausler, Peter, and Adrian Peace. 2006. Environmental Discourses. *Annual Review of Anthropology* 35: 457–79.

Myers, Daniel J., and Daniel M. Cress, eds. 2004. *Authority in Contention—Research in Social Movements, Conflicts and Change.* Vol. 25. Oxford, UK: Elsevier.

Nagel, Joane. 1994. Constructing Ethnicity: Creating and Recreating Ethnic Identity and Culture. *Social Problems* 41 (1): 152–76.

Naples, Nancy. 2002. Materialist Feminist Discourse Analysis and Social Movement Research: Mapping the Changing Context for "Community Control." In *Social Movements: Identity, Culture, and the State,* ed. N. Whittier, D. S. Meyer, and B. Robnett, 226–46. New York: Oxford University Press.

———. 2003. *Feminism and Method: Ethnography, Discourse Analysis, and Activist Research.* New York: Routledge.

Nepstad, Sharon E. 2004. Disciples and Dissenters: Tactical Choice and Consequences in the Plowshares Movement. In *Research in Social Movements, Conflict and Change,* Vol. 25, ed. D. J. Myers and D. M. Cress, 130–59. Oxford, UK: Elsevier Science/JAI Press.

Nikolaev, Alexander G., and Douglas V. Porpora. 2007. Talking War: How Elite U.S. Newspaper Editorials and Opinion Pieces Debated the Attack on Iraq. *Sociological Focus* 40 (1): 6–25.

Nussbaum, Martha. 2001. *Upheavals of Thought: The Intelligence of Emotions.* Cambridge, UK: Cambridge University Press.

Oliver, Pamela E., and Hank Johnston. 2000. What a Good Idea! Ideology and Frames in Social Movement Research. *Mobilization* 5 (1): 37–54.

Pagnucco, Ron. 1996. A Comparison of the Political Behavior of Faith-Based and Secular Peace Groups. In *Disruptive Religion: The Force of Faith in Social Movement Activism,* ed. C. Smith, 205–22. New York: Routledge.

Pagnucco, Ron, and Jackie Smith. 1993. The Peace Movement and the Formation of U.S. Foreign Policy. *Peace & Change* 18 (2): 157–81.

Pei, Minxin. 2003. The Paradoxes of American Nationalism. *Foreign Policy* (May–June): 1–7. www.foreignpolicy.com (accessed October 1, 2005).

Petonito, Gina. 2000. Racial Discourse and Enemy Construction. In *Social Conflicts and Collective Identities,* ed. P. G. Coy and L. M. Woehrle, 19–40. New York: Rowman & Littlefield.

Pew Research Center. 2001. *Military Action a Higher Priority Than Homeland Defense.* The Pew Research Center for the People and the Press. http://people-press.org/reports/display.php3?PageID=101 (accessed March 1, 2007).

Polletta, Francesca. 2006. *It Was Like a Fever: Storytelling in Protest and Politics.* Chicago: University of Chicago Press.

Polletta, Francesca, and Edwin Amenta. 2001. Conclusion: Second That Emotion? Lessons From Once Novel Concepts in Social Movement Research. In *Passionate Politics: Emotions and Social Movements*, ed. J. Goodwin, J. M. Jasper, and F. Polletta, 303–16. Chicago: University of Chicago Press.

Program on International Policy Attitudes. 2006. Polling the Nations: Program on International Policy Attitudes. http://poll.orspub.com (accessed June 23, 2006).

Ramsey, David S. 2004. From Babel on: "The City on a Hill" in the Age of Global Village. *Language and Culture Research Series* 3:219–44.

Reagan, Ronald. 1988. Address to the Nation on Aid to the Nicaraguan Democratic Resistance. February 2. www.reagan.utexas.edu/archives/speeches/1988/020288e.htm (accessed June 23, 2008).

Risse, Thomas, Stephen C. Ropp, and Kathryn Sikkink. 1999. The Socialization of International Human Rights Norms into Domestic Practices: Introduction. In *The Power of Human Rights: International Norms and Domestic Change*, ed. T. Risse, S. C. Ropp, and K. Sikkink, 1–38. New York: Cambridge University Press.

Robnett, Belinda. 1997. *How Long? How Long?: African-American Women in the Struggle for Civil Rights*. New York: Oxford University Press.

Rohlinger, Deana A. 2002. Framing the Abortion Debate: Organizational Resources, Media Strategies, and Movement-Countermovement Dynamics. *Sociological Quarterly* 43 (4): 479–507.

Roszak, Theodore. 1968. *The Making of a Counterculture*. Garden City, N.Y.: Doubleday Anchor.

Rothman, Franklin D., and Pamela E. Oliver. 1999. From Local to Global: The Anti-Dam Movement in Southern Brazil, 1979–1992. *Mobilization* 4 (1): 41–57.

Rupp, Leila J., and Verta Taylor. 1987. *Survival in the Doldrums: The American Women's Rights Movement*. New York: Oxford University Press.

Ryan, Charlotte. 1991. *Prime Time Activism: Media Strategies for Grassroots Organizing*. Boston: South End Press.

Sandberg, Sveinung. 2006. Fighting Neo-liberalism with Neo-liberal Discourse: ATTAC Norway, Foucault and Collective Action Framing. *Social Movement Studies* 5 (3): 209–27.

Schatz, Robert T., and Ervin Staub. 1997. Manifestations of Blind and Constructive Patriotism: Personality Correlates and Individual-Group Relations. In *Patriotism in the Lives of Individuals and Nations*, ed. D. Bar-Tal and E. Staub, 229–46. Chicago: Nelson-Hall.

Schatz, Robert T., Ervin Staub, and Howard Lavine. 1999. On the Varieties of National Attachment: Blind versus Constitutional Patriotism. *Political Psychology* 20 (1): 151–74.

Schnittker, Jason, Jeremy Freese, and Brian Powell. 2003. Who Are Feminists and What Do They Believe? The Role of Generations. *American Sociological Review* 68 (August): 607–22.

Seidman, Steven. 1998. *Contested Knowledge: Social Theory in the Postmodern Era*. 2nd ed. Malden, Mass.: Blackwell Publishers.

Shapiro, Peter, ed. 1994. *The Citizen Soldier: A History of National Service in America*. College Park, Md.: Center for Political Leadership and Participation.

Smith, Anthony D. 1989. The Origins of Nations. *Ethnic and Racial Studies* 12:340–67.

Smith, Christian. 1996a. *Resisting Reagan: The U.S. Central America Peace Movement*. Chicago: The University of Chicago Press.

———. 1996b. Correcting a Curious Neglect, or Bringing Religion Back In. In *Disruptive Religion: The Force of Faith in Social Movement Activism*, ed. C. Smith, 1–25. New York: Routledge.

Smith, Jackie. 1995. Transnational Political Processes and the Human Rights Movement. *Research in Social Movements, Conflicts and Change* 18:185–219.

———. 2001. Globalizing Resistance: The Battle of Seattle and the Future of Social Movements. *Mobilization* 6 (1): 1–19.

———. 2002. Bridging Global Divides? Strategic Framing and Solidarity in Transnational Social Movement Organizations. *International Sociology* 17 (4): 505–28.

———. 2004. Exploring Connections between Global Integration and Political Mobilization. *Journal of World-Systems Research* 10 (1): 255–85.

———. 2006. Conversation with the authors, May.

Smith, Tom W. 1990. *Ethnic Images.* Chicago: NORC.

Smith, Tom W., Kenneth A. Rasinski, and Marianna Toce. 2001. *America Rebounds: A National Study of Public Opinion to the September 11th Terrorist Attacks.* Chicago: NORC.

Snow, David A. 2004a. Framing Processes, Ideology, and Discursive Fields. In *The Blackwell Companion to Social Movements,* ed. D. A. Snow, S. A. Soule, and H. Kriesi, 380–412. Malden, Mass.: Blackwell Publishing.

———. 2004b. Social Movements As Challenges to Authority: Resistance to an Emerging Conceptual Hegemony. *Research in Social Movements, Conflicts and Change* 25:3–25.

Snow, David A., and Robert D. Benford. 1988. Ideology, Frame Resonance and Participant Mobilization. In *International Social Movement Research,* Vol. 1, ed. B. Klandermans, H. Kriesi and S. Tarrow, 197–217. Greenwich, Conn.: JAI.

———. 1992. Master Frames and Cycles of Protest. In *Frontiers of Social Movement Theory,* ed. A. D. Morris and C. McClurg Mueller, 133–55. New Haven, Conn.: Yale University Press.

Snow, David A., E. B. Rochford Jr., Steven K. Worden, and Robert D. Benford. 1986. Frame Alignment Processes, Micromobilization, and Movement Participation. *American Sociological Review* 51 (4): 464–81.

Snyder, R. Claire. 1999. *Citizen-Soldiers and Manly Warriors: Military Service and Gender in the Civic Republican Tradition.* Lanham, Md.: Rowman & Littlefield.

Staggenborg, Suzanne. 1986. Coalition Work in the Pro-Choice Movement: Organizational and Environmental Opportunities and Obstacles. *Social Problems* 33 (5): 374–90.

Staub, Ervin. 1997. Blind Versus Constructive Patriotism: Moving from Embeddedness in the Group to Critical Loyalty and Action. In *Patriotism in the Lives of Individuals and Nations,* ed. Daniel Bar-Tal and Ervin Staub, 213–28. Chicago: Nelson-Hall.

Steinberg, Marc W. 1999. The Talk and Back Talk of Collective Action: A Dialogic Analysis of Repertoires of Discourse in Nineteenth-Century English Cotton Spinners. *American Journal of Sociology* 105 (3): 736–80.

Suskind, Ron. 2004. *The Price of Loyalty: George W. Bush, the White House, and the Education of Paul O'Neill.* New York: Simon & Schuster.

Swidler, Ann. 1986. Culture in Action: Symbols and Strategies. *American Sociological Review* 51 (2): 273–76.

Tarrow, Sidney. 1992. Mentalities, Political Cultures, and Collective Action Frames: Constructing Meaning Through Action. In *Frontiers of Social Movement Theory,* ed. A. D. Morris and C. McClurg Mueller, 174–202. New Haven, Conn.: Yale University Press.

———. 1998. *Power in Movement: Social Movements and Contentious Politics.* 2nd ed. New York: Cambridge University Press.

Taylor, Verta, and Nancy Whittier. 1992. Collective Identity in Social Movement Communities: Lesbian Feminist Mobilization. In *Frontiers of Social Movement Theory,* ed. A. D. Morris and C. McClurg Mueller, 104–30. New Haven, Conn.: Yale University Press.

———. 1995. Analytical Approaches to Social Movement Culture: The Culture of the Women's Movement. In *Social Movements and Culture,* ed. H. Johnston and B. Klandermans, 163–87. Minneapolis: University of Minnesota Press.

Tickner, J. Ann. 1992. *Gender in International Relations: Feminist Perspectives on Achieving Global Security.* New York: Columbia University Press.

Tilly, Charles. 1978. *From Mobilization to Revolution.* Reading, Pa.: Addison Wesley.

Urban, Hugh B. 2006. The Secrets of the Kingdom: Spiritual Discourse and Material Interests in the Bush Administration. *Discourse* 27 (1): 141–65.

Van Dijk, Teun A. 1993. Principles of Critical Discourse Analysis. *Discourse and Society* 4 (2): 249–83.

Van Evera, Stephen. 1994. Hypotheses on Nationalism and War. *International Security* 18:5–39.

Walton, Stuart. 2004. *A Natural History of Human Emotions.* 1st Grove Press ed. New York: Grove Press.

Weber, Max. 1947/1997. *The Theory of Social and Economic Organization.* New York: Free Press.

White, Ralph K. 1970. *Nobody Wanted War: Misperception in Vietnam and Other Wars.* Garden City, N.Y.: Anchor Books.

Whittier, Nancy. 2001. Emotional Strategies: The Collective Reconstruction and Display of Oppositional Emotions in the Movement Against Child Sexual Abuse. In *Passionate Politics: Emotions and Social Movements,* ed. J. Goodwin, J. M. Jasper, and F. Polletta, 233–50. Chicago: University of Chicago Press.

Williams, Raymond. 1977. *Marxism and Literature.* Oxford, UK: Oxford University Press.

———. 1982. *The Sociology of Culture.* New York: Schocken Books.

Williams, Rhys H. 1995. Constructing the Public Good: Social Movements and Cultural Resources. *Social Problems* 42 (1): 124–43.

———. 2002. From the "Beloved Community" to "Family Values": Religious Language, Symbolic Repertories, and Democratic Culture. In *Social Movements: Identity, Culture, and the State,* ed. N. Whittier, D. S. Meyer, and B. Robnett, 247–65. New York: Oxford University Press.

———. 2004. The Cultural Contexts of Collective Action: Constraints, Opportunities, and the Symbolic Life of Social Movements. In *The Blackwell Companion to Social Movements,* ed. D. A. Snow, S. A. Soule, and H. Kriesi, 91–115. Malden, Mass.: Blackwell Publishing.

Williams, Rhys H., and Susan M. Alexander. 1994. Religious Rhetoric in American Populism: Civil Religion as Movement Ideology. *Journal for the Scientific Study of Religion* 33(1): 1–15.

Williams, Rhys H., and N. J. Demerath III. 1991. Religion and Political Process in an American City. *American Sociological Review* 56 (4): 417–31.

Wills, Garry. 1990. *Under God: Religion and American Politics.* New York: Simon and Schuster.

Wittner, Lawrence S. 1984. *Rebels Against War: The American Peace Movement, 1933–1983.* Philadelphia: Temple University Press.

Woodward, Bob. 2002. *Bush at War.* New York: Simon & Schuster.

———. 2004. *Plan of Attack.* New York: Simon & Schuster.

Worth, Owen, and Carmen Kuhling. 2004. Counter-hegemony, Anti-globalisation and Culture in International Political Economy. *Capital and Class* (December): 31–42.

Wuthnow, Robert. 1988. *The Restructuring of American Religion: Society and Faith Since World War II.* Princeton, N.J.: Princeton University Press.

Yang, Guobin. 2000. Achieving Emotions in Collective Action: Emotional Processes and Movement Mobilization in the 1989 Chinese Student Movement. *Sociological Quarterly* 41 (4): 593–614.

Index

Page numbers in italic type refer to tables and photos.

About the Authors

Lynne M. Woehrle is associate professor of sociology at Mount Mary College, a Catholic college for women in Milwaukee, Wisconsin. She teaches sociology and coordinates a certificate in peacebuilding in the Department of Behavioral Science. Her research and teaching interests include peacebuilding, conflict analysis, gender analysis, and social movements working for peace and justice from the local to the global stage. She has served on the board of the Peace Studies Association, and as chair for the Section on Peace, War, and Social Conflict in the American Sociological Association. Her related research with one or more of the coauthors of this book includes articles that have appeared in *American Behavioral Scientist; Research in Social Movements, Conflicts, and Change; Peace Review; Social Problems; Sociological Perspectives; Sociological Research Online;* and *Sociological Spectrum.* Among her other publications are articles and chapters she has authored and coauthored that appeared in *Research in Social Movements, Conflicts and Change; Encyclopedia of Peace, Violence, and Conflict; Women's Studies Quarterly;* and the *Women and War Reader.* She is coeditor of *Teaching the Sociology of Peace, War, and Military Institutions* (2007). She also coedited the book *Social Conflicts and Collective Identities* (2000) with Patrick Coy. She is active in her community on issues and projects related to peace, the environment, human rights, and economic justice.

Patrick G. Coy is associate professor of political science and conflict management at Kent State University in Kent, Ohio, and director of the Center for Applied Conflict Management at KSU. His primary publications have focused on the Catholic Worker movement, Peace Brigades International, community mediation in the United States, the dynamics of international nonviolent accompaniment, and the U.S. peace movement. His research with one or more of the coauthors of this book includes articles that have appeared in *Peace Review; Research in Social Movements, Conflicts and Change; Sociological Perspectives; Sociological Spectrum; Social Problems; Sociological Research Online;* and *American Behavioral Scientist.* Other publications have appeared in *Mediation Quarterly, Peace and Change, The Sociological Quarterly,* and elsewhere. Coy frequently publishes op-eds in major daily newspapers, and he is the editor of numerous volumes of *Research in Social Movements, Conflicts and Change.* He also edited *A Revolution of the Heart: Essays on the Catholic Worker* (1988), and coedited *Social Conflicts and Collective Identities* (2000). He has served on the councils of the International Peace Research Association and the Peace History Society, as well as national chair of the Fellowship of Reconciliation. He is currently on the board of the Cleveland Mediation Center. Patrick Coy received the Distinguished Teaching Award of the College of Arts and Sciences at Kent State University in 2000, and he was also recently named as one the "101 Most Dangerous Academics in America" by right-wing pundit David Horowitz.

Gregory M. Maney is associate professor of sociology at Hofstra University in Hempstead, New York. His research and teaching examine social movements, the dynamics of intergroup conflict, and effective strategies for promoting peace. Funded by the United States Institute of Peace, his dissertation focused upon transnational dimensions of conflict in Northern Ireland. His published research with the coauthors of this book includes articles that have appeared in *American Behavioral Scientist; Peace Review; Research in Social Movements, Conflicts and Change; Sociological Perspectives; Social Problems;* and *Sociological Research Online.* Among other works, he has authored and coauthored articles that have appeared in the *American Journal of Sociology; International Journal of Conflict Management; Journal of Peace Research; Mobilization; Research in Social Movements, Conflict and Change; Social Problems;* and *Sociological Methods and Research.* He has recently received grants from the Sociological Initiatives Foundation and the American Sociological Association to conduct community-based studies assessing the roles of local governments and residents in conflicts surrounding day labor markets on Long Island. He has served as chair of both the membership and nomination committees of the Peace, War, and Social Conflict Section of the American Sociological Association. He is currently serving on the council of the Collective Behavior and Social Movements Section of the ASA. He has conducted numerous workshops on community organizing and peacebuilding for grassroots community organizations. He is active in his community on several interrelated social justice issues and projects.